# The 30-Minute
# Mediterranean Cookbook

1800 Quick, Delicious & Healthy Mediterranean Recipes for Living and Eating Well Every Day with 21-DAY MEAL PLAN

Annette L. Oberlin

# CONTENTS

## Vegetable Mains And Meatless Recipes ..............................29

# Beans , Grains, And Pastas Recipes ................................. 43

## Sides , Salads, And Soups Recipes ................................................ 57

# Poultry And Meats Recipes ................................................ 82

# Introduction

Welcome to "The 30-Minute Mediterranean Cookbook with 21-DAY MEAL PLAN." My name is Annette L. Oberlin, and I am a passionate home cook who loves creating healthy and delicious meals for my family and friends. In this cookbook, I have compiled some of my favorite Mediterranean recipes that are quick, easy, and nutritious. I have also included a 21-day meal plan to help you get started on your healthy eating journey.

I wrote this cookbook to share my love of Mediterranean cuisine with others. The Mediterranean diet is known for its health benefits, including reducing the risk of heart disease, stroke, and diabetes. However, many people think that eating healthy means sacrificing taste and flavor. That's why I created this cookbook to show that healthy eating can be delicious, satisfying, and easy.

In this cookbook, you will find 1800 recipes that are simple, flavorful, and nutritious. All the recipes can be made in 30 minutes or less, making them perfect for busy weeknights. The recipes are organized into chapters, including breakfast, snacks, salads, soups, meatless dishes, seafood, poultry, meat, and desserts.

In addition to the recipes, I have also included a 21-day meal plan to help you kickstart your healthy eating journey. The meal plan includes three meals and two snacks per day, with a mix of vegetarian and non-vegetarian options. Each day's meals are balanced and designed to provide you with the necessary nutrients to fuel your day.

"The 30-Minute Mediterranean Cookbook with 21-DAY MEAL PLAN" is a comprehensive guide to healthy and delicious Mediterranean cuisine. With 1800 quick and easy recipes and a 21-day meal plan, this cookbook is perfect for anyone who wants to eat healthy but doesn't want to sacrifice taste and flavor. Whether you're a seasoned cook or a beginner, this cookbook has something for everyone. So, grab your apron and let's get cooking!

# What is the Mediterranean diet exactly?

The Mediterranean diet is a dietary pattern that is based on the traditional foods and flavors of the Mediterranean region, which includes countries such as Greece, Italy, and Spain.

This way of eating emphasizes the consumption of whole, plant-based foods, such as fruits, vegetables, legumes, and nuts, as well as healthy fats like olive oil and fatty fish. It also includes moderate consumption of lean proteins, such as poultry and dairy, and limited intake of processed and unhealthy foods, like refined sugars and trans fats.

The Mediterranean diet has been associated with a variety of health benefits, including reduced risk of chronic diseases such as heart disease, diabetes, and some cancers. It is also considered a sustainable and environmentally friendly way of eating, as it emphasizes the consumption of locally sourced, seasonal foods.

While the specific foods and proportions may vary depending on the country and region, the Mediterranean diet is generally characterized by a high intake of fruits, vegetables, whole grains, and olive oil, and a low intake of red meat and processed foods. It is often described as a balanced and flexible approach to eating, with a focus on wholesome, nutrient-dense foods.

# What are the health benefits of following a Mediterranean diet?

- **Heart health**

The Mediterranean diet has been extensively studied and shown to reduce the risk of heart disease. It emphasizes the consumption of heart-healthy foods such as fruits, vegetables, whole grains, legumes, fish, and olive oil, while limiting processed foods, red meat, and unhealthy fats.

- **Reduced risk of chronic diseases**

Following a Mediterranean diet has been linked to a lower risk of developing chronic conditions such as type 2 diabetes, certain types of cancer (e.g., breast and colorectal cancer), and neurodegenerative diseases like Alzheimer's and Parkinson's.

- **Weight management**

The Mediterranean diet emphasizes whole, minimally processed foods and encourages moderate portions. It incorporates plenty of fruits, vegetables, and whole grains, which are low in calories but high in fiber, helping you feel full and satisfied.

- **Improved cognitive function**

Several studies have found that adhering to a Mediterranean diet is associated with better cognitive performance and a reduced risk of cognitive decline. The high intake of fruits, vegetables, whole grains, fish, and healthy fats may promote brain health and protect against age-related cognitive impairment.

- **Anti-inflammatory effects**

Chronic inflammation is linked to various health issues, including heart disease, obesity, and certain types of cancer. The Mediterranean diet, rich in fruits, vegetables, whole grains, and olive oil, contains numerous anti-inflammatory compounds that may help reduce inflammation in the body.

- **Longevity**

Following a Mediterranean diet has been associated with a longer lifespan and a reduced risk of premature death. The combination of its beneficial effects on heart health, chronic disease prevention, weight management, and overall well-being likely contributes to this effect.

## What foods should be limited or avoided on the Mediterranean diet?

The Mediterranean diet emphasizes whole, minimally processed foods and is known for its numerous health benefits. However, there are certain foods that are recommended to be limited or avoided altogether in order to fully reap the benefits of this dietary pattern. Some of these foods include:

- **Red meat**

While the Mediterranean diet is not strictly vegetarian, it places a greater emphasis on plant-based proteins such as legumes, nuts, and fish. Red meat, particularly processed meat, is high in saturated fat and has been linked to an increased risk of heart disease and certain cancers.

- **Processed foods**

The Mediterranean diet emphasizes whole, minimally processed foods such as fruits, vegetables, whole grains, and lean proteins. Processed foods, on the other hand, are often high in added sugars, salt, and unhealthy fats, which can contribute to chronic diseases such as obesity, diabetes, and heart disease.

- **Refined grains**

The Mediterranean diet emphasizes whole grains such as brown rice, quinoa, and whole wheat bread. Refined grains, on the other hand, have been stripped of their fiber and nutrients, and can cause blood sugar spikes and crashes.

- **Added sugars**

The Mediterranean diet is low in added sugars, which have been linked to numerous health problems such as obesity, diabetes, and heart disease. Instead, natural sweeteners such as honey or fresh fruit are used to add sweetness to dishes.

- **Saturated and trans fats**

The Mediterranean diet emphasizes healthy fats such as olive oil, nuts, and fatty fish, which have been shown to be beneficial for heart health. Saturated and trans fats, on the other hand, can raise cholesterol levels and increase the risk of heart disease.

# Breakfast Recipes

## Vegetable Polenta With Fried Eggs

Servings:4
Cooking Time:35 Minutes
**Ingredients:**
- 2 tbsp butter
- ½ tsp sea salt
- 1 cup polenta
- 4 eggs
- 2 spring onions, chopped
- 1 bell pepper, chopped
- 1 zucchini, chopped
- 1 tsp ginger-garlic paste
- 1 ½ cups vegetable broth
- ¼ tsp chili flakes, crushed
- 2 tbsp basil leaves, chopped

**Directions:**
1. Melt 1 tbsp of the butter in a skillet over medium heat. Place in spring onions, ginger-garlic paste, bell pepper, and zucchini and sauté for 5 minutes; set aside.
2. Pour the broth and 1 ½ cups of water in a pot and bring to a boil. Gradually whisk in polenta to avoid chunks, lower the heat, and simmer for 4-5 minutes. Keep whisking until it begins to thicken. Cook covered for 20 minutes, stirring often. Add the zucchini mixture, chili flakes, and salt and stir.
3. Heat the remaining butter in a skillet. Break the eggs and fry them until set and well cooked. Divide the polenta between bowls, top with fried eggs and basil, and serve.

**Nutrition Info:**
- Info Per Serving: Calories: 295;Fat: 12g;Protein: 11g;Carbs: 36g.

## Feta And Spinach Frittata

Servings:2
Cooking Time: 15 Minutes
**Ingredients:**
- 4 large eggs, beaten
- 2 tablespoons fresh chopped herbs, such as rosemary, thyme, oregano, basil or 1 teaspoon dried herbs
- ¼ teaspoon salt
- Freshly ground black pepper, to taste
- 4 tablespoons extra-virgin olive oil, divided
- 1 cup fresh spinach, arugula, kale, or other leafy greens
- 4 ounces quartered artichoke hearts, rinsed, drained, and thoroughly dried
- 8 cherry tomatoes, halved
- ½ cup crumbled soft goat cheese

**Directions:**
1. Preheat the broiler to Low.
2. In a small bowl, combine the beaten eggs, herbs, salt, and pepper and whisk well with a fork. Set aside.

3. In an ovenproof skillet, heat 2 tablespoons of olive oil over medium heat. Add the spinach, artichoke hearts, and cherry tomatoes and sauté until just wilted, 1 to 2 minutes.
4. Pour in the egg mixture and let it cook undisturbed over medium heat for 3 to 4 minutes, until the eggs begin to set on the bottom.
5. Sprinkle the goat cheese across the top of the egg mixture and transfer the skillet to the oven.
6. Broil for 4 to 5 minutes, or until the frittata is firm in the center and golden brown on top.
7. Remove from the oven and run a rubber spatula around the edge to loosen the sides. Slice the frittata in half and serve drizzled with the remaining 2 tablespoons of olive oil.

**Nutrition Info:**
- Info Per Serving: Calories: 529;Fat: 46.5g;Protein: 21.4g;Carbs: 7.1g.

## Artichoke & Spinach Frittata

Servings:4
Cooking Time:55 Minutes
**Ingredients:**
- 4 oz canned artichokes, chopped
- 2 tsp olive oil
- ½ cup whole milk
- 8 eggs
- 1 cup spinach, chopped
- 1 garlic clove, minced
- ½ cup Parmesan, crumbled
- 1 tsp oregano, dried
- 1 Jalapeño pepper, minced
- Salt to taste

**Directions:**
1. Preheat oven to 360 F. Warm the olive oil in a skillet over medium heat and sauté garlic and spinach for 3 minutes.
2. Beat the eggs in a bowl. Stir in artichokes, milk, Parmesan cheese, oregano, jalapeño pepper, and salt. Add in spinach mixture and toss to combine. Transfer to a greased baking dish and bake for 20 minutes until golden and bubbling. Slice into wedges and serve.

**Nutrition Info:**
- Info Per Serving: Calories: 190;Fat: 14g;Protein: 10g;Carbs: 5g.

## Pecorino Bulgur & Spinach Cupcakes

Servings:6
Cooking Time:45 Minutes
**Ingredients:**
- 2 eggs, whisked
- 1 cup bulgur
- 3 cups water
- 1 cup spinach, torn

- 2 spring onions, chopped
- ¼ cup Pecorino cheese, grated
- ½ tsp garlic powder
- Sea salt and pepper to taste
- ½ tsp dried oregano

**Directions:**

1. Preheat the oven to 340 °F. Grease a muffin tin with cooking spray. Warm 2 cups of salted water in a saucepan over medium heat and add in bulgur. Bring to a boil and cook for 10-15 minutes. Remove to a bowl and fluff with a fork. Stir in spinach, spring onions, eggs, Pecorino cheese, garlic powder, salt, pepper, and oregano. Divide between muffin holes and bake for 25 minutes. Serve chilled.

**Nutrition Info:**

- Info Per Serving: Calories: 280;Fat: 12g;Protein: 5g;Carbs: 9g.

# Pistachio Muesli Pots With Pomegranate

Servings:2
Cooking Time:10 Minutes
**Ingredients:**

- ½ cup old-fashioned oats
- ¼ cup shelled pistachios
- 3 tbsp sesame seeds
- 2 tbsp chia seeds
- ¾ cup milk
- ½ cup Greek yogurt
- 2 tsp honey
- ½ cup pomegranate seeds

**Directions:**

1. Mix the oats, pistachios, sesame seeds, chia seeds, milk, yogurt, and honey in a medium bowl. Divide the mixture between two mason jars. Top with pomegranate seeds. Cover the jar with lids and place in the refrigerator. Serve.

**Nutrition Info:**

- Info Per Serving: Calories: 502;Fat: 24g;Protein: 17g;Carbs: 60g.

# Granola & Berry Parfait

Servings:2
Cooking Time:5 Minutes
**Ingredients:**

- 2 cups berries
- 1 ½ cups Greek yogurt
- 1 tbsp powdered sugar
- ¼ cup granola

**Directions:**

1. Divide between two bowls a layer of berries, yogurt, and powdered sugar. Scatter with granola and serve.

**Nutrition Info:**

- Info Per Serving: Calories: 244;Fat: 11g;Protein: 21g;Carbs: 13g.

# Basic Tortilla De Patatas

Servings:4
Cooking Time:35 Minutes
**Ingredients:**

- 1 ½ lb gold potatoes, peeled and sliced
- ½ cup olive oil
- 1 sweet onion, thinly sliced
- 8 eggs
- ½ dried oregano
- Salt to taste

**Directions:**

1. Heat the olive oil in a skillet over medium heat. Fry the potatoes for 8-10 minutes, stirring often. Add in onion, oregano, and salt and cook for 5-6 minutes until the potatoes are tender and slightly golden; set aside.

2. In a bowl, beat the eggs with a pinch of salt. Add in the potato mixture and mix well. Pour into the skillet and cook for about 10-12 minutes. Flip the tortilla using a plate, and cook for 2 more minutes until nice and crispy. Slice and serve.

**Nutrition Info:**

- Info Per Serving: Calories: 440;Fat: 34g;Protein: 14g;Carbs: 22g.

# Chickpea Lettuce Wraps

Servings:2
Cooking Time: 0 Minutes
**Ingredients:**

- 1 can chickpeas, drained and rinsed well
- 1 celery stalk, diced
- ½ shallot, minced
- 1 green apple, cored and diced
- 3 tablespoons tahini (sesame paste)
- 2 teaspoons freshly squeezed lemon juice
- 1 teaspoon raw honey
- 1 teaspoon Dijon mustard
- Dash salt
- Filtered water, to thin
- 4 romaine lettuce leaves

**Directions:**

1. In a medium bowl, stir together the chickpeas, celery, shallot, apple, tahini, lemon juice, honey, mustard, and salt. If needed, add some water to thin the mixture.

2. Place the romaine lettuce leaves on a plate. Fill each with the chickpea filling, using it all. Wrap the leaves around the filling. Serve immediately.

**Nutrition Info:**

- Info Per Serving: Calories: 397;Fat: 15.1g;Protein: 15.1g;Carbs: 53.1g.

# Za'atar Pizza

Servings:4
Cooking Time: 1o To 12 Minutes
**Ingredients:**
- 1 sheet puff pastry
- ¼ cup extra-virgin olive oil
- ⅓ cup za'atar seasoning

**Directions:**
1. Preheat the oven to 350ºF. Line a baking sheet with parchment paper.
2. Place the puff pastry on the prepared baking sheet. Cut the pastry into desired slices.
3. Brush the pastry with the olive oil. Sprinkle with the za'atar seasoning.
4. Put the pastry in the oven and bake for 10 to 12 minutes, or until edges are lightly browned and puffed up.
5. Serve warm.

**Nutrition Info:**
- Info Per Serving: Calories: 374;Fat: 30.0g;Protein: 3.0g;Carbs: 20.0g.

# Vegetable & Cheese Frittata

Servings:4
Cooking Time:30 Minutes
**Ingredients:**
- 2 tbsp olive oil
- ½ lb cauliflower florets
- ½ cup skimmed milk
- 6 eggs
- 1 red bell pepper, chopped
- ½ cup fontina cheese, grated
- ½ tsp red pepper
- ½ tsp turmeric
- Salt and black pepper to taste

**Directions:**
1. Preheat oven to 360°F. In a bowl, beat the eggs with milk. Add in fontina cheese, red pepper, turmeric, salt, and pepper. Mix in red bell pepper. Warm olive oil in a skillet over medium heat, pour in the egg mixture and cook for 4-5 minutes. Set aside.
2. Blanch the cauliflower florets in a pot for 5 minutes until tender. Spread over the egg mixture. Place the skillet in the oven and bake for 15 minutes or until golden brown. Allow cooling for a few minutes before slicing. Serve warm.

**Nutrition Info:**
- Info Per Serving: Calories: 312;Fat: 18g;Protein: 21g;Carbs: 17g.

# Parsley Tomato Eggs

Servings:6
Cooking Time:25 Minutes
**Ingredients:**
- 2 tbsp olive oil
- 1 onion, chopped
- 2 garlic cloves, minced
- 2 cans tomatoes, diced
- 6 large eggs
- ½ cup fresh chives, chopped

**Directions:**
1. Warm the olive oil in a large skillet over medium heat. Add the onion and garlic and cook for 3 minutes, stirring occasionally. Pour in the tomatoes with their juices o and cook for 3 minutes until bubbling.
2. Crack one egg into a small custard cup. With a large spoon, make six indentations in the tomato mixture. Gently pour the first cracked egg into one indentation and repeat, cracking the remaining eggs, one at a time, into the custard cup and pouring one into each indentation. Cover the skillet and cook for 6-8 minutes. Top with chives and serve.

**Nutrition Info:**
- Info Per Serving: Calories: 123;Fat: 8g;Protein: 7g;Carbs: 4g.

# Banana & Chocolate Porridge

Servings:4
Cooking Time:20 Minutes
**Ingredients:**
- 2 bananas
- 4 dried apricots, chopped
- 1 cup barley, soaked
- 2 tbsp flax seeds
- 1 tbsp cocoa powder
- 1 cup coconut milk
- ¼ tsp mint leaves
- 2 oz dark chocolate bars, grated
- 2 tbsp coconut flakes

**Directions:**
1. Place the barley in a saucepan along with the flaxseeds and two cups of water. Bring to a boil, then lower the heat and simmer for 12 minutes, stirring often.
2. Meanwhile, in a food processor, blend bananas, cocoa powder, coconut milk, apricots, and mint leaves until smooth. Once the barley is ready, stir in chocolate. Add in banana mixture. Garnish with coconut flakes. Serve.

**Nutrition Info:**
- Info Per Serving: Calories: 476;Fat: 22g;Protein: 10g;Carbs: 65g.

# Falafel Balls With Tahini Sauce

Servings:4
Cooking Time: 20 Minutes
**Ingredients:**
- Tahini Sauce:
- ½ cup tahini
- 2 tablespoons lemon juice
- ¼ cup finely chopped flat-leaf parsley
- 2 cloves garlic, minced
- ½ cup cold water, as needed
- Falafel:
- 1 cup dried chickpeas, soaked overnight, drained
- ¼ cup chopped flat-leaf parsley

- ¼ cup chopped cilantro
- 1 large onion, chopped
- 1 teaspoon cumin
- ½ teaspoon chili flakes
- 4 cloves garlic
- 1 teaspoon sea salt
- 5 tablespoons almond flour
- 1½ teaspoons baking soda, dissolved in 1 teaspoon water
- 2 cups peanut oil
- 1 medium bell pepper, chopped
- 1 medium tomato, chopped
- 4 whole-wheat pita breads

**Directions:**
1. Make the Tahini Sauce:
2. Combine the ingredients for the tahini sauce in a small bowl. Stir to mix well until smooth.
3. Wrap the bowl in plastic and refrigerate until ready to serve.
4. Make the Falafel:
5. Put the chickpeas, parsley, cilantro, onion, cumin, chili flakes, garlic, and salt in a food processor. Pulse to mix well but not puréed.
6. Add the flour and baking soda to the food processor, then pulse to form a smooth and tight dough.
7. Put the dough in a large bowl and wrap in plastic. Refrigerate for at least 2 hours to let it rise.
8. Divide and shape the dough into walnut-sized small balls.
9. Pour the peanut oil in a large pot and heat over high heat until the temperature of the oil reaches 375ºF.
10. Drop 6 balls into the oil each time, and fry for 5 minutes or until golden brown and crispy. Turn the balls with a strainer to make them fried evenly.
11. Transfer the balls on paper towels with the strainer, then drain the oil from the balls.
12. Roast the pita breads in the oven for 5 minutes or until golden brown, if needed, then stuff the pitas with falafel balls and top with bell peppers and tomatoes. Drizzle with tahini sauce and serve immediately.

**Nutrition Info:**
- Info Per Serving: Calories: 574;Fat: 27.1g;Protein: 19.8g;Carbs: 69.7g.

# Power Green Smoothie

Servings:1
Cooking Time:10 Minutes
**Ingredients:**
- 1 tbsp extra-virgin olive oil
- 1 avocado, peeled and pitted
- 1 cup milk
- ½ cup watercress
- ½ cup baby spinach leaves
- ½ cucumber, peeled and seeded
- 10 mint leaves, stems removed

- ½ lemon, juiced

**Directions:**
1. In a blender, mix avocado, milk, baby spinach, watercress, cucumber, olive oil, mint, and lemon juice and blend until smooth and creamy. Add more milk or water to achieve your desired consistency. Serve chilled or at room temperature.

**Nutrition Info:**
- Info Per Serving: Calories: 330;Fat: 30.2g;Protein: 4g;Carbs: 19g.

# Chia & Almond Oatmeal

Servings:2
Cooking Time:10 Min + Chilling Time
**Ingredients:**
- ¼ tsp almond extract
- ½ cup milk
- ½ cup rolled oats
- 2 tbsp almonds, sliced
- 2 tbsp sugar
- 1 tsp chia seeds
- ¼ tsp ground cardamom
- ¼ tsp ground cinnamon

**Directions:**
1. Combine the milk, oats, almonds, sugar, chia seeds, cardamom, almond extract, and cinnamon in a mason jar and shake well. Keep in the refrigerator for 4 hours. Serve.

**Nutrition Info:**
- Info Per Serving: Calories: 131;Fat: 6.2g;Protein: 4.9g;Carbs: 17g.

# Sunday Pancakes In Berry Sauce

Servings:4
Cooking Time:20 Minutes
**Ingredients:**
- Pancakes
- 6 tbsp olive oil
- 1 cup flour
- 1 tsp baking powder
- ¼ tsp salt
- 2 large eggs
- 1 lemon, zested and juiced
- ½ tsp vanilla extract
- ½ tsp dark rum
- Berry Sauce
- 1 cup mixed berries
- 3 tbsp sugar
- 1 tbsp lemon juice
- ½ tsp vanilla extract

**Directions:**
1. In a large bowl, combine the flour, baking powder, and salt and whisk to break up any clumps. Add 4 tablespoons of olive oil, eggs, lemon zest and juice, rum, and vanilla extract and whisk to combine well. Brush a frying pan with butter

over medium heat and cook the pancakes for 5-7 minutes, flipping once until bubbles begin to form.

2.  To make the sauce, pour the mixed berries, lemon juice, vanilla, and sugar in a small saucepan over medium heat. Cook for 3-4 minutes until bubbly, adding a little water if the mixture is too thick. Mash the berries with a fork and stir until smooth. Pour over the pancakes and serve.

**Nutrition Info:**

*   Info Per Serving: Calories: 275;Fat: 26g;Protein: 4g;Carbs: 8g.

## Creamy Breakfast Bulgur With Berries

Servings:2
Cooking Time: 10 Minutes
**Ingredients:**

*   ½ cup medium-grain bulgur wheat
*   1 cup water
*   Pinch sea salt
*   ¼ cup unsweetened almond milk
*   1 teaspoon pure vanilla extract
*   ¼ teaspoon ground cinnamon
*   1 cup fresh berries of your choice

**Directions:**

1.  Put the bulgur in a medium saucepan with the water and sea salt, and bring to a boil.

2.  Cover, remove from heat, and let stand for 10 minutes until water is absorbed.

3.  Stir in the milk, vanilla, and cinnamon until fully incorporated. Divide between 2 bowls and top with the fresh berries to serve.

**Nutrition Info:**

*   Info Per Serving: Calories: 173;Fat: 1.6g;Protein: 5.7g;Carbs: 34.0g.

## Maple-vanilla Yogurt With Walnuts

Servings:4
Cooking Time:10 Minutes
**Ingredients:**

*   2 cups Greek yogurt
*   ¾ cup maple syrup
*   1 cup walnuts, chopped
*   1 tsp vanilla extract
*   2 tsp cinnamon powder

**Directions:**

1.  Combine yogurt, walnuts, vanilla, maple syrup, and cinnamon powder in a bowl. Let sit in the fridge for 10 minutes.

**Nutrition Info:**

*   Info Per Serving: Calories: 400;Fat: 25g;Protein: 11g;Carbs: 40g.

## Hummus Toast With Pine Nuts & Ricotta

Servings:2
Cooking Time:5 Minutes
**Ingredients:**

*   2 whole-wheat bread slices, toasted
*   1 tsp water
*   1 tbsp hummus
*   2 tsp ricotta cheese, crumbled
*   ½ lemon, juiced
*   2 tsp pine nuts

**Directions:**

1.  Whisk hummus, water, and lemon juice in a bowl and spread over toasted slices. Sprinkle ricotta cheese and pine nuts.

**Nutrition Info:**

*   Info Per Serving: Calories: 150;Fat: 8g;Protein: 6g;Carbs: 15g.

## Vegetable & Hummus Bowl

Servings:4
Cooking Time:15 Minutes
**Ingredients:**

*   2 tbsp butter
*   2 tbsp olive oil
*   3 cups green cabbage, shredded
*   3 cups kale, chopped
*   1 lb asparagus, chopped
*   ½ cup hummus
*   1 avocado, sliced
*   4 boiled eggs, sliced
*   1 tbsp balsamic vinegar
*   1 garlic clove, minced
*   2 tsp yellow mustard
*   Salt and black pepper to taste

**Directions:**

1.  Melt butter in a skillet over medium heat and sauté asparagus for 5 minutes. Mix the olive oil, balsamic vinegar, garlic, yellow mustard, salt, and pepper in a bowl. Spoon the hummus onto the center of a salad bowl and arrange in the asparagus, kale, cabbage, and avocado. Top with the egg slices. Drizzle with the dressing and serve.

**Nutrition Info:**

*   Info Per Serving: Calories: 392;Fat: 31g;Protein: 14g;Carbs: 22g.

## Lime Watermelon Yogurt Smoothie

Servings:6
Cooking Time:5 Minutes
**Ingredients:**

*   ½ cup almond milk
*   2 cups watermelon, cubed
*   ½ cup Greek yogurt
*   ½ tsp lime zest

**Directions:**

1. In a food processor, blend watermelon, almond milk, lime zest, and yogurt until smooth. Serve into glasses.

**Nutrition Info:**

- Info Per Serving: Calories: 260;Fat: 10g;Protein: 2g;Carbs: 6g.

# Cherry Tomato & Zucchini Scrambled Eggs

Servings:4

Cooking Time:15 Minutes

**Ingredients:**

- 2 tbsp olive oil
- 6 cherry tomatoes, halved
- ½ cup chopped zucchini
- ½ chopped green bell pepper
- 8 eggs, beaten
- 1 shallot, chopped
- 1 tbsp chopped fresh parsley
- 1 tbsp chopped fresh basil
- Salt and black pepper to taste

**Directions:**

1. Warm oil in a pan over medium heat. Place in zucchini, green bell peppers, salt, black pepper, and shallot. Cook for 4-5 minutes to sweat the shallot. Stir in tomatoes, parsley, and basil.

2. Cook for a minute and top with the beaten eggs. Lower the heat and cook for 6-7 minutes until the eggs are set but not runny. Remove to a platter to serve.

**Nutrition Info:**

- Info Per Serving: Calories: 205;Fat: 15g;Protein: 12g;Carbs: 4g.

# Super Cheeses And Mushroom Tart

Servings:4

Cooking Time: 1 Hour 30 Minutes

**Ingredients:**

- Crust:
- 1¾ cups almond flour
- 1 tablespoon raw honey
- ¾ teaspoon sea salt
- ¼ cup extra-virgin olive oil
- ⅓ cup water
- Filling:
- 2 tablespoons extra-virgin olive oil, divided
- 1 pound white mushrooms, trimmed and sliced thinly
- Sea salt, to taste
- 1 garlic clove, minced
- 2 teaspoons minced fresh thyme
- ¼ cup shredded Mozzarella cheese
- ½ cup grated Parmesan cheese
- 4 ounces part-skim ricotta cheese
- Ground black pepper, to taste
- 2 tablespoons ground basil

**Directions:**

1. Make the Crust:
2. Preheat the oven to 350ºF.
3. Combine the flour, honey, salt and olive oil in a large bowl. Stir to mix well. Gently mix in the water until a smooth dough forms.
4. Drop walnut-size clumps from the dough in the single layer on a tart pan. Press the clumps to coat the bottom of the pan.
5. Bake the crust in the preheated oven for 50 minutes or until firm and browned. Rotate the pan halfway through.
6. Make the Filling:
7. While baking the crust, heat 1 tablespoon of olive oil in a nonstick skillet over medium-high heat until shimmering.
8. Add the mushrooms and sprinkle with ½ teaspoon of salt. Sauté for 15 minutes or until tender.
9. Add the garlic and thyme and sauté for 30 seconds or until fragrant.
10. Make the Tart:
11. Meanwhile, combine the cheeses, salt, ground black pepper, and 1 tablespoon of olive oil in a bowl. Stir to mix well.
12. Spread the cheese mixture over the crust, then top with the mushroom mixture.
13. Bake in the oven for 20 minutes or until the cheeses are frothy and the tart is heated through. Rotate the pan halfway through the baking time.
14. Remove the tart from the oven. Allow to cool for at least 10 minutes, then sprinkle with basil. Slice to serve.

**Nutrition Info:**

- Info Per Serving: Calories: 530;Fat: 26.6g;Protein: 11.7g;Carbs: 63.5g.

# Tomato & Avocado Toast

Servings:2

Cooking Time:15 Minutes

**Ingredients:**

- 3 tbsp olive oil
- 2 tbsp ground flaxseed
- ½ tsp baking powder
- 2 large eggs
- Salt and black pepper to taste
- ½ tsp garlic powder
- 1 avocado, peeled and sliced
- 5 chopped cherry tomatoes
- 1 tsp cilantro, chopped

**Directions:**

1. Place the flaxseed and baking powder in a bowl and mix, breaking up any lumps in the baking powder. Add eggs, salt, pepper, and garlic powder. Whisk well. Let sit for 2 minutes.

2. Warm 1 tablespoon of the olive oil in a small skillet over medium heat. Pour in the egg mixture cook for 2-3 minutes until the eggs are set on the bottom. Using a rubber spatula, scrape down the sides to allow the uncooked egg to reach the bottom. Cook for another 2-3 minutes.

3. Flip like a pancake and cook for 1-2 more minutes. Allow to cool slightly. Slice into 2 pieces. Top each toast with avocado slices, cherry tomatoes, and cilantro and drizzle with the remaining olive oil.

**Nutrition Info:**
- Info Per Serving: Calories: 287;Fat: 25g;Protein: 9g;Carbs: 10g.

## Basil Cheese Omelet

Servings:2
Cooking Time:20 Minutes
**Ingredients:**
- 1 tbsp olive oil
- ½ pint cherry tomatoes
- 2 garlic cloves, minced
- 5 large eggs, beaten
- 3 tbsp milk
- Salt and black pepper to taste
- 2 tbsp fresh oregano, minced
- 2 tbsp fresh basil, minced
- 2 oz ricotta cheese, crumbled

**Directions:**
1. Warm the olive oil in a skillet over medium heat. Add the cherry tomatoes. Reduce the heat, cover the pan, and let the tomatoes soften. When the tomatoes are mostly softened and broken down, remove the lid, add garlic and continue to sauté.
2. In a bowl, combine the eggs, milk, salt, pepper, and herbs and whisk well to combine. Increase the heat to medium, pour the egg mixture over the tomatoes and garlic, and then sprinkle with ricotta cheese. Cook for 7-8 minutes, flipping once until the eggs are set. Run a spatula around the edge of the pan to make sure they won't stick. Serve warm.

**Nutrition Info:**
- Info Per Serving: Calories: 394;Fat: 29.6g;Protein: 26g;Carbs: 6g.

## Energy Nut Smoothie

Servings:1
Cooking Time:10 Minutes
**Ingredients:**
- 1 tbsp extra-virgin olive oil
- ½ cup Greek yogurt
- ½ cup almond milk
- ½ orange, zested and juiced
- 1 tbsp pistachios, chopped
- 1 tsp honey
- ½ tsp ground allspice
- ¼ tsp ground cinnamon
- ¼ tsp vanilla extract

**Directions:**
1. Place the yogurt, almond milk, orange zest and juice, olive oil, pistachios, honey, allspice, cinnamon, and vanilla in a blender and pulse until smooth and creamy. Add a little water to achieve your desired consistency. Serve in a chilled glass.

**Nutrition Info:**
- Info Per Serving: Calories: 264;Fat: 22.2g;Protein: 6g;Carbs: 12g.

## Classic Spanish Tortilla With Tuna

Servings:4
Cooking Time:30 Minutes
**Ingredients:**
- 7 oz canned tuna packed in water, flaked
- 2 plum tomatoes, seeded and diced
- 2 tbsp olive oil
- 6 large eggs, beaten
- 2 small potatoes, diced
- 2 green onions, chopped
- 1 roasted red bell pepper, sliced
- 1 tsp dried tarragon

**Directions:**
1. Preheat your broiler to high. Heat the olive oil in a skillet over medium heat. Fry the potatoes for 7 minutes until slightly soft. Add the green onions and cook for 3 minutes. Stir in the tuna, tomatoes, peppers, tarragon, and eggs. Cook for 8-10 minutes until the eggs are bubbling from the bottom and the bottom is slightly brown. Place the skillet under the preheated broiler for 5-6 minutes or until the middle is set and the top is slightly brown. Serve sliced into wedges.

**Nutrition Info:**
- Info Per Serving: Calories: 422;Fat: 21g;Protein: 14g;Carbs: 46g.

## Fluffy Almond Flour Pancakes With Strawberries

Servings:4
Cooking Time: 15 Minutes
**Ingredients:**
- 1 cup plus 2 tablespoons unsweetened almond milk
- 1 cup almond flour
- 2 large eggs, whisked
- ⅓ cup honey
- 1 teaspoon baking soda
- ¼ teaspoon salt
- 2 tablespoons extra-virgin olive oil
- 1 cup sliced strawberries

**Directions:**
1. Combine the almond milk, almond flour, whisked eggs, honey, baking soda, and salt in a large bowl and whisk to incorporate.
2. Heat the olive oil in a large skillet over medium-high heat.
3. Make the pancakes: Pour ⅓ cup of batter into the hot skillet and swirl the pan so the batter covers the bottom evenly. Cook for 2 to 3 minutes until the pancake turns golden brown around the edges. Gently flip the pancake with a spatula and cook for 2 to 3 minutes until cooked through. Repeat with the remaining batter.

4. Serve the pancakes with the sliced strawberries on top.
**Nutrition Info:**
- Info Per Serving: Calories: 298;Fat: 11.7g;Protein: 11.8g;Carbs: 34.8g.

# Detox Juice

Servings:1
Cooking Time:5 Minutes
**Ingredients:**
- ½ grapefruit
- ½ lemon
- 3 cups cavolo nero
- 1 cucumber
- ¼ cup fresh parsley leaves
- ¼ pineapple, cut into wedges
- ½ green apple
- 1 tsp grated fresh ginger

**Directions:**
1. In a mixer, place the cavolo nero, parsley, cucumber, pineapple, grapefruit, apple, lemon, and ginger and pulse until smooth. Serve in a tall glass.

**Nutrition Info:**
- Info Per Serving: Calories: 255;Fat: 0.9g;Protein: 9.5g;Carbs: 60g.

# Almond Iced-coffee

Servings:1
Cooking Time:5 Minutes
**Ingredients:**
- 1 cup brewed black coffee, warm
- 1 tbsp olive oil
- 1 tsp MCT oil
- 1 tbsp heavy cream
- ½ tsp almond extract
- ½ tsp ground cinnamon

**Directions:**
1. Pour the warm coffee (not hot) into a blender. Add the olive oil, heavy cream, MCT oil, almond extract, and cinnamon. Blend well until smooth and creamy. Drink warm and enjoy.

**Nutrition Info:**
- Info Per Serving: Calories: 128;Fat: 14.2g;Protein: 0g;Carbs: 0g.

# Roasted Tomato Panini

Servings:2
Cooking Time: 3 Hours 6 Minutes
**Ingredients:**
- 2 teaspoons olive oil
- 4 Roma tomatoes, halved
- 4 cloves garlic
- 1 tablespoon Italian seasoning
- Sea salt and freshly ground pepper, to taste
- 4 slices whole-grain bread
- 4 basil leaves
- 2 slices fresh Mozzarella cheese

**Directions:**
1. Preheat the oven to 250ºF. Grease a baking pan with olive oil.
2. Place the tomatoes and garlic in the baking pan, then sprinkle with Italian seasoning, salt, and ground pepper. Toss to coat well.
3. Roast in the preheated oven for 3 hours or until the tomatoes are lightly wilted.
4. Preheat the panini press.
5. Make the panini: Place two slices of bread on a clean work surface, then top them with wilted tomatoes. Sprinkle with basil and spread with Mozzarella cheese. Top them with remaining two slices of bread.
6. Cook the panini for 6 minutes or until lightly browned and the cheese melts. Flip the panini halfway through the cooking.
7. Serve immediately.

**Nutrition Info:**
- Info Per Serving: Calories: 323;Fat: 12.0g;Protein: 17.4g;Carbs: 37.5g.

# Baked Ricotta With Honey Pears

Servings:4
Cooking Time: 22 To 25 Minutes
**Ingredients:**
- 1 container whole-milk ricotta cheese
- 2 large eggs
- ¼ cup whole-wheat pastry flour
- 1 tablespoon sugar
- 1 teaspoon vanilla extract
- ¼ teaspoon ground nutmeg
- 1 pear, cored and diced
- 2 tablespoons water
- 1 tablespoon honey
- Nonstick cooking spray

**Directions:**
1. Preheat the oven to 400ºF. Spray four ramekins with nonstick cooking spray.
2. Beat together the ricotta, eggs, flour, sugar, vanilla, and nutmeg in a large bowl until combined. Spoon the mixture into the ramekins.
3. Bake in the preheated oven for 22 to 25 minutes, or until the ricotta is just set.
4. Meanwhile, in a small saucepan over medium heat, simmer the pear in the water for 10 minutes, or until slightly softened. Remove from the heat, and stir in the honey.
5. Remove the ramekins from the oven and cool slightly on a wire rack. Top the ricotta ramekins with the pear and serve.

**Nutrition Info:**
- Info Per Serving: Calories: 329;Fat: 19.0g;Protein: 17.0g;Carbs: 23.0g.

# Couscous & Cucumber Bowl

Servings:4
Cooking Time:15 Minutes
**Ingredients:**
- 2 tbsp olive oil
- ¾ cup couscous
- 1 cup water
- 1 yellow onion, chopped
- 2 garlic cloves, minced
- 2 cups canned chickpeas
- Salt to taste
- 15 oz canned tomatoes, diced
- 1 cucumber, cut into ribbons
- ½ cup black olives, chopped
- 1 tbsp lemon juice
- 1 tbsp mint leaves, chopped

**Directions:**
1.  Cover the couscous with salted boiling water, cover, and let it sit for about 5 minutes. Then fluff with a fork and set aside.
2.  Warm the olive oil in a skillet over medium heat and sauté onion and garlic for 3 minutes until soft. Stir in chickpeas, salt, and tomatoes for 1-2 minutes. Turn off the heat and mix in olives, couscous, and lemon juice. Transfer to a bowl and top with cucumber ribbons and mint to serve.

**Nutrition Info:**
- Info Per Serving: Calories: 350;Fat: 11g;Protein: 12g;Carbs: 50g.

# Breakfast Pancakes With Berry Sauce

Servings:4
Cooking Time: 10 Minutes
**Ingredients:**
- Pancakes:
- 1 cup almond flour
- 1 teaspoon baking powder
- ¼ teaspoon salt
- 6 tablespoon extra-virgin olive oil, divided
- 2 large eggs, beaten
- Zest and juice of 1 lemon
- ½ teaspoon vanilla extract
- Berry Sauce:
- 1 cup frozen mixed berries
- 1 tablespoon water, plus more as needed
- ½ teaspoon vanilla extract

**Directions:**
1.  Make the Pancakes
2.  In a large bowl, combine the almond flour, baking powder, and salt and stir to break up any clumps.
3.  Add 4 tablespoons olive oil, beaten eggs, lemon zest and juice, and vanilla extract and stir until well mixed.
4.  Heat 1 tablespoon of olive oil in a large skillet. Spoon about 2 tablespoons of batter for each pancake. Cook until

bubbles begin to form, 4 to 5 minutes. Flip and cook for another 2 to 3 minutes. Repeat with the remaining 1 tablespoon of olive oil and batter.
5.  Make the Berry Sauce
6.  Combine the frozen berries, water, and vanilla extract in a small saucepan and heat over medium-high heat for 3 to 4 minutes until bubbly, adding more water as needed. Using the back of a spoon or fork, mash the berries and whisk until smooth.
7.  Serve the pancakes with the berry sauce.

**Nutrition Info:**
- Info Per Serving: Calories: 275;Fat: 26.0g;Protein: 4.0g;Carbs: 8.0g.

# Sweet Banana Pancakes With Strawberries

Servings:4
Cooking Time:15 Minutes
**Ingredients:**
- 2 tbsp olive oil
- 1 cup flour
- 1 cup + 2 tbsp milk
- 2 eggs, beaten
- ⅓ cup honey
- 1 tsp baking soda
- ¼ tsp salt
- 1 sliced banana
- 1 cup sliced strawberries
- 1 tbsp maple syrup

**Directions:**
1.  Mix together the flour, milk, eggs, honey, baking soda, and salt in a bowl. Warm the olive oil in a skillet over medium heat and pour in ⅓ cup of the pancake batter. Cook for 2-3 minutes. Add half of the fresh fruit and flip to cook for 2-3 minutes on the other side until cooked through. Top with the remaining fruit, drizzle with maple syrup and serve.

**Nutrition Info:**
- Info Per Serving: Calories: 415;Fat: 24g;Protein: 12g;Carbs: 46g.

# Poached Egg & Avocado Toasts

Servings:4
Cooking Time:15 Minutes
**Ingredients:**
- 4 bread slices, toasted
- 4 eggs
- 2 avocados, chopped
- ¼ cup chopped fresh cilantro
- 3 tbsp red wine vinegar
- 1 lemon, juiced and zested
- 1 garlic clove, minced
- Salt and black pepper to taste
- 1 tsp hot sauce

**Directions:**

1. Puree avocados, cilantro, lemon juice, lemon zest, garlic, 2 tbsp of vinegar, salt, black pepper, and hot sauce with an immersion blender in a bowl until smooth. Bring to a boil salted water in a pot over high heat.
2. Add in the remaining vinegar and a pinch of salt. Drop the eggs, one at a time, and poach for 2-3 minutes until the whites are set and yolks are cooked. Remove with a perforated spoon to a paper towel to drain. Spread the avocado mash on the bread toasts and top with poached eggs to serve.

**Nutrition Info:**
- Info Per Serving: Calories: 296;Fat: 24.3g;Protein: 8g;Carbs: 14g.

## Roasted Vegetable Panini

Servings:4
Cooking Time: 15 Minutes
**Ingredients:**
- 2 tablespoons extra-virgin olive oil, divided
- 1½ cups diced broccoli
- 1 cup diced zucchini
- ¼ cup diced onion
- ¼ teaspoon dried oregano
- ⅛ teaspoon kosher or sea salt
- ⅛ teaspoon freshly ground black pepper
- 1 jar roasted red peppers, drained and finely chopped
- 2 tablespoons grated Parmesan or Asiago cheese
- 1 cup fresh Mozzarella, sliced
- 1 whole-grain Italian loaf, cut into 4 equal lengths
- Cooking spray

**Directions:**
1. Place a large, rimmed baking sheet in the oven. Preheat the oven to 450ºF with the baking sheet inside.
2. In a large bowl, stir together 1 tablespoon of the oil, broccoli, zucchini, onion, oregano, salt and pepper.
3. Remove the baking sheet from the oven and spritz the baking sheet with cooking spray. Spread the vegetable mixture on the baking sheet and roast for 5 minutes, stirring once halfway through cooking.
4. Remove the baking sheet from the oven. Stir in the red peppers and Parmesan cheese.
5. In a large skillet over medium-high heat, heat the remaining 1 tablespoon of the oil.
6. Cut open each section of bread horizontally, but don't cut all the way through. Fill each with the vegetable mix (about ½ cup), and layer 1 ounce of sliced Mozzarella cheese on top. Close the sandwiches, and place two of them on the skillet. Place a heavy object on top and grill for 2½ minutes. Flip the sandwiches and grill for another 2½ minutes.
7. Repeat the grilling process with the remaining two sandwiches.
8. Serve hot.

**Nutrition Info:**
- Info Per Serving: Calories: 116;Fat: 4.0g;Protein: 12.0g;Carbs: 9.0g.

## Apple & Date Smoothie

Servings:1
Cooking Time:5 Minutes
**Ingredients:**
- 1 apple, peeled and chopped
- ½ cup milk
- 4 dates
- 1 tsp ground cinnamon

**Directions:**
1. In a blender, place the milk, ½ cup of water, dates, cinnamon, and apple. Blitz until smooth. Let chill in the fridge for 30 minutes. Serve in a tall glass.

**Nutrition Info:**
- Info Per Serving: Calories: 486;Fat: 29g;Protein: 4.2g;Carbs: 63g.

## Bell Pepper & Cheese Egg Scramble

Servings:4
Cooking Time:20 Minutes
**Ingredients:**
- ½ cup fresh mozzarella cheese, crumbled
- 2 tsp olive oil
- 1 cup bell peppers, chopped
- 2 garlic cloves, minced
- 6 large eggs, beaten
- Salt to taste
- 2 tbsp fresh cilantro, chopped

**Directions:**
1. Warm the olive oil in a large skillet over medium heat. Add the peppers and sauté for 5 minutes, stirring occasionally. Add the garlic and cook for 1 minute. Stir in the eggs and salt and cook for 2-3 minutes until the eggs begin to set on the bottom. Top with mozzarella cheese and cook the eggs for about 2 more minutes, stirring slowly, until the eggs are soft-set and custardy. Sprinkle with cilantro and serve.

**Nutrition Info:**
- Info Per Serving: Calories: 259;Fat: 16g;Protein: 29g;Carbs: 2g.

## Spinach Cheese Pie

Servings:8
Cooking Time: 25 Minutes
**Ingredients:**
- 2 tablespoons extra-virgin olive oil
- 1 onion, chopped
- 1 pound frozen spinach, thawed
- ¼ teaspoon ground nutmeg
- ¼ teaspoon garlic salt
- ¼ teaspoon freshly ground black pepper
- 4 large eggs, divided
- 1 cup grated Parmesan cheese, divided
- 2 puff pastry doughs, at room temperature
- 4 hard-boiled eggs, halved
- Nonstick cooking spray

**Directions:**

1. Preheat the oven to 350ºF. Spritz a baking sheet with nonstick cooking spray and set aside.

2. Heat a large skillet over medium-high heat. Add the olive oil and onion and sauté for about 5 minutes, stirring occasionally, or until translucent.

3. Squeeze the excess water from the spinach, then add to the skillet and cook, uncovered, so that any excess water from the spinach can evaporate.

4. Season with the nutmeg, garlic salt, and black pepper. Remove from heat and set aside to cool.

5. Beat 3 eggs in a small bowl. Add the beaten eggs and ½ cup of Parmesan cheese to the spinach mixture, stirring well.

6. Roll out the pastry dough on the prepared baking sheet. Layer the spinach mixture on top of the dough, leaving 2 inches around each edge.

7. Once the spinach is spread onto the pastry dough, evenly place the hard-boiled egg halves throughout the pie, then cover with the second pastry dough. Pinch the edges closed.

8. Beat the remaining 1 egg in the bowl. Brush the egg wash over the pastry dough.

9. Bake in the preheated oven for 15 to 20 minutes until golden brown.

10. Sprinkle with the remaining ½ cup of Parmesan cheese. Cool for 5 minutes before cutting and serving.

**Nutrition Info:**

- Info Per Serving: Calories: 417;Fat: 28.0g;Protein: 17.0g;Carbs: 25.0g.

## Egg & Spinach Pie

Servings:8
Cooking Time:30 Minutes
**Ingredients:**

- 2 tbsp olive oil
- 1 onion, chopped
- 1 lb spinach, chopped
- Salt and black pepper to taste
- ¼ tsp ground nutmeg
- 4 large eggs
- 1 cup grated Pecorino cheese
- 2 puff pastry doughs, at room temperature
- 4 hard-boiled eggs, halved

**Directions:**

1. Preheat the oven to 350 °F. Warm the oil in a large skillet over medium heat. Sauté onion for 5 minutes until translucent. Add the spinach and cook for 5 minutes until wilted. Add the garlic salt, pepper, and nutmeg. Set aside to cool.

2. Whish 3 eggs in a small bowl. Pour them over the cooled spinach mixture and sprinkle with ½ cup Pecorino cheese. Roll out one of the pastry doughs on a greased baking sheet.

3. Spread the spinach mix on top, leaving 2 inches around each edge. Top with hard-boiled egg halves, then cover with the second pastry dough. Pinch the edges closed. Beat the

remaining egg into a small bowl. Brush the egg wash over the top of the pie. Bake for 15-20 minutes until golden.

**Nutrition Info:**

- Info Per Serving: Calories: 417;Fat: 28g;Protein: 7g;Carbs: 25g.

## Mozzarella & Olive Cakes

Servings:6
Cooking Time:25 Minutes
**Ingredients:**

- 4 tbsp olive oil, softened
- ¼ cup mozzarella, shredded
- ¼ cup black olives, chopped
- ½ cup milk
- 1 egg, beaten
- 1 cup cornflour
- 1 tsp baking powder
- 3 sun-dried tomatoes, chopped
- 2 tbsp fresh cilantro, chopped
- ¼ tsp kosher salt

**Directions:**

1. Preheat oven to 360 °F. In a bowl, whisk the egg with milk and olive oil. In a separate bowl, mix the salt, cornflour, cilantro, and baking powder. Combine the wet ingredients with the dry mixture. Stir in black olives, tomatoes, and mozzarella cheese. Pour the mixture into greased ramekins and bake for 18-20 minutes or until cooked and golden.

**Nutrition Info:**

- Info Per Serving: Calories: 189;Fat: 11.7g;Protein: 4g;Carbs: 19g.

## Tomato And Egg Scramble

Servings:4
Cooking Time: 20 Minutes
**Ingredients:**

- 2 tablespoons extra-virgin olive oil
- ¼ cup finely minced red onion
- 1½ cups chopped fresh tomatoes
- 2 garlic cloves, minced
- ½ teaspoon dried thyme
- ½ teaspoon dried oregano
- 8 large eggs
- ½ teaspoon salt
- ¼ teaspoon freshly ground black pepper
- ¾ cup crumbled feta cheese
- ¼ cup chopped fresh mint leaves

**Directions:**

1. Heat the olive oil in a large skillet over medium heat.

2. Sauté the red onion and tomatoes in the hot skillet for 10 to 12 minutes, or until the tomatoes are softened.

3. Stir in the garlic, thyme, and oregano and sauté for 2 to 4 minutes, or until the garlic is fragrant.

4. Meanwhile, beat the eggs with the salt and pepper in a medium bowl until frothy.

5. Pour the beaten eggs into the skillet and reduce the heat to low. Scramble
6. for 3 to 4 minutes, stirring constantly, or until the eggs are set.
7. Remove from the heat and scatter with the feta cheese and mint. Serve warm.

**Nutrition Info:**
- Info Per Serving: Calories: 260;Fat: 21.9g;Protein: 10.2g;Carbs: 5.8g.

# Spicy Tofu Tacos With Cherry Tomato Salsa

Servings:4
Cooking Time: 11 Minutes
**Ingredients:**
- Cherry Tomato Salsa:
- ¼ cup sliced cherry tomatoes
- ½ jalapeño, deseeded and sliced
- Juice of 1 lime
- 1 garlic clove, minced
- Sea salt and freshly ground black pepper, to taste
- 2 teaspoons extra-virgin olive oil
- Spicy Tofu Taco Filling:
- 4 tablespoons water, divided
- ½ cup canned black beans, rinsed and drained
- 2 teaspoons fresh chopped chives, divided
- ¾ teaspoon ground cumin, divided
- ¾ teaspoon smoked paprika, divided
- Dash cayenne pepper (optional)
- ¼ teaspoon sea salt
- ¼ teaspoon freshly ground black pepper
- 1 teaspoon extra-virgin olive oil
- 6 ounces firm tofu, drained, rinsed, and pressed
- 4 corn tortillas
- ¼ avocado, sliced
- ¼ cup fresh cilantro

**Directions:**
1. Make the Cherry Tomato Salsa:
2. Combine the ingredients for the salsa in a small bowl. Stir to mix well. Set aside until ready to use.
3. Make the Spicy Tofu Taco Filling:
4. Add 2 tablespoons of water into a saucepan, then add the black beans and sprinkle with 1 teaspoon of chives, ½ teaspoon of cumin, ¼ teaspoon of smoked paprika, and cayenne. Stir to mix well.
5. Cook for 5 minutes over medium heat until heated through, then mash the black beans with the back of a spoon. Turn off the heat and set aside.
6. Add remaining water into a bowl, then add the remaining chives, cumin, and paprika. Sprinkle with cayenne, salt, and black pepper. Stir to mix well. Set aside.
7. Heat the olive oil in a nonstick skillet over medium heat until shimmering.

8. Add the tofu and drizzle with taco sauce, then sauté for 5 minutes or until the seasoning is absorbed. Remove the tofu from the skillet and set aside.
9. Warm the tortillas in the skillet for 1 minutes or until heated through.
10. Transfer the tortillas onto a large plate and top with tofu, mashed black beans, avocado, cilantro, then drizzle the tomato salsa over. Serve immediately.

**Nutrition Info:**
- Info Per Serving: Calories: 240;Fat: 9.0g;Protein: 11.6g;Carbs: 31.6g.

# Warm Bulgur Breakfast Bowls With Fruits

Servings:6
Cooking Time: 15 Minutes
**Ingredients:**
- 2 cups unsweetened almond milk
- 1½ cups uncooked bulgur
- 1 cup water
- ½ teaspoon ground cinnamon
- 2 cups frozen (or fresh, pitted) dark sweet cherries
- 8 dried (or fresh) figs, chopped
- ½ cup chopped almonds
- ¼ cup loosely packed fresh mint, chopped

**Directions:**
1. Combine the milk, bulgur, water, and cinnamon in a medium saucepan, stirring, and bring just to a boil.
2. Cover, reduce the heat to medium-low, and allow to simmer for 10 minutes, or until the liquid is absorbed.
3. Turn off the heat, but keep the pan on the stove, and stir in the frozen cherries (no need to thaw), figs, and almonds. Cover and let the hot bulgur thaw the cherries and partially hydrate the figs, about 1 minute.
4. Fold in the mint and stir to combine, then serve.

**Nutrition Info:**
- Info Per Serving: Calories: 207;Fat: 6.0g;Protein: 8.0g;Carbs: 32.0g.

# Lemon Cardamom Buckwheat Pancakes

Servings:2
Cooking Time:20 Minutes
**Ingredients:**
- ½ cup buckwheat flour
- ½ tsp cardamom
- ½ tsp baking powder
- ½ cup milk
- ¼ cup plain Greek yogurt
- 1 egg
- 1 tsp lemon zest
- 1 tbsp honey

**Directions:**
1. Mix the buckwheat flour, cardamom, and baking powder in a medium bowl. Whisk the milk, yogurt, egg,

lemon zest, and honey in another bowl. Add the wet ingredients to the dry ingredients and stir until the batter is smooth.

2. Spray a frying pan with non-stick cooking oil and cook the pancakes over medium heat until the edges begin to brown. Flip and cook on the other side for 3 more minutes. Serve.

**Nutrition Info:**

- Info Per Serving: Calories: 196;Fat: 6g;Protein: 10g;Carbs: 27g.

## Morning Zinger Smoothie

Servings:2

Cooking Time:5 Minutes

**Ingredients:**

- 1 green apple, chopped
- 2 cups spinach
- 1 avocado, peeled and diced
- 1 tsp honey
- 1 kiwi, peeled
- 2 cups almond milk

**Directions:**

1. Place spinach, apple, avocado, honey, kiwi, and almond milk in a food processor and blend until smooth. Serve chilled.

**Nutrition Info:**

- Info Per Serving: Calories: 170;Fat: 11g;Protein: 3g;Carbs: 22g.

## Crustless Tiropita (greek Cheese Pie)

Servings:6

Cooking Time: 35 To 40 Minutes

**Ingredients:**

- 4 tablespoons extra-virgin olive oil, divided
- ½ cup whole-milk ricotta cheese
- 1¼ cups crumbled feta cheese
- 1 tablespoon chopped fresh dill
- 2 tablespoons chopped fresh mint
- ½ teaspoon lemon zest
- ¼ teaspoon freshly ground black pepper
- 2 large eggs
- ½ teaspoon baking powder

**Directions:**

1. Preheat the oven to 350ºF. Coat the bottom and sides of a baking dish with 2 tablespoons of olive oil. Set aside.

2. Mix together the ricotta and feta cheese in a medium bowl and stir with a fork until well combined. Add the dill, mint, lemon zest, and black pepper and mix well.

3. In a separate bowl, whisk together the eggs and baking powder. Pour the whisked eggs into the bowl of cheese mixture. Blend well.

4. Slowly pour the mixture into the coated baking dish and drizzle with the remaining 2 tablespoons of olive oil.

5. Bake in the preheated oven for about 35 to 40 minutes, or until the pie is browned around the edges and cooked through.

6. Cool for 5 minutes before slicing into wedges.

**Nutrition Info:**

- Info Per Serving: Calories: 181;Fat: 16.6g;Protein: 7.0g;Carbs: 1.8g.

## Avocado Toast With Goat Cheese

Servings:2

Cooking Time: 2 To 3 Minutes

**Ingredients:**

- 2 slices whole-wheat thin-sliced bread
- ½ avocado
- 2 tablespoons crumbled goat cheese
- Salt, to taste

**Directions:**

1. Toast the bread slices in a toaster for 2 to 3 minutes on each side until browned.

2. Scoop out the flesh from the avocado into a medium bowl and mash it with a fork to desired consistency. Spread the mash onto each piece of toast.

3. Scatter the crumbled goat cheese on top and season as needed with salt.

4. Serve immediately.

**Nutrition Info:**

- Info Per Serving: Calories: 136;Fat: 5.9g;Protein: 5.0g;Carbs: 17.5g.

## Easy Pizza Pockets

Servings:2

Cooking Time: 0 Minutes

**Ingredients:**

- ½ cup tomato sauce
- ½ teaspoon oregano
- ½ teaspoon garlic powder
- ½ cup chopped black olives
- 2 canned artichoke hearts, drained and chopped
- 2 ounces pepperoni, chopped
- ½ cup shredded Mozzarella cheese
- 1 whole-wheat pita, halved

**Directions:**

1. In a medium bowl, stir together the tomato sauce, oregano, and garlic powder.

2. Add the olives, artichoke hearts, pepperoni, and cheese. Stir to mix.

3. Spoon the mixture into the pita halves and serve.

**Nutrition Info:**

- Info Per Serving: Calories: 375;Fat: 23.5g;Protein: 17.1g;Carbs: 27.1g.

# Vegetable Mains And Meatless Recipes

## Simple Zoodles

Servings:2
Cooking Time: 5 Minutes
**Ingredients:**
- 2 tablespoons avocado oil
- 2 medium zucchinis, spiralized
- ¼ teaspoon salt
- Freshly ground black pepper, to taste

**Directions:**
1. Heat the avocado oil in a large skillet over medium heat until it shimmers.
2. Add the zucchini noodles, salt, and black pepper to the skillet and toss to coat. Cook for 1 to 2 minutes, stirring constantly, until tender.
3. Serve warm.

**Nutrition Info:**
- Info Per Serving: Calories: 128;Fat: 14.0g;Protein: 0.3g;Carbs: 0.3g.

## Sweet Mustard Cabbage Hash

Servings:4
Cooking Time:30 Minutes
**Ingredients:**
- 1 head Savoy cabbage, shredded
- 3 tbsp olive oil
- 1 onion, finely chopped
- 2 garlic cloves, minced
- ½ tsp fennel seeds
- ¼ cup red wine vinegar
- 1 tbsp mustard powder
- 1 tbsp honey
- Salt and black pepper to taste

**Directions:**
1. Warm olive oil in a pan over medium heat and sauté onion, fennel seeds, cabbage, salt, and pepper for 8-9 minutes.
2. In a bowl, mix vinegar, mustard, and honey; set aside. Sauté garlic in the pan for 30 seconds. Pour in vinegar mixture and cook for 10-15 minutes until the liquid reduces by half.

**Nutrition Info:**
- Info Per Serving: Calories: 181;Fat: 12g;Protein: 3.4g;Carbs: 19g.

## Baked Veggie Medley

Servings:4
Cooking Time:70 Minutes
**Ingredients:**
- 2 tbsp olive oil
- ½ lb green beans, trimmed
- 1 tomato, chopped
- 1 potato, sliced
- ½ tbsp tomato paste
- 2 tbsp chopped fresh parsley
- 1 tsp sweet paprika
- 1 onion, sliced
- 1 cup mushrooms, sliced
- 1 celery stalk, chopped
- 1 red bell pepper, sliced
- 1 eggplant, sliced
- ½ cup vegetable broth
- Salt and black pepper to taste

**Directions:**
1. Preheat oven to 375°F. Warm oil in a skillet over medium heat and sauté onion, bell pepper, celery, and mushrooms for 5 minutes until tender. Stir in paprika and tomato paste for 1 minute. Pour in the vegetable broth and stir. Combine the remaining ingredients in a baking pan and mix in the sautéed vegetable. Bake covered with foil for 40-50 minutes.

**Nutrition Info:**
- Info Per Serving: Calories: 175;Fat: 8g;Protein: 5.2g;Carbs: 25.2g.

## Vegetable And Tofu Scramble

Servings:2
Cooking Time: 10 Minutes
**Ingredients:**
- 2 tablespoons extra-virgin olive oil
- ½ red onion, finely chopped
- 1 cup chopped kale
- 8 ounces mushrooms, sliced
- 8 ounces tofu, cut into pieces
- 2 garlic cloves, minced
- Pinch red pepper flakes
- ½ teaspoon sea salt
- ⅛ teaspoon freshly ground black pepper

**Directions:**
1. Heat the olive oil in a medium nonstick skillet over medium-high heat until shimmering.
2. Add the onion, kale, and mushrooms to the skillet and cook for about 5 minutes, stirring occasionally, or until the vegetables start to brown.
3. Add the tofu and stir-fry for 3 to 4 minutes until softened.
4. Stir in the garlic, red pepper flakes, salt, and black pepper and cook for 30 seconds.
5. Let the mixture cool for 5 minutes before serving.

**Nutrition Info:**
- Info Per Serving: Calories: 233;Fat: 15.9g;Protein: 13.4g;Carbs: 11.9g.

# Garlicky Broccoli Rabe

Servings:4
Cooking Time: 5 To 6 Minutes
**Ingredients:**
- 14 ounces broccoli rabe, trimmed and cut into 1-inch pieces
- 2 teaspoons salt, plus more for seasoning
- Black pepper, to taste
- 2 tablespoons extra-virgin olive oil
- 3 garlic cloves, minced
- ¼ teaspoon red pepper flakes

**Directions:**
1. Bring 3 quarts water to a boil in a large saucepan. Add the broccoli rabe and 2 teaspoons of the salt to the boiling water and cook for 2 to 3 minutes, or until wilted and tender.
2. Drain the broccoli rabe. Transfer to ice water and let sit until chilled. Drain again and pat dry.
3. In a skillet over medium heat, heat the oil and add the garlic and red pepper flakes. Sauté for about 2 minutes, or until the garlic begins to sizzle.
4. Increase the heat to medium-high. Stir in the broccoli rabe and cook for about 1 minute, or until heated through, stirring constantly. Season with salt and pepper.
5. Serve immediately.

**Nutrition Info:**
- Info Per Serving: Calories: 87;Fat: 7.3g;Protein: 3.4g;Carbs: 4.0g.

# Sautéed Spinach And Leeks

Servings:2
Cooking Time: 8 Minutes
**Ingredients:**
- 3 tablespoons olive oil
- 2 garlic cloves, crushed
- 2 leeks, chopped
- 2 red onions, chopped
- 9 ounces fresh spinach
- 1 teaspoon kosher salt
- ½ cup crumbled goat cheese

**Directions:**
1. Coat the bottom of the Instant Pot with the olive oil.
2. Add the garlic, leek, and onions and stir-fry for about 5 minutes, on Sauté mode.
3. Stir in the spinach. Sprinkle with the salt and sauté for an additional 3 minutes, stirring constantly.
4. Transfer to a plate and scatter with the goat cheese before serving.

**Nutrition Info:**
- Info Per Serving: Calories: 447;Fat: 31.2g;Protein: 14.6g;Carbs: 28.7g.

# Zoodles With Beet Pesto

Servings:2
Cooking Time: 50 Minutes
**Ingredients:**
- 1 medium red beet, peeled, chopped
- ½ cup walnut pieces
- ½ cup crumbled goat cheese
- 3 garlic cloves
- 2 tablespoons freshly squeezed lemon juice
- 2 tablespoons plus 2 teaspoons extra-virgin olive oil, divided
- ¼ teaspoon salt
- 4 small zucchinis, spiralized

**Directions:**
1. Preheat the oven to 375°F.
2. Wrap the chopped beet in a piece of aluminum foil and seal well.
3. Roast in the preheated oven for 30 to 40 minutes until tender.
4. Meanwhile, heat a skillet over medium-high heat until hot. Add the walnuts and toast for 5 to 7 minutes, or until fragrant and lightly browned.
5. Remove the cooked beets from the oven and place in a food processor. Add the toasted walnuts, goat cheese, garlic, lemon juice, 2 tablespoons of olive oil, and salt. Pulse until smoothly blended. Set aside.
6. Heat the remaining 2 teaspoons of olive oil in a large skillet over medium heat. Add the zucchini and toss to coat in the oil. Cook for 2 to 3 minutes, stirring gently, or until the zucchini is softened.
7. Transfer the zucchini to a serving plate and toss with the beet pesto, then serve.

**Nutrition Info:**
- Info Per Serving: Calories: 423;Fat: 38.8g;Protein: 8.0g;Carbs: 17.1g.

# Stuffed Portobello Mushroom With Tomatoes

Servings:4
Cooking Time: 15 Minutes
**Ingredients:**
- 4 large portobello mushroom caps
- 3 tablespoons extra-virgin olive oil
- Salt and freshly ground black pepper, to taste
- 4 sun-dried tomatoes
- 1 cup shredded mozzarella cheese, divided
- ½ to ¾ cup low-sodium tomato sauce

**Directions:**
1. Preheat the broiler on high.
2. Arrange the mushroom caps on a baking sheet and drizzle with olive oil. Sprinkle with salt and pepper.
3. Broil for 1o minutes, flipping the mushroom caps halfway through, until browned on the top.

4. Remove from the broil. Spoon 1 tomato, 2 tablespoons of cheese, and 2 to 3 tablespoons of sauce onto each mushroom cap.

5. Return the mushroom caps to the broiler and continue broiling for 2 to 3 minutes.

6. Cool for 5 minutes before serving.

**Nutrition Info:**
- Info Per Serving: Calories: 217;Fat: 15.8g;Protein: 11.2g;Carbs: 11.7g.

## Easy Zucchini Patties

Servings:2
Cooking Time: 5 Minutes
**Ingredients:**
- 2 medium zucchinis, shredded
- 1 teaspoon salt, divided
- 2 eggs
- 2 tablespoons chickpea flour
- 1 tablespoon chopped fresh mint
- 1 scallion, chopped
- 2 tablespoons extra-virgin olive oil

**Directions:**
1. Put the shredded zucchini in a fine-mesh strainer and season with ½ teaspoon of salt. Set aside.

2. Beat together the eggs, chickpea flour, mint, scallion, and remaining ½ teaspoon of salt in a medium bowl.

3. Squeeze the zucchini to drain as much liquid as possible. Add the zucchini to the egg mixture and stir until well incorporated.

4. Heat the olive oil in a large skillet over medium-high heat.

5. Drop the zucchini mixture by spoonful into the skillet. Gently flatten the zucchini with the back of a spatula.

6. Cook for 2 to 3 minutes or until golden brown. Flip and cook for an additional 2 minutes.

7. Remove from the heat and serve on a plate.

**Nutrition Info:**
- Info Per Serving: Calories: 264;Fat: 20.0g;Protein: 9.8g;Carbs: 16.1g.

## Grilled Eggplant "steaks" With Sauce

Servings:6
Cooking Time:20 Minutes
**Ingredients:**
- 2 lb eggplants, sliced lengthways
- 6 tbsp olive oil
- 5 garlic cloves, minced
- 1 tsp dried oregano
- ½ tsp red pepper flakes
- ½ cup Greek yogurt
- 3 tbsp chopped fresh parsley
- 1 tsp grated lemon zest
- 2 tsp lemon juice
- 1 tsp ground cumin

- Salt and black pepper to taste

**Directions:**
1. In a bowl, whisk half of the olive oil, yogurt, parsley, lemon zest and juice, cumin, and salt; set aside until ready to serve. Preheat your grill to High. Rub the eggplant steaks with the remaining olive oil, oregano, salt, and pepper. Grill them for 4-6 minutes per side until browned and tender; transfer to a serving platter. Drizzle yogurt sauce over eggplant.

**Nutrition Info:**
- Info Per Serving: Calories: 112;Fat: 7g;Protein: 2.6g;Carbs: 11.3g.

## Mini Crustless Spinach Quiches

Servings:6
Cooking Time: 20 Minutes
**Ingredients:**
- 2 tablespoons extra-virgin olive oil
- 1 onion, finely chopped
- 2 cups baby spinach
- 2 garlic cloves, minced
- 8 large eggs, beaten
- ¼ cup unsweetened almond milk
- ½ teaspoon sea salt
- ¼ teaspoon freshly ground black pepper
- 1 cup shredded Swiss cheese
- Cooking spray

**Directions:**
1. Preheat the oven to 375ºF. Spritz a 6-cup muffin tin with cooking spray. Set aside.

2. In a large skillet over medium-high heat, heat the olive oil until shimmering. Add the onion and cook for about 4 minutes, or until soft. Add the spinach and cook for about 1 minute, stirring constantly, or until the spinach softens. Add the garlic and sauté for 30 seconds. Remove from the heat and let cool.

3. In a medium bowl, whisk together the eggs, milk, salt and pepper.

4. Stir the cooled vegetables and the cheese into the egg mixture. Spoon the mixture into the prepared muffin tins. Bake for about 15 minutes, or until the eggs are set.

5. Let rest for 5 minutes before serving.

**Nutrition Info:**
- Info Per Serving: Calories: 218;Fat: 17.0g;Protein: 14.0g;Carbs: 4.0g.

## Creamy Sweet Potatoes And Collards

Servings:2
Cooking Time: 35 Minutes
**Ingredients:**
- 1 tablespoon avocado oil
- 3 garlic cloves, chopped
- 1 yellow onion, diced
- ½ teaspoon crushed red pepper flakes

- 1 large sweet potato, peeled and diced
- 2 bunches collard greens, stemmed, leaves chopped into 1-inch squares
- 1 can diced tomatoes with juice
- 1 can red kidney beans or chickpeas, drained and rinsed
- 1½ cups water
- ½ cup unsweetened coconut milk
- Salt and black pepper, to taste

**Directions:**

1. In a large, deep skillet over medium heat, melt the avocado oil.
2. Add the garlic, onion, and red pepper flakes and cook for 3 minutes. Stir in the sweet potato and collards.
3. Add the tomatoes with their juice, beans, water, and coconut milk and mix well. Bring the mixture just to a boil.
4. Reduce the heat to medium-low, cover, and simmer for about 30 minutes, or until softened.
5. Season to taste with salt and pepper and serve.

**Nutrition Info:**

- Info Per Serving: Calories: 445;Fat: 9.6g;Protein: 18.1g;Carbs: 73.1g.

## Chili Vegetable Skillet

Servings:4
Cooking Time:30 Minutes
**Ingredients:**

- 1 cup condensed cream of mushroom soup
- 1 ½ lb eggplants, cut into chunks
- 1 cup cremini mushrooms, sliced
- 4 tbsp olive oil
- 1 carrot, thinly sliced
- 1 can tomatoes
- ½ cup red onion, thinly sliced
- 2 garlic cloves, minced
- 1 tsp fresh rosemary
- 1 tsp chili pepper
- Salt and black pepper to taste
- 2 tbsp parsley, chopped
- ¼ cup Parmesan cheese, grated

**Directions:**

1. Warm the olive oil in a skillet over medium heat. Add in the eggplant and cook until golden brown on all sides, about 5 minutes; set aside. Add in the carrot, onion, and mushrooms and sauté for 4 more minutes to the same skillet. Add in garlic, rosemary, and chili pepper. Cook for another 30-40 seconds. Add in 1 cup of water, cream of mushroom soup, and tomatoes. Bring to a boil and lower the heat; simmer covered for 5 minutes. Mix in sautéed eggplants and parsley and cook for 10 more minutes. Sprinkle with salt and black pepper. Serve topped with Parmesan cheese.

**Nutrition Info:**

- Info Per Serving: Calories: 261;Fat: 18.7g;Protein: 5g;Carbs: 23g.

## Greek-style Eggplants

Servings:4
Cooking Time:25 Minutes
**Ingredients:**

- 1 ½ lb eggplants, sliced into rounds
- ¼ cup olive oil
- Salt and black pepper to taste
- 4 tsp balsamic vinegar
- 1 tbsp capers, minced
- 1 garlic clove, minced
- ½ tsp lemon zest
- ½ tsp fresh oregano, minced
- 3 tbsp fresh mint, minced

**Directions:**

1. Preheat oven to 420ºF. Arrange the eggplant rounds on a greased baking dish and drizzle with some olive oil. Sprinkle with salt and pepper. Bake for 10-12 per side until mahogany lightly charred. Whisk remaining olive oil, balsamic vinegar, capers, garlic, lemon zest, oregano, salt, and pepper together in a bowl. Drizzle the mixture all over the eggplants and sprinkle with mint. Serve and enjoy!

**Nutrition Info:**

- Info Per Serving: Calories: 111;Fat: 9.2g;Protein: 1.2g;Carbs: 7g.

## Veggie-stuffed Portabello Mushrooms

Servings:6
Cooking Time: 24 To 25 Minutes
**Ingredients:**

- 3 tablespoons extra-virgin olive oil, divided
- 1 cup diced onion
- 2 garlic cloves, minced
- 1 large zucchini, diced
- 3 cups chopped mushrooms
- 1 cup chopped tomato
- 1 teaspoon dried oregano
- ¼ teaspoon kosher salt
- ¼ teaspoon crushed red pepper
- 6 large portabello mushrooms, stems and gills removed
- Cooking spray
- 4 ounces fresh Mozzarella cheese, shredded

**Directions:**

1. In a large skillet over medium heat, heat 2 tablespoons of the oil. Add the onion and sauté for 4 minutes. Stir in the garlic and sauté for 1 minute.
2. Stir in the zucchini, mushrooms, tomato, oregano, salt and red pepper. Cook for 10 minutes, stirring constantly. Remove from the heat.
3. Meanwhile, heat a grill pan over medium-high heat.
4. Brush the remaining 1 tablespoon of the oil over the portabello mushroom caps. Place the mushrooms, bottom-side down, on the grill pan. Cover with a sheet of aluminum foil sprayed with nonstick cooking spray. Cook for 5 minutes.

5. Flip the mushroom caps over, and spoon about ½ cup of the cooked vegetable mixture into each cap. Top each with about 2½ tablespoons of the Mozzarella.

6. Cover and grill for 4 to 5 minutes, or until the cheese is melted.

7. Using a spatula, transfer the portabello mushrooms to a plate. Let cool for about 5 minutes before serving.

**Nutrition Info:**
- Info Per Serving: Calories: 111;Fat: 4.0g;Protein: 11.0g;Carbs: 11.0g.

# Asparagus & Mushroom Farro

Servings:2
Cooking Time:40 Minutes
**Ingredients:**
- ½ oz dried porcini mushrooms, soaked
- 2 tbsp olive oil
- 1 cup hot water
- 3 cups vegetable stock
- ½ large onion, minced
- 1 garlic clove
- 1 cup fresh mushrooms, sliced
- ½ cup farro
- ½ cup dry white wine
- ½ tsp dried thyme
- ½ tsp dried marjoram
- 4 oz asparagus, chopped
- 2 tbsp grated Parmesan cheese

**Directions:**
1. Drain the soaked mushrooms, reserving the liquid, and cut them into slices. Warm the olive oil in a saucepan oven over medium heat. Sauté the onion, garlic, and soaked and fresh mushrooms for 8 minutes. Stir in the farro for 1-2 minutes. Add the wine, thyme, marjoram, reserved mushroom liquid, and a ladleful of stock. Bring it to a boil.

2. Lower the heat and cook for about 20 minutes, stirring occasionally and adding another ladleful of stock, until the farro is cooked through but not overcooked. Stir in the asparagus and the remaining stock. Cook for 3-5 more minutes or until the asparagus is softened. Sprinkle with Parmesan cheese and serve warm.

**Nutrition Info:**
- Info Per Serving: Calories: 341;Fat: 16g;Protein: 13g;Carbs: 26g.

# Simple Braised Carrots

Servings:4
Cooking Time:20 Minutes
**Ingredients:**
- 2 tbsp butter
- 1 lb carrots, cut into sticks
- ¾ cup water
- ¼ cup orange juice
- 1 tbsp honey
- Salt and white pepper to taste
- 1 tsp rosemary leaves

**Directions:**
1. Combine all the ingredients, except for the carrots and rosemary, in a heavy saucepan over medium heat and bring to a boil. Add carrots and cover. Turn the heat to a simmer and continue to cook for 5–8 minutes until carrots are soft when pierced with a knife. Remove the carrots to a serving plate. Then, increase heat to high and bring the liquid to a boil. Boil until the liquid has reduced and syrupy, about 4 minutes. Drizzle the sauce over the carrots and sprinkle with rosemary. Serve warm.

**Nutrition Info:**
- Info Per Serving: Calories: 122;Fat: 6g;Protein: 1g;Carbs: 17g.

# Brussels Sprouts Linguine

Servings:4
Cooking Time: 25 Minutes
**Ingredients:**
- 8 ounces whole-wheat linguine
- ⅓ cup plus 2 tablespoons extra-virgin olive oil, divided
- 1 medium sweet onion, diced
- 2 to 3 garlic cloves, smashed
- 8 ounces Brussels sprouts, chopped
- ½ cup chicken stock
- ⅓ cup dry white wine
- ½ cup shredded Parmesan cheese
- 1 lemon, quartered

**Directions:**
1. Bring a large pot of water to a boil and cook the pasta for about 5 minutes, or until al dente. Drain the pasta and reserve 1 cup of the pasta water. Mix the cooked pasta with 2 tablespoons of the olive oil. Set aside.

2. In a large skillet, heat the remaining ⅓ cup of the olive oil over medium heat. Add the onion to the skillet and sauté for about 4 minutes, or until tender. Add the smashed garlic cloves and sauté for 1 minute, or until fragrant.

3. Stir in the Brussels sprouts and cook covered for 10 minutes. Pour in the chicken stock to prevent burning. Once the Brussels sprouts have wilted and are fork-tender, add white wine and cook for about 5 minutes, or until reduced.

4. Add the pasta to the skillet and add the pasta water as needed.

5. Top with the Parmesan cheese and squeeze the lemon over the dish right before eating.

**Nutrition Info:**
- Info Per Serving: Calories: 502;Fat: 31.0g;Protein: 15.0g;Carbs: 50.0g.

# Vegan Lentil Bolognese

Servings:2
Cooking Time: 50 Minutes
**Ingredients:**
- 1 medium celery stalk
- 1 large carrot
- ½ large onion
- 1 garlic clove

- 2 tablespoons olive oil
- 1 can crushed tomatoes
- 1 cup red wine
- ½ teaspoon salt, plus more as needed
- ½ teaspoon pure maple syrup
- 1 cup cooked lentils (prepared from ½ cup dry)

**Directions:**
1. Add the celery, carrot, onion, and garlic to a food processor and process until everything is finely chopped.
2. In a Dutch oven, heat the olive oil over medium-high heat. Add the chopped mixture and sauté for about 10 minutes, stirring occasionally, or until the vegetables are lightly browned.
3. Stir in the tomatoes, wine, salt, and maple syrup and bring to a boil.
4. Once the sauce starts to boil, cover, and reduce the heat to medium-low. Simmer for 30 minutes, stirring occasionally, or until the vegetables are softened.
5. Stir in the cooked lentils and cook for an additional 5 minutes until warmed through.
6. Taste and add additional salt, if needed. Serve warm.

**Nutrition Info:**
- Info Per Serving: Calories: 367;Fat: 15.0g;Protein: 13.7g;Carbs: 44.5g.

# Stuffed Portobello Mushrooms With Spinach

Servings:4
Cooking Time: 20 Minutes
**Ingredients:**
- 8 large portobello mushrooms, stems removed
- 3 teaspoons extra-virgin olive oil, divided
- 1 medium red bell pepper, diced
- 4 cups fresh spinach
- ¼ cup crumbled feta cheese

**Directions:**
1. Preheat the oven to 450ºF.
2. Using a spoon to scoop out the gills of the mushrooms and discard them. Brush the mushrooms with 2 teaspoons of olive oil.
3. Arrange the mushrooms (cap-side down) on a baking sheet. Roast in the preheated oven for 20 minutes.
4. Meantime, in a medium skillet, heat the remaining olive oil over medium heat until it shimmers.
5. Add the bell pepper and spinach and sauté for 8 to 10 minutes, stirring occasionally, or until the spinach is wilted.
6. Remove the mushrooms from the oven to a paper towel-lined plate. Using a spoon to stuff each mushroom with the bell pepper and spinach mixture. Scatter the feta cheese all over.
7. Serve immediately.

**Nutrition Info:**
- Info Per Serving: Calories: 115;Fat: 5.9g;Protein: 7.2g;Carbs: 11.5g.

# Zucchini Ribbons With Ricotta

Servings:4
Cooking Time:10 Minutes
**Ingredients:**
- 3 tbsp olive oil
- 1 garlic clove, minced
- 1 tsp lemon zest
- 1 tbsp lemon juice
- 4 zucchinis, cut into ribbons
- Salt and black pepper to taste
- 2 tbsp chopped fresh parsley
- ½ ricotta cheese, crumbled

**Directions:**
1. Whisk 2 tablespoons oil, garlic, salt, pepper, and lemon zest, and lemon juice in a bowl. Warm the remaining olive oil in a skillet over medium heat. Season the zucchini ribbons with salt and pepper and add them to the skillet; cook for 3-4 minutes per side. Transfer to a serving bowl and drizzle with the dressing, sprinkle with parsley and cheese and serve.

**Nutrition Info:**
- Info Per Serving: Calories: 134;Fat: 2g;Protein: 2g;Carbs: 4g.

# Parmesan Stuffed Zucchini Boats

Servings:4
Cooking Time: 15 Minutes
**Ingredients:**
- 1 cup canned low-sodium chickpeas, drained and rinsed
- 1 cup no-sugar-added spaghetti sauce
- 2 zucchinis
- ¼ cup shredded Parmesan cheese

**Directions:**
1. Preheat the oven to 425ºF.
2. In a medium bowl, stir together the chickpeas and spaghetti sauce.
3. Cut the zucchini in half lengthwise and scrape a spoon gently down the length of each half to remove the seeds.
4. Fill each zucchini half with the chickpea sauce and top with one-quarter of the Parmesan cheese.
5. Place the zucchini halves on a baking sheet and roast in the oven for 15 minutes.
6. Transfer to a plate. Let rest for 5 minutes before serving.

**Nutrition Info:**
- Info Per Serving: Calories: 139;Fat: 4.0g;Protein: 8.0g;Carbs: 20.0g.

# Fried Eggplant Rolls

Servings:4
Cooking Time: 10 Minutes
**Ingredients:**
- 2 large eggplants, trimmed and cut lengthwise into ¼-inch-thick slices
- 1 teaspoon salt
- 1 cup shredded ricotta cheese
- 4 ounces goat cheese, shredded
- ¼ cup finely chopped fresh basil
- ½ teaspoon freshly ground black pepper
- Olive oil spray

**Directions:**
1. Add the eggplant slices to a colander and season with salt. Set aside for 15 to 20 minutes.
2. Mix together the ricotta and goat cheese, basil, and black pepper in a large bowl and stir to combine. Set aside.
3. Dry the eggplant slices with paper towels and lightly mist them with olive oil spray.
4. Heat a large skillet over medium heat and lightly spray it with olive oil spray.
5. Arrange the eggplant slices in the skillet and fry each side for 3 minutes until golden brown.
6. Remove from the heat to a paper towel-lined plate and rest for 5 minutes.
7. Make the eggplant rolls: Lay the eggplant slices on a flat work surface and top each slice with a tablespoon of the prepared cheese mixture. Roll them up and serve immediately.

**Nutrition Info:**
- Info Per Serving: Calories: 254;Fat: 14.9g;Protein: 15.3g;Carbs: 18.6g.

# Roasted Vegetables

Servings:2
Cooking Time: 35 Minutes
**Ingredients:**
- 6 teaspoons extra-virgin olive oil, divided
- 12 to 15 Brussels sprouts, halved
- 1 medium sweet potato, peeled and cut into 2-inch cubes
- 2 cups fresh cauliflower florets
- 1 medium zucchini, cut into 1-inch rounds
- 1 red bell pepper, cut into 1-inch slices
- Salt, to taste

**Directions:**
1. Preheat the oven to 425ºF.
2. Add 2 teaspoons of olive oil, Brussels sprouts, sweet potato, and salt to a large bowl and toss until they are completely coated.
3. Transfer them to a large roasting pan and roast for 10 minutes, or until the Brussels sprouts are lightly browned.
4. Meantime, combine the cauliflower florets with 2 teaspoons of olive oil and salt in a separate bowl.
5. Remove from the oven. Add the cauliflower florets to the roasting pan and roast for 10 minutes more.

6. Meanwhile, toss the zucchini and bell pepper with the remaining olive oil in a medium bowl until well coated. Season with salt.
7. Remove the roasting pan from the oven and stir in the zucchini and bell pepper. Continue roasting for 15 minutes, or until the vegetables are fork-tender.
8. Divide the roasted vegetables between two plates and serve warm.

**Nutrition Info:**
- Info Per Serving: Calories: 333;Fat: 16.8g;Protein: 12.2g;Carbs: 37.6g.

# Baked Vegetable Stew

Servings:6
Cooking Time:70 Minutes
**Ingredients:**
- 1 can diced tomatoes, drained with juice reserved
- 3 tbsp olive oil
- 1 onion, chopped
- 2 tbsp fresh oregano, minced
- 1 tsp paprika
- 4 garlic cloves, minced
- 1 ½ lb green beans, sliced
- 1 lb Yukon Gold potatoes, peeled and chopped
- 1 tbsp tomato paste
- Salt and black pepper to taste
- 3 tbsp fresh basil, chopped

**Directions:**
1. Preheat oven to 360°F. Warm the olive oil in a skillet over medium heat. Sauté onion and garlic for 3 minutes until softened. Stir in oregano and paprika for 30 seconds. Transfer to a baking dish and add in green beans, potatoes, tomatoes, tomato paste, salt, pepper, and 1 ½ cups of water; stir well. Bake for 40-50 minutes. Sprinkle with basil. Serve.

**Nutrition Info:**
- Info Per Serving: Calories: 121;Fat: 0.8g;Protein: 4.2g;Carbs: 26g.

# Chargrilled Vegetable Kebabs

Servings:4
Cooking Time:26 Minutes
**Ingredients:**
- 2 red bell peppers, cut into squares
- 2 zucchinis, sliced into half-moons
- 6 portobello mushroom caps, quartered
- ¼ cup olive oil
- 1 tsp Dijon mustard
- 1 tsp fresh rosemary, chopped
- 1 garlic clove, minced
- Salt and black pepper to taste
- 2 red onions, cut into wedges

**Directions:**
1. Preheat your grill to High. Mix the olive oil, mustard, rosemary, garlic, salt, and pepper in a bowl. Reserve half of the oil mixture for serving. Thread the vegetables in alternating order onto metal skewers and brush them with

35

the remaining oil mixture. Grill them for about 15 minutes until browned, turning occasionally. Transfer the kebabs to a serving platter and remove the skewers. Drizzle with reserved oil mixture and serve.

**Nutrition Info:**

- Info Per Serving: Calories: 96;Fat: 9.2g;Protein: 1.1g;Carbs: 3.6g.

# Roasted Celery Root With Yogurt Sauce

Servings:6
Cooking Time:50 Minutes
**Ingredients:**

- 3 tbsp olive oil
- 3 celery roots, sliced
- Salt and black pepper to taste
- ¼ cup plain yogurt
- ¼ tsp grated lemon zest
- 1 tsp lemon juice
- 1 tsp sesame seeds, toasted
- 1 tsp coriander seeds, crushed
- ¼ tsp dried thyme
- ¼ tsp chili powder
- ¼ cup fresh cilantro, chopped

**Directions:**

1. Preheat oven to 425ºF. Place the celery slices on a baking sheet. Sprinkle them with olive oil, salt, and pepper. Roast for 25-30 minutes. Flip each piece and continue to roast for 10-15 minutes until celery root is very tender and sides touching sheet are browned. Transfer celery to a serving platter.
2. Whisk yogurt, lemon zest and juice, and salt together in a bowl. In a separate bowl, combine sesame seeds, coriander seeds, thyme, chili powder, and salt. Drizzle celery root with yogurt sauce and sprinkle with seed mixture and cilantro.

**Nutrition Info:**

- Info Per Serving: Calories: 75;Fat: 7.5g;Protein: 0.7g;Carbs: 1.8g.

# Tahini & Feta Butternut Squash

Servings:6
Cooking Time:50 Minutes
**Ingredients:**

- 3 lb butternut squash, peeled, halved lengthwise, and seeded
- 3 tbsp olive oil
- Salt and black pepper to taste
- 2 tbsp fresh thyme, chopped
- 1 tbsp tahini
- 1 ½ tsp lemon juice
- 1 tsp honey
- 1 oz feta cheese, crumbled
- ¼ cup pistachios, chopped

**Directions:**

1. Preheat oven to 425ºF. Slice the squash halves crosswise into ½-inch-thick pieces. Toss them with 2 tablespoons of olive oil, salt, and pepper and arrange them on a greased baking sheet in an even layer. Roast for 45-50 minutes or until golden and tender. Transfer squash to a serving platter. Whisk tahini, lemon juice, honey, remaining oil, and salt together in a bowl. Drizzle squash with tahini dressing and sprinkle with feta, pistachios, and thyme. Serve and enjoy!

**Nutrition Info:**

- Info Per Serving: Calories: 212;Fat: 12g;Protein: 4.1g;Carbs: 27g.

# Marinara Zoodles

Servings:4
Cooking Time:65 Minutes
**Ingredients:**

- 2 cans crushed tomatoes
- 2 tbsp olive oil
- 16 oz zucchini noodles
- 1 can diced tomatoes,
- 1 onion, chopped
- 4 garlic cloves, minced
- 1 tbsp dried Italian seasoning
- 1 tsp dried oregano
- Sea salt to taste
- ¼ tsp red pepper flakes
- ¼ cup Romano cheese, grated

**Directions:**

1. Warm olive oil in a pot over medium heat and sauté onion and garlic for 5 minutes, stirring frequently until fragrant. Pour in tomatoes, oregano, Italian seasoning, salt, and red pepper flakes. Bring just to a boil, then lower the heat, and simmer for 10-15 minutes. Stir in the zucchini noodles and cook for 3-4 minutes until the noodles are slightly softened. Scatter with Romano cheese and serve.

**Nutrition Info:**

- Info Per Serving: Calories: 209;Fat: 9g;Protein: 8.1g;Carbs: 27.8g.

# Roasted Artichokes

Servings:4
Cooking Time:50 Minutes
**Ingredients:**

- 4 artichokes, stalk trimmed and large leaves removed
- 2 lemons, freshly squeezed
- 4 tbsp extra-virgin olive oil
- 4 cloves garlic, chopped
- 1 tsp fresh rosemary
- 1 tsp fresh basil
- 1 tsp fresh parsley
- 1 tsp fresh oregano
- Salt and black pepper to taste
- 1 tsp red pepper flakes
- 1 tsp paprika

**Directions:**

1. Preheat oven to 395°F. In a small bowl, thoroughly combine the garlic with herbs and spices; set aside. Cut the artichokes in half vertically and scoop out the fibrous choke to expose the heart with a teaspoon.

2. Rub the lemon juice all over the entire surface of the artichoke halves. Arrange them on a parchment-lined baking dish, cut side up, and brush them evenly with olive oil. Stuff the cavities with the garlic/herb mixture. Cover them with aluminum foil and bake for 30 minutes. Discard the foil and bake for another 10 minutes until lightly charred. Serve.

**Nutrition Info:**

- Info Per Serving: Calories: 220;Fat: 14g;Protein: 6g;Carbs: 21g.

# Zoodles With Walnut Pesto

Servings:4

Cooking Time: 10 Minutes

**Ingredients:**

- 4 medium zucchinis, spiralized
- ¼ cup extra-virgin olive oil, divided
- 1 teaspoon minced garlic, divided
- ½ teaspoon crushed red pepper
- ¼ teaspoon freshly ground black pepper, divided
- ¼ teaspoon kosher salt, divided
- 2 tablespoons grated Parmesan cheese, divided
- 1 cup packed fresh basil leaves
- ¾ cup walnut pieces, divided

**Directions:**

1. In a large bowl, stir together the zoodles, 1 tablespoon of the olive oil, ½ teaspoon of the minced garlic, red pepper, ⅛ teaspoon of the black pepper and ⅛ teaspoon of the salt. Set aside.

2. Heat ½ tablespoon of the oil in a large skillet over medium-high heat. Add half of the zoodles to the skillet and cook for 5 minutes, stirring constantly. Transfer the cooked zoodles into a bowl. Repeat with another ½ tablespoon of the oil and the remaining zoodles. When done, add the cooked zoodles to the bowl.

3. Make the pesto: In a food processor, combine the remaining ½ teaspoon of the minced garlic, ⅛ teaspoon of the black pepper and ⅛ teaspoon of the salt, 1 tablespoon of the Parmesan, basil leaves and ¼ cup of the walnuts. Pulse until smooth and then slowly drizzle the remaining 2 tablespoons of the oil into the pesto. Pulse again until well combined.

4. Add the pesto to the zoodles along with the remaining 1 tablespoon of the Parmesan and the remaining ½ cup of the walnuts. Toss to coat well.

5. Serve immediately.

**Nutrition Info:**

- Info Per Serving: Calories: 166;Fat: 16.0g;Protein: 4.0g;Carbs: 3.0g.

# Sautéed Cabbage With Parsley

Servings:4

Cooking Time: 12 To 14 Minutes

**Ingredients:**

- 1 small head green cabbage, cored and sliced thin
- 2 tablespoons extra-virgin olive oil, divided
- 1 onion, halved and sliced thin
- ¾ teaspoon salt, divided
- ¼ teaspoon black pepper
- ¼ cup chopped fresh parsley
- 1½ teaspoons lemon juice

**Directions:**

1. Place the cabbage in a large bowl with cold water. Let sit for 3 minutes. Drain well.

2. Heat 1 tablespoon of the oil in a skillet over medium-high heat until shimmering. Add the onion and ¼ teaspoon of the salt and cook for 5 to 7 minutes, or until softened and lightly browned. Transfer to a bowl.

3. Heat the remaining 1 tablespoon of the oil in now-empty skillet over medium-high heat until shimmering. Add the cabbage and sprinkle with the remaining ½ teaspoon of the salt and black pepper. Cover and cook for about 3 minutes, without stirring, or until cabbage is wilted and lightly browned on bottom.

4. Stir and continue to cook for about 4 minutes, uncovered, or until the cabbage is crisp-tender and lightly browned in places, stirring once halfway through cooking. Off heat, stir in the cooked onion, parsley and lemon juice.

5. Transfer to a plate and serve.

**Nutrition Info:**

- Info Per Serving: Calories: 117;Fat: 7.0g;Protein: 2.7g;Carbs: 13.4g.

# Cauliflower Rice Risotto With Mushrooms

Servings:4

Cooking Time: 10 Minutes

**Ingredients:**

- 1 teaspoon extra-virgin olive oil
- ½ cup chopped portobello mushrooms
- 4 cups cauliflower rice
- ½ cup half-and-half
- ¼ cup low-sodium vegetable broth
- 1 cup shredded Parmesan cheese

**Directions:**

1. In a medium skillet, heat the olive oil over medium-low heat until shimmering.

2. Add the mushrooms and stir-fry for 3 minutes.

3. Stir in the cauliflower rice, half-and-half, and vegetable broth. Cover and bring to a boil over high heat for 5 minutes, stirring occasionally.

4. Add the Parmesan cheese and stir to combine. Continue cooking for an additional 3 minutes until the cheese is melted.

5. Divide the mixture into four bowls and serve warm.

* Info Per Serving: Calories: 167;Fat: 10.7g;Protein: 12.1g;Carbs: 8.1g.

# Zucchini Crisp

Servings:2
Cooking Time: 20 Minutes
**Ingredients:**
* 4 zucchinis, sliced into ½-inch rounds
* ½ cup unsweetened almond milk
* 1 teaspoon fresh lemon juice
* 1 teaspoon arrowroot powder
* ½ teaspoon salt, divided
* ½ cup whole wheat bread crumbs
* ¼ cup nutritional yeast
* ¼ cup hemp seeds
* ½ teaspoon garlic powder
* ¼ teaspoon crushed red pepper
* ¼ teaspoon black pepper

**Directions:**
1. Preheat the oven to 375ºF. Line two baking sheets with parchment paper and set aside.
2. Put the zucchini in a medium bowl with the almond milk, lemon juice, arrowroot powder, and ¼ teaspoon of salt. Stir to mix well.
3. In a large bowl with a lid, thoroughly combine the bread crumbs, nutritional yeast, hemp seeds, garlic powder, crushed red pepper and black pepper. Add the zucchini in batches and shake until the slices are evenly coated.
4. Arrange the zucchini on the prepared baking sheets in a single layer.
5. Bake in the preheated oven for about 20 minutes, or until the zucchini slices are golden brown.
6. Season with the remaining ¼ teaspoon of salt before serving.

**Nutrition Info:**
* Info Per Serving: Calories: 255;Fat: 11.3g;Protein: 8.6g;Carbs: 31.9g.

# Garlicky Zucchini Cubes With Mint

Servings:4
Cooking Time: 10 Minutes
**Ingredients:**
* 3 large green zucchinis, cut into ½-inch cubes
* 3 tablespoons extra-virgin olive oil
* 1 large onion, chopped
* 3 cloves garlic, minced
* 1 teaspoon salt
* 1 teaspoon dried mint

**Directions:**
1. Heat the olive oil in a large skillet over medium heat.
2. Add the onion and garlic and sauté for 3 minutes, stirring constantly, or until softened.
3. Stir in the zucchini cubes and salt and cook for 5 minutes, or until the zucchini is browned and tender.

4. Add the mint to the skillet and toss to combine, then continue cooking for 2 minutes.
5. Serve warm.

**Nutrition Info:**
* Info Per Serving: Calories: 146;Fat: 10.6g;Protein: 4.2g;Carbs: 11.8g.

# Tradicional Matchuba Green Beans

Servings:4
Cooking Time:15 Minutes
**Ingredients:**
* 1 ¼ lb narrow green beans, trimmed
* 3 tbsp butter, melted
* 1 cup Moroccan matbucha
* 2 green onions, chopped
* Salt and black pepper to taste

**Directions:**
1. Steam the green beans in a pot for 5-6 minutes until tender. Remove to a bowl, reserving the cooking liquid. In a skillet over medium heat, melt the butter. Add in green onions, salt, and black pepper and cook until fragrant. Lower the heat and put in the green beans along with some of the reserved water. Simmer for 3-4 minutes. Serve the green beans with the Sabra Moroccan matbucha as a dip.

**Nutrition Info:**
* Info Per Serving: Calories: 125;Fat: 8.6g;Protein: 2.2g;Carbs: 9g.

# Homemade Vegetarian Moussaka

Servings:4
Cooking Time:80 Minutes
**Ingredients:**
* 2 tbsp olive oil
* 1 yellow onion, chopped
* 2 garlic cloves, chopped
* 2 eggplants, halved
* ½ cup vegetable broth
* Salt and black pepper to taste
* ½ tsp paprika
* ¼ cup parsley, chopped
* 1 tsp basil, chopped
* 1 tsp hot sauce
* 1 tomato, chopped
* 2 tbsp tomato puree
* 6 Kalamata olives, chopped
* ½ cup feta cheese, crumbled

**Directions:**
1. Preheat oven to 360ºF. Remove the tender center part of the eggplants and chop it. Arrange the eggplant halves on a baking tray and drizzle with some olive oil. Roast for 35-40 minutes.
2. Warm the remaining olive oil in a skillet over medium heat and add eggplant flesh, onion, and garlic and sauté for 5 minutes until tender. Stir in the vegetable broth, salt, pepper, basil, hot sauce, paprika, tomato, and tomato puree. Lower the heat and simmer for 10-15 minutes. Once the eggplants

are ready, remove them from the oven and fill them with the mixture. Top with Kalamata olives and feta cheese. Return to the oven and bake for 10-15 minutes. Sprinkle with parsley.

**Nutrition Info:**
- Info Per Serving: Calories: 223;Fat: 14g;Protein: 6.9g;Carbs: 23g.

# Cauliflower Hash With Carrots

Servings:4
Cooking Time: 10 Minutes
**Ingredients:**
- 3 tablespoons extra-virgin olive oil
- 1 large onion, chopped
- 1 tablespoon minced garlic
- 2 cups diced carrots
- 4 cups cauliflower florets
- ½ teaspoon ground cumin
- 1 teaspoon salt

**Directions:**
1. In a large skillet, heat the olive oil over medium heat.
2. Add the onion and garlic and sauté for 1 minute. Stir in the carrots and stir-fry for 3 minutes.
3. Add the cauliflower florets, cumin, and salt and toss to combine.
4. Cover and cook for 3 minutes until lightly browned. Stir well and cook, uncovered, for 3 to 4 minutes, until softened.
5. Remove from the heat and serve warm.

**Nutrition Info:**
- Info Per Serving: Calories: 158;Fat: 10.8g;Protein: 3.1g;Carbs: 14.9g.

# Tomatoes Filled With Tabbouleh

Servings:4
Cooking Time:25 Minutes
**Ingredients:**
- 3 tbsp olive oil, divided
- 8 medium tomatoes
- ½ cup water
- ½ cup bulgur wheat
- 1 ½ cups minced parsley
- ⅓ cup minced fresh mint
- 2 scallions, chopped
- 1 tsp sumac
- Salt and black pepper to taste
- 1 lemon, zested

**Directions:**
1. Place the bulgur wheat and 2 cups of salted water in a pot and bring to a boil. Lower the heat and simmer for 10 minutes or until tender. Remove the pot from the heat and cover with a lid. Let it sit for 15 minutes.
2. Preheat the oven to 400ºF. Slice off the top of each tomato and scoop out the pulp and seeds using a spoon into a sieve set over a bowl. Drain and discard any excess liquid; chop the remaining pulp and place it in a large mixing bowl.

Add in parsley, mint, scallions, sumac, lemon zest, lemon juice, bulgur, pepper, and salt, and mix well.
3. Spoon the filling into the tomatoes and place the lids on top. Drizzle with olive oil and bake for 15-20 minutes until the tomatoes are tender. Serve and enjoy!

**Nutrition Info:**
- Info Per Serving: Calories: 160;Fat: 7g;Protein: 5g;Carbs: 22g.

# Eggplant And Zucchini Gratin

Servings:6
Cooking Time: 19 Minutes
**Ingredients:**
- 2 large zucchinis, finely chopped
- 1 large eggplant, finely chopped
- ¼ teaspoon kosher salt
- ¼ teaspoon freshly ground black pepper
- 3 tablespoons extra-virgin olive oil, divided
- ¾ cup unsweetened almond milk
- 1 tablespoon all-purpose flour
- ⅓ cup plus 2 tablespoons grated Parmesan cheese, divided
- 1 cup chopped tomato
- 1 cup diced fresh Mozzarella
- ¼ cup fresh basil leaves

**Directions:**
1. Preheat the oven to 425ºF.
2. In a large bowl, toss together the zucchini, eggplant, salt and pepper.
3. In a large skillet over medium-high heat, heat 1 tablespoon of the oil. Add half of the veggie mixture to the skillet. Stir a few times, then cover and cook for about 4 minutes, stirring occasionally. Pour the cooked veggies into a baking dish. Place the skillet back on the heat, add 1 tablespoon of the oil and repeat with the remaining veggies. Add the veggies to the baking dish.
4. Meanwhile, heat the milk in the microwave for 1 minute. Set aside.
5. Place a medium saucepan over medium heat. Add the remaining 1 tablespoon of the oil and flour to the saucepan. Whisk together until well blended.
6. Slowly pour the warm milk into the saucepan, whisking the entire time. Continue to whisk frequently until the mixture thickens a bit. Add ⅓ cup of the Parmesan cheese and whisk until melted. Pour the cheese sauce over the vegetables in the baking dish and mix well.
7. Fold in the tomatoes and Mozzarella cheese. Roast in the oven for 10 minutes, or until the gratin is almost set and not runny.
8. Top with the fresh basil leaves and the remaining 2 tablespoons of the Parmesan cheese before serving.

**Nutrition Info:**
- Info Per Serving: Calories: 122;Fat: 5.0g;Protein: 10.0g;Carbs: 11.0g.

## Sautéed Mushrooms With Garlic & Parsley

Servings:6
Cooking Time:15 Minutes
**Ingredients:**

- 3 tbsp butter
- 2 lb cremini mushrooms, sliced
- 2 tbsp garlic, minced
- Salt and black pepper to taste
- 1 tbsp fresh parsley, chopped

**Directions:**

1. Melt the butter in a skillet over medium heat. Cook the garlic for 1-2 minutes until soft. Stir in the mushrooms and season with salt. Sauté for 7-8 minutes, stirring often. Remove to a serving dish. Top with pepper and parsley to serve.

**Nutrition Info:**

- Info Per Serving: Calories: 183;Fat: 9g;Protein: 8.9g;Carbs: 10.1g.

## Creamy Polenta With Mushrooms

Servings:2
Cooking Time: 30 Minutes
**Ingredients:**

- ½ ounce dried porcini mushrooms (optional but recommended)
- 2 tablespoons olive oil
- 1 pound baby bella (cremini) mushrooms, quartered
- 1 large shallot, minced
- 1 garlic clove, minced
- 1 tablespoon flour
- 2 teaspoons tomato paste
- ½ cup red wine
- 1 cup mushroom stock (or reserved liquid from soaking the porcini mushrooms, if using)
- ½ teaspoon dried thyme
- 1 fresh rosemary sprig
- 1½ cups water
- ½ teaspoon salt
- ⅓ cup instant polenta
- 2 tablespoons grated Parmesan cheese

**Directions:**

1. If using the dried porcini mushrooms, soak them in 1 cup of hot water for about 15 minutes to soften them. When they're softened, scoop them out of the water, reserving the soaking liquid. Mince the porcini mushrooms.
2. Heat the olive oil in a large sauté pan over medium-high heat. Add the mushrooms, shallot, and garlic, and sauté for 10 minutes, or until the vegetables are wilted and starting to caramelize.
3. Add the flour and tomato paste, and cook for another 30 seconds. Add the red wine, mushroom stock or porcini soaking liquid, thyme, and rosemary. Bring the mixture to a boil, stirring constantly until it thickens. Reduce the heat and let it simmer for 10 minutes.

4. Meanwhile, bring the water to a boil in a saucepan and add salt.
5. Add the instant polenta and stir quickly while it thickens. Stir in the Parmesan cheese. Taste and add additional salt, if needed. Serve warm.

**Nutrition Info:**

- Info Per Serving: Calories: 450;Fat: 16.0g;Protein: 14.1g;Carbs: 57.8g.

## Eggplant Rolls In Tomato Sauce

Servings:4
Cooking Time:60 Minutes
**Ingredients:**

- 2 tbsp olive oil
- 1 ½ cups ricotta cheese
- 2 cans diced tomatoes
- 1 shallot, finely chopped
- 2 garlic cloves, minced
- 1 tbsp Italian seasoning
- 1 tsp dried oregano
- 2 eggplants
- ½ cup grated mozzarella
- Salt to taste
- ¼ tsp red pepper flakes

**Directions:**

1. Preheat oven to 350ºF. Warm olive oil in a pot over medium heat and sauté shallot and garlic for 3 minutes until tender and fragrant. Mix in tomatoes, oregano, Italian seasoning, salt, and red flakes and simmer for 6 minutes.
2. Cut the eggplants lengthwise into 1,5-inch slices and season with salt. Grill them for 2-3 minutes per side until softened. Place them on a plate and spoon 2 tbsp of ricotta cheese. Wrap them and arrange on a greased baking dish. Pour over the sauce and scatter with the mozzarella cheese. Bake for 15-20 minutes until golden-brown and bubbling.

**Nutrition Info:**

- Info Per Serving: Calories: 362;Fat: 17g;Protein: 19g;Carbs: 38g.

## Zucchini And Artichokes Bowl With Farro

Servings:4
Cooking Time: 10 Minutes
**Ingredients:**

- ⅓ cup extra-virgin olive oil
- ⅓ cup chopped red onions
- ½ cup chopped red bell pepper
- 2 garlic cloves, minced
- 1 cup zucchini, cut into ½-inch-thick slices
- ½ cup coarsely chopped artichokes
- ½ cup canned chickpeas, drained and rinsed
- 3 cups cooked farro
- Salt and freshly ground black pepper, to taste
- ½ cup crumbled feta cheese, for serving (optional)
- ¼ cup sliced olives, for serving (optional)

- 2 tablespoons fresh basil, chiffonade, for serving (optional)
- 3 tablespoons balsamic vinegar, for serving (optional)

**Directions:**

1. Heat the olive oil in a large skillet over medium heat until it shimmers.
2. Add the onions, bell pepper, and garlic and sauté for 5 minutes, stirring occasionally, until softened.
3. Stir in the zucchini slices, artichokes, and chickpeas and sauté for about 5 minutes until slightly tender.
4. Add the cooked farro and toss to combine until heated through. Sprinkle the salt and pepper to season.
5. Divide the mixture into bowls. Top each bowl evenly with feta cheese, olive slices, and basil and sprinkle with the balsamic vinegar, if desired.

**Nutrition Info:**

- Info Per Serving: Calories: 366;Fat: 19.9g;Protein: 9.3g;Carbs: 50.7g.

## Buttery Garlic Green Beans

Servings:6
Cooking Time:25 Minutes

**Ingredients:**

- 2 tbsp butter
- 1 lb green beans, trimmed
- 4 cups water
- 6 garlic cloves, minced
- 1 shallot, chopped
- Celery salt to taste
- ½ tsp red pepper flakes

**Directions:**

1. Pour 4 cups of water in a pot over high heat and bring to a boil. Cut the green beans in half crosswise. Reduce the heat and add in the green beans. Simmer for 6-8 minutes until crisp-tender but still vibrant green. Drain beans and set aside.
2. Melt the butter in a pan over medium heat and sauté garlic and shallot for 3 minutes until the garlic is slightly browned and fragrant. Stir in the beans and season with celery salt. Cook for 2–3 minutes. Serve topped with red pepper flakes.

**Nutrition Info:**

- Info Per Serving: Calories: 65;Fat: 4g;Protein: 2g;Carbs: 7g.

## Stir-fried Kale With Mushrooms

Servings:4
Cooking Time:10 Minutes

**Ingredients:**

- 1 cup cremini mushrooms, sliced
- 4 tbsp olive oil
- 1 small red onion, chopped
- 2 cloves garlic, thinly sliced
- 1 ½ lb curly kale
- 2 tomatoes, chopped
- 1 tsp dried oregano

- 1 tsp dried basil
- ½ tsp dried rosemary
- ½ tsp dried thyme
- Salt and black pepper to taste

**Directions:**

1. Warm the olive oil in a saucepan over medium heat. Sauté the onion and garlic for about 3 minutes or until they are softened. Add in the mushrooms, kale, and tomatoes, stirring to promote even cooking. Turn the heat to a simmer, add in the spices and cook for 5-6 minutes until the kale wilt.

**Nutrition Info:**

- Info Per Serving: Calories: 221;Fat: 16g;Protein: 9g;Carbs: 19g.

## Moroccan Tagine With Vegetables

Servings:2
Cooking Time: 40 Minutes

**Ingredients:**

- 2 tablespoons olive oil
- ½ onion, diced
- 1 garlic clove, minced
- 2 cups cauliflower florets
- 1 medium carrot, cut into 1-inch pieces
- 1 cup diced eggplant
- 1 can whole tomatoes with their juices
- 1 can chickpeas, drained and rinsed
- 2 small red potatoes, cut into 1-inch pieces
- 1 cup water
- 1 teaspoon pure maple syrup
- ½ teaspoon cinnamon
- ½ teaspoon turmeric
- 1 teaspoon cumin
- ½ teaspoon salt
- 1 to 2 teaspoons harissa paste

**Directions:**

1. In a Dutch oven, heat the olive oil over medium-high heat. Sauté the onion for 5 minutes, stirring occasionally, or until the onion is translucent.
2. Stir in the garlic, cauliflower florets, carrot, eggplant, tomatoes, and potatoes. Using a wooden spoon or spatula to break up the tomatoes into smaller pieces.
3. Add the chickpeas, water, maple syrup, cinnamon, turmeric, cumin, and salt and stir to incorporate. Bring the mixture to a boil.
4. Once it starts to boil, reduce the heat to medium-low. Stir in the harissa paste, cover, allow to simmer for about 40 minutes, or until the vegetables are softened. Taste and adjust seasoning as needed.
5. Let the mixture cool for 5 minutes before serving.

**Nutrition Info:**

- Info Per Serving: Calories: 293;Fat: 9.9g;Protein: 11.2g;Carbs: 45.5g.

## Garlic-butter Asparagus With Parmesan

Servings: 2
Cooking Time: 8 Minutes
**Ingredients:**

- 1 cup water
- 1 pound asparagus, trimmed
- 2 cloves garlic, chopped
- 3 tablespoons almond butter
- Salt and ground black pepper, to taste
- 3 tablespoons grated Parmesan cheese

**Directions:**

1. Pour the water into the Instant Pot and insert a trivet.
2. Put the asparagus on a tin foil add the butter and garlic. Season to taste with salt and pepper.
3. Fold over the foil and seal the asparagus inside so the foil doesn't come open. Arrange the asparagus on the trivet.
4. Secure the lid. Select the Manual mode and set the cooking time for 8 minutes at High Pressure.
5. Once cooking is complete, do a quick pressure release. Carefully open the lid.
6. Unwrap the foil packet and serve sprinkled with the Parmesan cheese.

**Nutrition Info:**

- Info Per Serving: Calories: 243;Fat: 15.7g;Protein: 12.3g;Carbs: 15.3g.

## Cauliflower Cakes With Goat Cheese

Servings: 4
Cooking Time: 50 Minutes
**Ingredients:**

- ¼ cup olive oil
- 10 oz cauliflower florets
- 1 tsp ground turmeric
- 1 tsp ground coriander
- Salt and black pepper to taste
- ½ tsp ground mustard seeds
- 4 oz Goat cheese, softened
- 2 scallions, sliced thin
- 1 large egg, lightly beaten
- 2 garlic cloves, minced
- 1 tsp grated lemon zest
- 4 lemon wedges
- ¼ cup flour

**Directions:**

1. Preheat oven to 420°F. In a bowl, whisk 1 tablespoon oil, turmeric, coriander, salt, ground mustard, and pepper. Add in the cauliflower and toss to coat. Transfer to a greased baking sheet and spread it in a single layer. Roast for 20-25 minutes until cauliflower is well browned and tender. Transfer the cauliflower to a large bowl and mash it coarsely with a potato masher. Stir in Goat cheese, scallions, egg, garlic, and lemon zest until well combined. Sprinkle flour over cauliflower mixture and stir to incorporate. Shape the mixture into 10-12 cakes and place them on a sheet pan. Chill to firm, about 30 minutes. Warm the remaining olive oil in a skillet over medium heat. Fry the cakes for 5-6 minutes on each side until deep golden brown and crisp. Serve with lemon wedges.

**Nutrition Info:**

- Info Per Serving: Calories: 320;Fat: 25g;Protein: 13g;Carbs: 12g.

## Baked Tomatoes And Chickpeas

Servings: 4
Cooking Time: 40 To 45 Minutes
**Ingredients:**

- 1 tablespoon extra-virgin olive oil
- ½ medium onion, chopped
- 3 garlic cloves, chopped
- ¼ teaspoon ground cumin
- 2 teaspoons smoked paprika
- 2 cans chickpeas, drained and rinsed
- 4 cups halved cherry tomatoes
- ½ cup plain Greek yogurt, for serving
- 1 cup crumbled feta cheese, for serving

**Directions:**

1. Preheat the oven to 425ºF.
2. Heat the olive oil in an ovenproof skillet over medium heat.
3. Add the onion and garlic and sauté for about 5 minutes, stirring occasionally, or until tender and fragrant.
4. Add the paprika and cumin and cook for 2 minutes. Stir in the chickpeas and tomatoes and allow to simmer for 5 to 10 minutes.
5. Transfer the skillet to the preheated oven and roast for 25 to 30 minutes, or until the mixture bubbles and thickens.
6. Remove from the oven and serve topped with yogurt and crumbled feta cheese.

**Nutrition Info:**

- Info Per Serving: Calories: 411;Fat: 14.9g;Protein: 20.2g;Carbs: 50.7g.

# Beans , Grains, And Pastas Recipes

## Instant Pot Pork With Rice

Servings:4
Cooking Time:35 Minutes
**Ingredients:**
- 3 tbsp olive oil
- 1 lb pork stew meat, cubed
- Salt and black pepper to taste
- 2 chicken broth
- 1 leek, sliced
- 1 onion, chopped
- 1 carrot, sliced
- 1 cup brown rice
- 2 garlic cloves, minced
- 2 tbsp cilantro, chopped

**Directions:**
1. Set your Instant Pot to Sauté and heat the olive oil. Place in pork and cook for 4-5 minutes, stirring often. Add in onion, leek, garlic, and carrot and sauté for 3 more minutes. Stir in brown rice for 1 minute and pour in chicken broth; return the pork. Lock the lid in place, select Manual, and cook for 20 minutes on High. When done, do a quick pressure release. Adjust the seasoning and serve topped with cilantro.

**Nutrition Info:**
- Info Per Serving: Calories: 310;Fat: 16g;Protein: 23g;Carbs: 18g.

## Lemony Farro And Avocado Bowl

Servings:4
Cooking Time: 25 Minutes
**Ingredients:**
- 1 tablespoon plus 2 teaspoons extra-virgin olive oil, divided
- ½ medium onion, chopped
- 1 carrot, shredded
- 2 garlic cloves, minced
- 1 cup pearled farro
- 2 cups low-sodium vegetable soup
- 2 avocados, peeled, pitted, and sliced
- Zest and juice of 1 small lemon
- ¼ teaspoon sea salt

**Directions:**
1. Heat 1 tablespoon of olive oil in a saucepan over medium-high heat until shimmering.
2. Add the onion and sauté for 5 minutes or until translucent.
3. Add the carrot and garlic and sauté for 1 minute or until fragrant.
4. Add the farro and pour in the vegetable soup. Bring to a boil over high heat. Reduce the heat to low. Put the lid on and simmer for 20 minutes or until the farro is al dente.

5. Transfer the farro in a large serving bowl, then fold in the avocado slices. Sprinkle with lemon zest and salt, then drizzle with lemon juice and 2 teaspoons of olive oil.
6. Stir to mix well and serve immediately.

**Nutrition Info:**
- Info Per Serving: Calories: 210;Fat: 11.1g;Protein: 4.2g;Carbs: 27.9g.

## Roasted Butternut Squash And Zucchini With Penne

Servings:6
Cooking Time: 30 Minutes
**Ingredients:**
- 1 large zucchini, diced
- 1 large butternut squash, peeled and diced
- 1 large yellow onion, chopped
- 2 tablespoons extra-virgin olive oil
- 1 teaspoon paprika
- ½ teaspoon garlic powder
- ½ teaspoon sea salt
- ½ teaspoon freshly ground black pepper
- 1 pound whole-grain penne
- ½ cup dry white wine
- 2 tablespoons grated Parmesan cheese

**Directions:**
1. Preheat the oven to 400ºF. Line a baking sheet with aluminum foil.
2. Combine the zucchini, butternut squash, and onion in a large bowl. Drizzle with olive oil and sprinkle with paprika, garlic powder, salt, and ground black pepper. Toss to coat well.
3. Spread the vegetables in the single layer on the baking sheet, then roast in the preheated oven for 25 minutes or until the vegetables are tender.
4. Meanwhile, bring a pot of water to a boil, then add the penne and cook for 14 minutes or until al dente. Drain the penne through a colander.
5. Transfer ½ cup of roasted vegetables in a food processor, then pour in the dry white wine. Pulse until smooth.
6. Pour the puréed vegetables in a nonstick skillet and cook with penne over medium-high heat for a few minutes to heat through.
7. Transfer the penne with the purée on a large serving plate, then spread the remaining roasted vegetables and Parmesan on top before serving.

**Nutrition Info:**
- Info Per Serving: Calories: 340;Fat: 6.2g;Protein: 8.0g;Carbs: 66.8g.

# Authentic Fettuccine A La Puttanesca

Servings:4
Cooking Time:20 Minutes
**Ingredients:**

- 2 tbsp extra-virgin olive oil
- 20 Kalamata olives, chopped
- ¼ cup fresh basil, chopped
- 4 garlic cloves, minced
- 2 anchovy fillets, chopped
- ¼ tsp red pepper flakes
- 3 tbsp capers
- 3 cans diced tomatoes
- 8 oz fettuccine pasta
- 2 tbsp Parmesan cheese, grated
- Salt and black pepper to taste

**Directions:**

1. Cook the fettuccine pasta according to pack instructions, drain and let it to cool. Warm olive oil in a skillet over medium heat and cook garlic and red flakes for 2 minutes. Add in capers, anchovies, olives, salt, and pepper and cook for another 2-3 minutes until the anchovies melt into the oil. Blend tomatoes in a food processor. Pour into the skillet and stir-fry for 5 minutes. Mix in basil and pasta. Serve garnished with Parmesan cheese.

**Nutrition Info:**

- Info Per Serving: Calories: 443;Fat: 14g;Protein: 18g;Carbs: 65g.

# Traditional Beef Lasagna

Servings:4
Cooking Time:70 Minutes
**Ingredients:**

- 2 tbsp olive oil
- 1 lb lasagne sheets
- 1 lb ground beef
- 1 white onion, chopped
- 1 tsp Italian seasoning
- Salt and black pepper to taste
- 1 cup marinara sauce
- ½ cup grated Parmesan cheese

**Directions:**

1. Preheat oven to 350° F. Warm olive oil in a skillet and add the beef and onion. Cook until the beef is brown, 7-8 minutes. Season with Italian seasoning, salt, and pepper. Cook for 1 minute and mix in the marinara sauce. Simmer for 3 minutes.

2. Spread a layer of the beef mixture in a lightly greased baking sheet and make a first single layer on the beef mixture. Top with a single layer of lasagna sheets. Repeat the layering two more times using the remaining ingredients in the same quantities. Sprinkle with Parmesan cheese. Bake in the oven until the cheese melts and is bubbly with the sauce, 20 minutes. Remove the lasagna, allow cooling for 2 minutes and dish onto serving plates. Serve warm.

**Nutrition Info:**

- Info Per Serving: Calories: 557;Fat: 29g;Protein: 60g;Carbs: 4g.

# Smoky Paprika Chickpeas

Servings:4
Cooking Time:30 Minutes
**Ingredients:**

- ¼ cup extra-virgin olive oil
- 4 garlic cloves, sliced thin
- ½ tsp red pepper flakes
- 1 onion, chopped fine
- Salt and black pepper to taste
- 1 tsp smoked paprika
- 2 cans chickpeas
- 1 cup chicken broth
- 2 tbsp minced fresh parsley
- 2 tsp lemon juice

**Directions:**

1. Warm 3 tbsp of olive oil in a skillet over medium heat. Cook garlic and pepper flakes until the garlic turns golden but not brown, about 3 minutes. Stir in onion and salt and cook until softened and lightly browned, 5 minutes. Stir in smoked paprika, chickpeas, and broth and bring to a boil. Simmer covered for 7 minutes until chickpeas are heated through.

2. Uncover, increase the heat to high, and continue to cook until nearly all liquid has evaporated, about 3 minutes. Remove and stir in parsley and lemon juice. Season with salt and pepper and drizzle with remaining olive oil. Serve warm.

**Nutrition Info:**

- Info Per Serving: Calories: 223;Fat: 11.4g;Protein: 7g;Carbs: 25g.

# Fofu Spaghetti Bolognese

Servings:4
Cooking Time:25 Minutes
**Ingredients:**

- 2 tbsp olive oil
- 16 oz spaghetti, broken in half
- 1 cup crumbled firm tofu
- 1 medium onion, chopped
- 2 celery stalks, chopped
- 1 garlic clove, minced
- 1 bay leaf
- 2 cups passata
- ¼ cup vegetable broth
- Salt and black pepper to taste
- 1 small bunch basil, chopped
- 1 cup grated Parmesan cheese

**Directions:**

1. In a pot of boiling water, cook the spaghetti pasta for 8-10 minutes until al dente. Drain and set aside.

2. Heat the olive oil in a large pot and cook the tofu until brown, 5 minutes. Stir in the onion, celery, and cook until

softened, 5 minutes. Add garlic, bay leaf and cook until fragrant, 30 seconds. Mix in passata, broth and season with salt and pepper. Cook until the sauce thickens, 8-10 minutes. Open the lid, stir in the basil and adjust the taste with salt and pepper. Divide the spaghetti between plates and top with the sauce. Sprinkle the Parmesan cheese and serve.

**Nutrition Info:**
- Info Per Serving: Calories: 424;Fat: 19g;Protein: 22g;Carbs: 31g.

# Oregano Chicken Risotto

Servings:4
Cooking Time:45 Minutes
**Ingredients:**
- 4 chicken thighs, bone-in and skin-on
- 2 tbsp olive oil
- 1 cup arborio rice
- 2 lemons, juiced
- 1 tsp oregano, dried
- 1 red onion, chopped
- Salt and black pepper to taste
- 2 garlic cloves, minced
- 2 ½ cups chicken stock
- 1 cup green olives, sliced
- 2 tbsp parsley, chopped
- ½ cup Parmesan, grated

**Directions:**
1. Warm the olive oil in a skillet over medium heat and brown chicken thighs skin-side down for 3-4 minutes, turn, and cook for 3 minutes. Remove to a plate. Place garlic and onion in the same skillet and sauté for 3 minutes. Stir in rice, salt, pepper, oregano, and lemon juice. Add 1 cup of chicken stock, reduce the heat and simmer the rice while stirring until it is absorbed. Add another cup of chicken broth and continue simmering until the stock is absorbed. Pour in the remaining chicken stock and return the chicken; cook until the rice is tender. Turn the heat off. Stir in Parmesan cheese and top with olives and parsley. Serve into plates. Enjoy!

**Nutrition Info:**
- Info Per Serving: Calories: 450;Fat: 19g;Protein: 26g;Carbs: 28g.

# Asparagus & Goat Cheese Rice Salad

Servings:4
Cooking Time:35 Minutes
**Ingredients:**
- 3 tbsp olive oil
- ½ cups brown rice
- Salt and black pepper to taste
- ½ lemon, zested and juiced
- 1 lb asparagus, chopped
- 1 shallot, minced
- 2 oz goat cheese, crumbled
- ¼ cup hazelnuts, toasted
- ¼ cup parsley, minced

**Directions:**

1. In a pot, bring 2 cups of water to a boil. Add rice, a pinch of salt, and cook until tender, 15-18 minutes, stirring occasionally. Drain the rice, spread onto a rimmed baking sheet, and drizzle with 1 tbsp of lemon juice. Let cool completely, 15 minutes.

2. Heat 1 tbsp of olive oil in a skillet over high heat. Add asparagus, salt, and pepper to taste and cook until asparagus is browned and crisp-tender, 4-5 minutes. Transfer to plate and let cool slightly. Whisk the remaining oil, lemon zest and juice, shallot in large a bowl. Add rice, asparagus, half of the goat cheese, half of the hazelnuts, and half of the parsley. Toss to combine and let sit for 10 minutes. Season with salt and pepper to taste. Sprinkle with the remaining goat cheese, hazelnuts, and parsley.

**Nutrition Info:**
- Info Per Serving: Calories: 185;Fat: 16g;Protein: 8g;Carbs: 24g.

# Eggplant & Chickpea Casserole

Servings:6
Cooking Time:75 Minutes
**Ingredients:**
- ¼ cup olive oil
- 2 onions, chopped
- 1 green bell pepper, chopped
- Salt and black pepper to taste
- 3 garlic cloves, minced
- 1 tsp dried oregano
- ½ tsp ground cumin
- 1 lb eggplants, cubed
- 1 can tomatoes, diced
- 2 cans chickpeas

**Directions:**
1. Preheat oven to 400° F. Warm the olive oil in a skillet over medium heat. Add the onions, bell pepper, salt, and pepper.
2. Cook for about 5 minutes until softened. Stir in garlic, oregano, and cumin for about 30 seconds until fragrant. Transfer to a baking dish and add the eggplants, tomatoes, and chickpeas and stir. Place in the oven and bake for 45-60 minutes, shaking the dish twice during cooking. Serve.

**Nutrition Info:**
- Info Per Serving: Calories: 260;Fat: 12g;Protein: 8g;Carbs: 33.4g.

# Ricotta & Olive Rigatoni

Servings:4
Cooking Time:25 Minutes
**Ingredients:**
- 2 tbsp extra-virgin olive oil
- 1 lb rigatoni
- ½ lb Ricotta cheese, crumbled
- 3/4 cup black olives, chopped
- 10 sun-dried tomatoes, sliced
- 1 tbsp dried oregano
- Black pepper to taste

## Directions:

1. Bring to a boil salted water in a pot over high heat. Add the rigatoni and cook according to package directions; drain. Heat the olive oil in a large saucepan over medium heat. Add the rigatoni, ricotta, olives, and sun-dried tomatoes. Toss mixture to combine and cook 2–3 minutes or until cheese just starts to melt. Season with oregano and pepper.

## Nutrition Info:

- Info Per Serving: Calories: 383;Fat: 28g;Protein: 15g;Carbs: 21g.

## Small Pasta And Beans Pot

Servings:2
Cooking Time: 15 Minutes

### Ingredients:

- 1 pound small whole wheat pasta
- 1 can diced tomatoes, juice reserved
- 1 can cannellini beans, drained and rinsed
- 2 tablespoons no-salt-added tomato paste
- 1 red or yellow bell pepper, chopped
- 1 yellow onion, chopped
- 1 tablespoon Italian seasoning mix
- 3 garlic cloves, minced
- ¼ teaspoon crushed red pepper flakes, optional
- 1 tablespoon extra-virgin olive oil
- 5 cups water
- 1 bunch kale, stemmed and chopped
- ½ cup pitted Kalamata olives, chopped
- 1 cup sliced basil

### Directions:

1. Except for the kale, olives, and basil, combine all the ingredients in a pot. Stir to mix well. Bring to a boil over high heat. Stir constantly.
2. Reduce the heat to medium high and add the kale. Cook for 10 minutes or until the pasta is al dente. Stir constantly.
3. Transfer all of them on a large plate and serve with olives and basil on top.

### Nutrition Info:

- Info Per Serving: Calories: 357;Fat: 7.6g;Protein: 18.2g;Carbs: 64.5g.

## Swoodles With Almond Butter Sauce

Servings:4
Cooking Time: 20 Minutes

### Ingredients:

- Sauce:
- 1 garlic clove
- 1-inch piece fresh ginger, peeled and sliced
- ¼ cup chopped yellow onion
- ¾ cup almond butter
- 1 tablespoon tamari
- 1 tablespoon raw honey
- 1 teaspoon paprika
- 1 tablespoon fresh lemon juice
- ⅛ teaspoon ground red pepper

- Sea salt and ground black pepper, to taste
- ¼ cup water
- Swoodles:
- 2 large sweet potatoes, spiralized
- 2 tablespoons coconut oil, melted
- Sea salt and ground black pepper, to taste
- For Serving:
- ½ cup fresh parsley, chopped
- ½ cup thinly sliced scallions

### Directions:

1. Make the Sauce
2. Put the garlic, ginger, and onion in a food processor, then pulse to combine well.
3. Add the almond butter, tamari, honey, paprika, lemon juice, ground red pepper, salt, and black pepper to the food processor. Pulse to combine well. Pour in the water during the pulsing until the mixture is thick and smooth.
4. Make the Swoodles:
5. Preheat the oven to 425ºF. Line a baking sheet with parchment paper.
6. Put the spiralized sweet potato in a bowl, then drizzle with olive oil. Toss to coat well. Transfer them on the baking sheet. Sprinkle with salt and pepper.
7. Bake in the preheated oven for 20 minutes or until lightly browned and al dente. Check the doneness during the baking and remove any well-cooked swoodles.
8. Transfer the swoodles on a large plate and spread with sauce, parsley, and scallions. Toss to serve.

### Nutrition Info:

- Info Per Serving: Calories: 441;Fat: 33.6g;Protein: 12.0g;Carbs: 29.6g.

## Roasted Ratatouille Pasta

Servings:2
Cooking Time: 30 Minutes

### Ingredients:

- 1 small eggplant
- 1 small zucchini
- 1 portobello mushroom
- 1 Roma tomato, halved
- ½ medium sweet red pepper, seeded
- ½ teaspoon salt, plus additional for the pasta water
- 1 teaspoon Italian herb seasoning
- 1 tablespoon olive oil
- 2 cups farfalle pasta
- 2 tablespoons minced sun-dried tomatoes in olive oil with herbs
- 2 tablespoons prepared pesto

### Directions:

1. Slice the ends off the eggplant and zucchini. Cut them lengthwise into ½-inch slices.
2. Place the eggplant, zucchini, mushroom, tomato, and red pepper in a large bowl and sprinkle with ½ teaspoon of salt. Using your hands, toss the vegetables well so that they're covered evenly with the salt. Let them rest for about 10 minutes.

3. While the vegetables are resting, preheat the oven to 400°F. Line a baking sheet with parchment paper.

4. When the oven is hot, drain off any liquid from the vegetables and pat them dry with a paper towel. Add the Italian herb seasoning and olive oil to the vegetables and toss well to coat both sides.

5. Lay the vegetables out in a single layer on the baking sheet. Roast them for 15 to 20 minutes, flipping them over after about 10 minutes or once they start to brown on the underside. When the vegetables are charred in spots, remove them from the oven.

6. While the vegetables are roasting, fill a large saucepan with water. Add salt and cook the pasta until al dente, about 8 to 10 minutes. Drain the pasta, reserving ½ cup of the pasta water.

7. When cool enough to handle, cut the vegetables into large chunks and add them to the hot pasta.

8. Stir in the sun-dried tomatoes and pesto and toss everything well. Serve immediately.

**Nutrition Info:**
- Info Per Serving: Calories: 613;Fat: 16.0g;Protein: 23.1g;Carbs: 108.5g.

# Veggie & Egg Quinoa With Pancetta

Servings:4
Cooking Time:35 Minutes
**Ingredients:**
- 4 pancetta slices, cooked and crumbled
- 2 tbsp olive oil
- 1 small red onion, chopped
- 1 red bell pepper, chopped
- 1 sweet potato, grated
- 1 green bell pepper, chopped
- 2 garlic cloves, minced
- 1 cup mushrooms, sliced
- ½ cup quinoa
- 1 cup chicken stock
- 4 eggs, fried
- ¼ tsp red pepper flakes
- Salt and black pepper to taste

**Directions:**
1. Warm the olive oil in a skillet over medium heat and cook onion, garlic, bell peppers, sweet potato, and mushrooms for 5 minutes, stirring often. Stir in quinoa for another minute. Mix in stock, salt, and pepper for 15 minutes. Share into plates and serve topped with fried eggs, salt, pepper, red pepper flakes, and crumbled pancetta.

**Nutrition Info:**
- Info Per Serving: Calories: 310;Fat: 15g;Protein: 16g;Carbs: 26g.

# Cherry Tomato Cannellini Beans

Servings:4
Cooking Time:10 Minutes
**Ingredients:**
- 2 tbsp olive oil
- 15 oz canned cannellini beans
- 10 cherry tomatoes, halved
- 2 spring onions, chopped
- 1 tsp paprika
- Salt and black pepper to taste
- ½ tsp ground cumin
- 1 tbsp lime juice

**Directions:**
1. Place beans, cherry tomatoes, spring onions, olive oil, paprika, salt, pepper, cumin, and lime juice in a bowl and toss to combine. Transfer to the fridge for 10 minutes. Serve.

**Nutrition Info:**
- Info Per Serving: Calories: 300;Fat: 8g;Protein: 13g;Carbs: 26g.

# Chili Veggie & Pasta Bake

Servings:4
Cooking Time:45 Minutes
**Ingredients:**
- 1 cup sliced white button mushrooms
- 1 tbsp olive oil
- 16 oz penne
- 1 cup chopped bell peppers
- 1 yellow squash, chopped
- 1 red onion, sliced
- Salt and black pepper to taste
- ¼ tsp red chili flakes
- 1 cup marinara sauce
- 1 cup grated Pecorino cheese
- ¼ cup chopped fresh basil

**Directions:**
1. In a pot of boiling water, cook the penne pasta for 8-10 minutes until al dente. Drain and set aside.

2. Heat the olive oil in a pan and sauté the bell peppers, squash, onion, and mushrooms. Cook until softened, 5 minutes.

3. Season with salt, pepper, and red chili flakes. Mix in marinara sauce and cook for 5 minutes. Stir in the penne and spread the Pecorino cheese on top. Bake in the oven until the cheeses melt and golden brown on top, 15 minutes. Allow cooling for 2 minutes and dish onto serving plates. Serve warm topped with basil.

**Nutrition Info:**
- Info Per Serving: Calories: 248;Fat: 12g;Protein: 27g;Carbs: 5g.

# Rigatoni With Peppers & Mozzarella

Servings:4
Cooking Time:30 Min + Marinating Time
**Ingredients:**

- 1 lb fresh mozzarella cheese, cubed
- 3 tbsp olive oil
- ¼ cup chopped fresh chives
- ¼ cup basil, chopped
- ½ tsp red pepper flakes
- 1 tsp apple cider vinegar
- Salt and black pepper to taste
- 3 garlic cloves, minced
- 2 cups sliced onions
- 3 cups bell peppers, sliced
- 2 cups tomato sauce
- 8 oz rigatoni
- 1 tbsp butter
- ¼ cup grated Parmesan cheese

**Directions:**

1. Bring to a boil salted water in a pot over high heat. Add the rigatoni and cook according to package directions. Drain and set aside, reserving 1 cup of the cooking water. Combine the mozzarella, 1 tablespoon of olive oil, chives, basil, pepper flakes, apple cider vinegar, salt, and pepper. Let the cheese marinate for 30 minutes at room temperature.
2. Warm the remaining olive oil in a large skillet over medium heat. Stir-fry the garlic for 10 seconds and add the onions and peppers. Cook for 3-4 minutes, stirring occasionally until the onions are translucent. Pour in the tomato sauce, and reduce the heat to a simmer. Add the rigatoni and reserved cooking water and toss to coat. Heat off and adjust the seasoning with salt and pepper. Toss with marinated mozzarella cheese and butter. Sprinkle with Parmesan cheese and serve.

**Nutrition Info:**

- Info Per Serving: Calories: 434;Fat: 18g;Protein: 44g;Carbs: 27g.

# Two-bean Cassoulet

Servings:4
Cooking Time:40 Minutes
**Ingredients:**

- 2 tbsp olive oil
- 1 cup canned pinto beans
- 1 cup canned can kidney beans
- 2 red bell peppers, chopped
- 1 onion, chopped
- 1 celery stalk, chopped
- 2 garlic cloves, minced
- 1 can diced tomatoes
- 1 tbsp red pepper flakes
- 1 tsp ground cumin
- Salt and black pepper to taste
- ¼ tsp ground coriander

**Directions:**

1. Warm olive oil in a pot over medium heat and sauté bell peppers, celery, garlic, and onion for 5 minutes until tender. Stir in ground cumin, ground coriander, salt, and pepper for 1 minute. Pour in beans, tomatoes, and red pepper flakes. Bring to a boil, then decrease the heat and simmer for another 20 minutes. Serve immediately.

**Nutrition Info:**

- Info Per Serving: Calories: 361;Fat: 8.4g;Protein: 17g;Carbs: 56g.

# Ribollita (tuscan Bean Soup)

Servings:6
Cooking Time:1 Hour 45 Minutes
**Ingredients:**

- 3 tbsp olive oil
- Salt and black pepper to taste
- 2 cups canned cannellini beans
- 6 oz pancetta, chopped
- ¼ tsp red pepper flakes
- 1 onion, chopped
- 2 carrots, chopped
- 1 celery rib, chopped
- 3 garlic cloves, minced
- 4 cups chicken broth
- 1 lb lacinato kale, chopped
- 1 can diced tomatoes
- 1 rosemary sprig, chopped
- Crusty bread for serving

**Directions:**

1. Warm the olive oil in a skillet over medium heat and add the pancetta. Cook, stirring occasionally, until pancetta is lightly browned and fat has rendered, 5-6 minutes. Add onion, carrots, and celery and cook, stirring occasionally, until softened and lightly browned, 4-6 minutes. Stir in garlic and red pepper flakes and cook until fragrant, 1 minute.
2. Stir in broth, 2 cups of water, and beans and bring to a boil. Cover and simmer for 15 minutes. Stir in lacinato kale and tomatoes and cook for another 5 minutes. Sprinkle with rosemary and adjust the taste. Serve with crusty bread.

**Nutrition Info:**

- Info Per Serving: Calories: 385;Fat: 18g;Protein: 36g;Carbs: 25g.

# Power Green Barley Pilaf

Servings:6
Cooking Time:25 Minutes
**Ingredients:**

- 3 tbsp olive oil
- 1 small onion, chopped fine
- Salt and black pepper to taste
- 1 ½ cups pearl barley, rinsed
- 2 garlic cloves, minced
- ½ tsp dried thyme
- 2 ½ cups water

- ¼ cup parsley, minced
- 2 tbsp cilantro, chopped
- 1 ½ tsp lemon juice

**Directions:**

1. Warm the olive oil in a saucepan over medium heat. Stir-fry onion for 5 minutes until soft. Stir in barley, garlic, and thyme and cook, stirring frequently, until barley is lightly toasted and fragrant, 3-4 minutes. Stir in water and bring to a simmer. Reduce heat to low, cover, and simmer until barley is tender and water is absorbed, 25-35 minutes. Lay clean dish towel underneath the lid and let pilaf sit for 10 minutes. Add parsley, cilantro, and lemon juice and fluff gently with a fork to mix. Season with salt and pepper and serve warm.

**Nutrition Info:**

- Info Per Serving: Calories: 275;Fat: 21g;Protein: 12g;Carbs: 32g.

# Baked Rolled Oat With Pears And Pecans

Servings:6
Cooking Time: 30 Minutes

**Ingredients:**

- 2 tablespoons coconut oil, melted, plus more for greasing the pan
- 3 ripe pears, cored and diced
- 2 cups unsweetened almond milk
- 1 tablespoon pure vanilla extract
- ¼ cup pure maple syrup
- 2 cups gluten-free rolled oats
- ½ cup raisins
- ¾ cup chopped pecans
- ¼ teaspoon ground nutmeg
- 1 teaspoon ground cinnamon
- ½ teaspoon ground ginger
- ¼ teaspoon sea salt

**Directions:**

1. Preheat the oven to 350ºF. Grease a baking dish with melted coconut oil, then spread the pears in a single layer on the baking dish evenly.
2. Combine the almond milk, vanilla extract, maple syrup, and coconut oil in a bowl. Stir to mix well.
3. Combine the remaining ingredients in a separate large bowl. Stir to mix well. Fold the almond milk mixture in the bowl, then pour the mixture over the pears.
4. Place the baking dish in the preheated oven and bake for 30 minutes or until lightly browned and set.
5. Serve immediately.

**Nutrition Info:**

- Info Per Serving: Calories: 479;Fat: 34.9g;Protein: 8.8g;Carbs: 50.1g.

# Lemony Tuna Barley With Capers

Servings:4
Cooking Time:50 Minutes

**Ingredients:**

- 2 tbsp olive oil
- 3 cups chicken stock
- 10 oz canned tuna, flaked
- 1 cup barley
- Salt and black pepper to taste
- 12 cherry tomatoes, halved
- ½ cup pepperoncini, sliced
- ¼ cup capers, drained
- ½ lemon, juiced

**Directions:**

1. Boil chicken stock in a saucepan over medium heat and add in barley. Cook covered for 40 minutes. Fluff the barley and remove to a bowl. Stir in tuna, salt, pepper, tomatoes, pepperoncini, olive oil, capers, and lemon juice. Serve.

**Nutrition Info:**

- Info Per Serving: Calories: 260;Fat: 12g;Protein: 24g;Carbs: 17g.

# Mediterranean Lentils

Servings:2
Cooking Time: 24 Minutes

**Ingredients:**

- 1 tablespoon olive oil
- 1 small sweet or yellow onion, diced
- 1 garlic clove, diced
- 1 teaspoon dried oregano
- ½ teaspoon ground cumin
- ½ teaspoon dried parsley
- ½ teaspoon salt, plus more as needed
- ¼ teaspoon freshly ground black pepper, plus more as needed
- 1 tomato, diced
- 1 cup brown or green lentils
- 2½ cups vegetable stock
- 1 bay leaf

**Directions:**

1. Set your Instant Pot to Sauté and heat the olive oil until it shimmers.
2. Add the onion and cook for 3 to 4 minutes until soft. Turn off the Instant Pot and add the garlic, oregano, cumin, parsley, salt, and pepper. Cook until fragrant, about 1 minute.
3. Stir in the tomato, lentils, stock, and bay leaf.
4. Lock the lid. Select the Manual mode and set the cooking time for 18 minutes at High Pressure.
5. When the timer beeps, perform a natural pressure release for 10 minutes, then release any remaining pressure. Carefully open the lid.
6. Remove and discard the bay leaf. Taste and season with more salt and pepper, as needed. If there's too much liquid remaining, select Sauté and cook until it evaporates.
7. Serve warm.

**Nutrition Info:**

- Info Per Serving: Calories: 426;Fat: 8.1g;Protein: 26.2g;Carbs: 63.8g.

# Spinach & Olive Penne

Servings:4
Cooking Time:30 Minutes
**Ingredients:**

- 1 tbsp olive oil
- 8 oz uncooked penne
- 2 garlic cloves, minced
- ¼ tsp paprika
- 2 cups parsley, chopped
- 4 cups baby spinach
- ¼ tsp ground nutmeg
- Salt and black pepper to taste
- ⅓ cup green olives, sliced
- ⅓ cup Parmesan cheese, grated

**Directions:**

1. Cook the pasta according to the package directions in a large pot until almost al dente. Drain the pasta, and save ¼ cup of the cooking water. Meanwhile, heat the oil in a skillet over medium heat. Add the garlic and paprika, and cook for 30 seconds, stirring constantly. Stir in the parsley for 1 minute. Add the spinach, nutmeg, pepper, and salt, and keep stirring for 3 minutes until the spinach wilts. Add the pasta and the reserved water to the skillet. Stir in the olives, and cook for about 2 minutes until most of the pasta water has been absorbed. Sprinkle with Parmesan cheese and serve.

**Nutrition Info:**

- Info Per Serving: Calories: 273;Fat: 5g;Protein: 17g;Carbs: 48g.

# Lush Moroccan Chickpea, Vegetable, And Fruit Stew

Servings:6
Cooking Time: 6 Hours 4 Minutes
**Ingredients:**

- 1 large bell pepper, any color, chopped
- 6 ounces green beans, trimmed and cut into bite-size pieces
- 3 cups canned chickpeas, rinsed and drained
- 1 can diced tomatoes, with the juice
- 1 large carrot, cut into ¼-inch rounds
- 2 large potatoes, peeled and cubed
- 1 large yellow onion, chopped
- 1 teaspoon grated fresh ginger
- 2 garlic cloves, minced
- 1¾ cups low-sodium vegetable soup
- 1 teaspoon ground cumin
- 1 tablespoon ground coriander
- ¼ teaspoon ground red pepper flakes
- Sea salt and ground black pepper, to taste
- 8 ounces fresh baby spinach
- ¼ cup diced dried figs

- ¼ cup diced dried apricots
- 1 cup plain Greek yogurt

**Directions:**

1. Place the bell peppers, green beans, chicken peas, tomatoes and juice, carrot, potatoes, onion, ginger, and garlic in the slow cooker.
2. Pour in the vegetable soup and sprinkle with cumin, coriander, red pepper flakes, salt, and ground black pepper. Stir to mix well.
3. Put the slow cooker lid on and cook on high for 6 hours or until the vegetables are soft. Stir periodically.
4. Open the lid and fold in the spinach, figs, apricots, and yogurt. Stir to mix well.
5. Cook for 4 minutes or until the spinach is wilted. Pour them in a large serving bowl. Allow to cool for at least 20 minutes, then serve warm.

**Nutrition Info:**

- Info Per Serving: Calories: 611;Fat: 9.0g;Protein: 30.7g;Carbs: 107.4g.

# Mozzarella & Asparagus Pasta

Servings:6
Cooking Time:40 Minutes
**Ingredients:**

- 1 ½ lb asparagus, trimmed, cut into 1-inch
- 2 tbsp olive oil
- 8 oz orecchiette
- 2 cups cherry tomatoes, halved
- Salt and black pepper to taste
- 2 cups fresh mozzarella, drained and chopped
- ⅓ cup torn basil leaves
- 2 tbsp balsamic vinegar

**Directions:**

1. Preheat oven to 390° F. In a large pot, cook the pasta according to the directions. Drain, reserving ¼ cup of cooking water.
2. In the meantime, in a large bowl, toss in asparagus, cherry tomatoes, oil, pepper, and salt. Spread the mixture onto a rimmed baking sheet and bake for 15 minutes, stirring twice throughout cooking. Remove the veggies from the oven, and add the cooked pasta to the baking sheet. Mix with a few tbsp of pasta water to smooth the sauce and veggies. Slowly mix in the mozzarella and basil. Drizzle with the balsamic vinegar and serve in bowls.

**Nutrition Info:**

- Info Per Serving: Calories: 188;Fat: 11g;Protein: 14g;Carbs: 23g.

# Garlic And Parsley Chickpeas

Servings:4
Cooking Time: 18 To 20 Minutes
**Ingredients:**

- ¼ cup extra-virgin olive oil, divided
- 4 garlic cloves, sliced thinly
- ⅛ teaspoon red pepper flakes
- 1 onion, chopped finely

- ¼ teaspoon salt, plus more to taste
- Black pepper, to taste
- 2 cans chickpeas, rinsed
- 1 cup vegetable broth
- 2 tablespoons minced fresh parsley
- 2 teaspoons lemon juice

**Directions:**
1. Add 3 tablespoons of the olive oil, garlic, and pepper flakes to a skillet over medium heat. Cook for about 3 minutes, stirring constantly, or until the garlic turns golden but not brown.
2. Stir in the onion and ¼ teaspoon salt and cook for 5 to 7 minutes, or until softened and lightly browned.
3. Add the chickpeas and broth to the skillet and bring to a simmer. Reduce the heat to medium-low, cover, and cook for about 7 minutes, or until the chickpeas are cooked through and flavors meld.
4. Uncover, increase the heat to high and continue to cook for about 3 minutes more, or until nearly all liquid has evaporated.
5. Turn off the heat, stir in the parsley and lemon juice. Season to taste with salt and pepper and drizzle with remaining 1 tablespoon of the olive oil.
6. Serve warm.

**Nutrition Info:**
- Info Per Serving: Calories: 220;Fat: 11.4g;Protein: 6.5g;Carbs: 24.6g.

# Pistachio & Cherry Tomato Rice Pilaf

Servings:4
Cooking Time:30 Minutes
**Ingredients:**
- 2 tbsp olive oil
- 1 cup basmati rice
- 1 carrot, shredded
- ½ cup scallions, chopped
- 12 cherry tomatoes, halved
- 1 oz pistachios, crushed
- 2 cups vegetable broth
- 1 garlic clove, minced
- 1 tsp ground coriander
- 2 tbsp fresh parsley, chopped

**Directions:**
1. Heat olive oil in a saucepan over medium heat. Add in the carrot, garlic, and scallions and cook for 3-4 minutes, stirring often. Stir in the rice for 1-2 minutes. Pour in the vegetable broth. Bring to a quick boil and sprinkle with ground coriander. Lower the heat and simmer covered for 10-12 minutes until the liquid has absorbed. Fluff the rice with a fork and transfer to a serving plate. Top with cherry tomatoes and pistachios and sprinkle with parsley. Serve.

**Nutrition Info:**
- Info Per Serving: Calories: 305;Fat: 11.4g;Protein: 8g;Carbs: 44g.

# Tortellini & Cannellini With Meatballs

Servings:4
Cooking Time:30 Minutes
**Ingredients:**
- 2 tbsp parsley, chopped
- 12 oz fresh tortellini
- 3 tbsp olive oil
- 5 cloves garlic, minced
- ½ lb meatballs
- 1 can cannellini beans
- 1 can roasted tomatoes
- Salt and black pepper to taste

**Directions:**
1. Bring to a boil salted water in a pot over high heat. Add the tortellini and cook according to package directions. Drain and set aside. Warm the olive oil in a large skillet over medium heat and sauté the garlic for 1 minute. Stir in meatballs and brown for 4–5 minutes on all sides. Add the tomatoes and cannellini and continue to cook for 5 minutes or until heated through. Adjust the seasoning with salt and pepper. Stir in tortellini. Sprinkle with parsley and serve.

**Nutrition Info:**
- Info Per Serving: Calories: 578;Fat: 30g;Protein: 25g;Carbs: 58g.

# Cranberry And Almond Quinoa

Servings:2
Cooking Time: 10 Minutes
**Ingredients:**
- 2 cups water
- 1 cup quinoa, rinsed
- ¼ cup salted sunflower seeds
- ½ cup slivered almonds
- 1 cup dried cranberries

**Directions:**
1. Combine water and quinoa in the Instant Pot.
2. Secure the lid. Select the Manual mode and set the cooking time for 10 minutes at High Pressure.
3. Once cooking is complete, do a quick pressure release. Carefully open the lid.
4. Add sunflower seeds, almonds, and dried cranberries and gently mix until well combined.
5. Serve hot.

**Nutrition Info:**
- Info Per Serving: Calories: 445;Fat: 14.8g;Protein: 15.1g;Carbs: 64.1g.

# Harissa Vegetable Couscous

Servings:4
Cooking Time:60 Minutes
**Ingredients:**
- Salt and black pepper to taste 1 large sweet potato
- 2 red bell peppers, sliced
- 2 zucchini, chopped
- 1 garlic clove, minced
- 3 tbsp olive oil
- 1 tsp harissa paste
- 1 cup couscous
- 8 oz spinach leaves, torn
- ½ lemon, juiced

**Directions:**
1. Preheat oven to 350 F. Whisk the garlic, harissa paste, salt, pepper, and olive oil in a large bowl. Add all the vegetables, except for the spinach, and toss to coat. Transfer to a baking dish. Roast for 35-40 minutes until the vegetables are tender.
2. Cover the couscous in a bowl with 1 ½ cups of boiling water and plut a lid. Let stand for 5 minutes to absorb the water.Fluff the couscous with a fork, then stir through the spinach and the lemon zest and juice. Stir through the roasted vegetables. Serve immediately.

**Nutrition Info:**
- Info Per Serving: Calories: 301;Fat: 11g;Protein: 9g;Carbs: 43g.

# Creamy Saffron Chicken With Ziti

Servings:4
Cooking Time:35 Minutes
**Ingredients:**
- 3 tbsp butter
- 16 oz ziti
- 4 chicken breasts, cut into strips
- ½ tsp ground saffron threads
- 1 yellow onion, chopped
- 2 garlic cloves, minced
- 1 tbsp almond flour
- 1 pinch cardamom powder
- 1 pinch cinnamon powder
- 1 cup heavy cream
- 1 cup chicken stock
- ¼ cup chopped scallions
- 3 tbsp chopped parsley
- Salt and black pepper to taste

**Directions:**
1. In a pot of boiling water, cook the ziti pasta for 8-10 minutes until al dente. Drain and set aside.
2. Melt the butter in a large skillet, season the chicken with salt, black pepper, and cook in the oil until golden brown on the outside, 5 minutes. Stir in the saffron, onion, garlic and cook until the onion softens and the garlic and saffron are fragrant, 3 minutes. Stir in the almond flour, cardamom powder, and cinnamon powder, and cook for 1 minute to

exude some fragrance. Add the heavy cream, chicken stock and cook for 2 to 3 minutes. Adjust the taste with salt, pepper and mix in the ziti and scallions. Allow warming for 1-2 minutes and turn the heat off. Garnish with parsley.

**Nutrition Info:**
- Info Per Serving: Calories: 775;Fat: 48g;Protein: 73g;Carbs: 3g.

# Bean & Egg Noodles With Lemon Sauce

Servings:4
Cooking Time:20 Minutes
**Ingredients:**
- 3 tbsp olive oil
- 12 oz egg noodles
- 1 can diced tomatoes
- 1 can cannellini beans
- ½ cup heavy cream
- 1 cup vegetable stock
- 2 garlic cloves, minced
- 1 onion, chopped
- 1 cup spinach, chopped
- 1 tsp dill
- 1 tsp thyme
- ½ tsp red pepper, crushed
- 1 tsp lemon juice
- 1 tbsp fresh basil, chopped

**Directions:**
1. Warm the olive oil in a pot over medium heat. Add in onion and garlic and cook for 3 minutes until softened. Stir in dill, thyme, and red pepper for 1 minute. Add in spinach, vegetable stock, and tomatoes. Bring to a boil, add the egg noodles, cover, and lower the heat. Cook for 5-7 minutes. Put in beans and cook until heated through. Combine the heavy cream, lemon juice, and basil. Serve the dish with creamy lemon sauce on the side.

**Nutrition Info:**
- Info Per Serving: Calories: 641;Fat: 19g;Protein: 28g;Carbs: 92g.

# Israeli Couscous With Asparagus

Servings:6
Cooking Time: 25 Minutes
**Ingredients:**
- 1½ pounds asparagus spears, ends trimmed and stalks chopped into 1-inch pieces
- 1 garlic clove, minced
- 1 tablespoon extra-virgin olive oil
- ¼ teaspoon freshly ground black pepper
- 1¾ cups water
- 1 box uncooked whole-wheat or regular Israeli couscous
- ¼ teaspoon kosher salt
- 1 cup garlic-and-herb goat cheese, at room temperature

**Directions:**
1. Preheat the oven to 425ºF.

2. In a large bowl, stir together the asparagus, garlic, oil, and pepper. Spread the asparagus on a large, rimmed baking sheet and roast for 10 minutes, stirring a few times. Remove the pan from the oven, and spoon the asparagus into a large serving bowl. Set aside.

3. While the asparagus is roasting, bring the water to a boil in a medium saucepan. Add the couscous and season with salt, stirring well.

4. Reduce the heat to medium-low. Cover and cook for 12 minutes, or until the water is absorbed.

5. Pour the hot couscous into the bowl with the asparagus. Add the goat cheese and mix thoroughly until completely melted.

6. Serve immediately.

**Nutrition Info:**

- Info Per Serving: Calories: 103;Fat: 2.0g;Protein: 6.0g;Carbs: 18.0g.

## Spicy Bean Rolls

Servings:4
Cooking Time:25 Minutes
**Ingredients:**

- 1 tbsp olive oil
- 1 red onion, chopped
- 2 garlic cloves, minced
- 1 green bell pepper, sliced
- 2 cups canned cannellini beans
- 1 red chili pepper, chopped
- 1 tbsp cilantro, chopped
- 1 tsp cumin, ground
- Salt and black pepper to taste
- 4 whole-wheat tortillas
- 1 cup mozzarella, shredded

**Directions:**
1. Warm the olive oil in a skillet over medium heat and sauté onion for 3 minutes. Stir in garlic, bell pepper, cannellini beans, red chili pepper, cilantro, cumin, salt, and pepper and cook for 15 minutes. Spoon bean mixture on each tortilla and top with cheese. Roll up and serve right away.

**Nutrition Info:**

- Info Per Serving: Calories: 680;Fat: 15g;Protein: 38g;Carbs: 75g.

## Simple Lentil Risotto

Servings:2
Cooking Time: 20 Minutes
**Ingredients:**

- ½ tablespoon olive oil
- ½ medium onion, chopped
- ½ cup dry lentils, soaked overnight
- ½ celery stalk, chopped
- 1 sprig parsley, chopped
- ½ cup Arborio (short-grain Italian) rice
- 1 garlic clove, lightly mashed
- 2 cups vegetable stock

**Directions:**
1. Press the Sauté button to heat your Instant Pot.
2. Add the oil and onion to the Instant Pot and sauté for 5 minutes.
3. Add all the remaining ingredients to the Instant Pot.
4. Secure the lid. Select the Manual mode and set the cooking time for 15 minutes at High Pressure.
5. Once cooking is complete, do a natural pressure release for 20 minutes, then release any remaining pressure. Carefully open the lid.
6. Stir and serve hot.

**Nutrition Info:**

- Info Per Serving: Calories: 261;Fat: 3.6g;Protein: 10.6g;Carbs: 47.1g.

## Raspberry & Nut Quinoa

Servings:4
Cooking Time:5 Minutes
**Ingredients:**

- 1 tbsp honey
- 2 cups almond milk
- 2 cups quinoa, cooked
- ½ tsp cinnamon powder
- 1 cup raspberries
- ¼ cup walnuts, chopped

**Directions:**
1. Combine quinoa, milk, cinnamon powder, honey, raspberries, and walnuts in a bowl. Serve in individual bowls.

**Nutrition Info:**

- Info Per Serving: Calories: 300;Fat: 15g;Protein: 5g;Carbs: 15g.

## Roasted Pepper Brown Rice

Servings:6
Cooking Time:1 Hour 50 Minutes
**Ingredients:**

- 2 tbsp Pecorino-Romano cheese, grated
- ¾ cup roasted red peppers, chopped
- 4 tsp olive oil
- 2 onions, finely chopped
- Salt and black pepper to taste
- 1 ½ cups vegetable broth
- 1 ½ cups brown rice, rinsed
- 1 lemon, cut into wedges

**Directions:**
1. Preheat oven to 375° F. Heat oil in a pot over medium heat until sizzling. Stir-fry the onions for 10-12 minutes until soft. Season with salt. Stir in 2 cups of water and broth and bring to a boil. Add in rice, cover, and transfer the pot to the oven. Cook until the rice is tender and liquid absorbed, 50-65 minutes. Remove from the oven. Sprinkle with red peppers and let sit for 5 minutes. Season to taste and stir in Pecorino-Romano cheese. Serve with lemon wedges.

**Nutrition Info:**

- Info Per Serving: Calories: 308;Fat: 10g;Protein: 11g;Carbs: 52g.

# Home-style Beef Ragu Rigatoni

Servings:6
Cooking Time:2 Hours
**Ingredients:**
- 1 tbsp olive oil
- 1 ½ lb bone-in short ribs
- Salt and black pepper to taste
- 1 onion, finely chopped
- 3 garlic cloves, minced
- 1 tsp fresh thyme, minced
- ½ tsp ground cinnamon
- A pinch of ground cloves
- ½ cup dry red wine
- 1 can tomatoes, diced
- 1 lb rigatoni
- 2 tbsp fresh parsley, minced
- 2 tbsp Pecorino cheese, grated

**Directions:**
1. Season the ribs with salt and pepper. Heat oil in a large skillet and brown the ribs on all sides, 7-10 minutes; transfer to a plate. Remove all but 1 tsp fat from skillet, add onion, and stir-fry over medium heat for 5 minutes. Stir in garlic, thyme, cinnamon, and cloves and cook until fragrant, 40 seconds. Pour in the wine, scraping off any browned bits, and simmer until almost evaporated, 2 minutes. Stir in tomatoes and their juice.
2. Nestle ribs into the sauce along with any accumulated juices and bring to a simmer. Lower the heat, cover and let simmer, turning the ribs from time to time until the meat is very tender and falling off bones, 2 hours. Transfer the ribs to cutting board, let cool slightly, then shred it using 2 forks; discard excess fat and bones.
3. Skim excess fat from the surface of the sauce with a spoon. Stir shredded meat and any accumulated juices into the sauce and bring to a simmer over medium heat. Season to taste. Meanwhile, bring a large pot filled with salted water to a boil and cook pasta until al dente. Reserve ½ cup of the cooking water, drain pasta and return it to pot. Add sauce and parsley and toss to combine. Season to taste and adjust consistency with reserved cooking water as needed. Serve with freshly grated Pecorino cheese.

**Nutrition Info:**
- Info Per Serving: Calories: 415;Fat: 11g;Protein: 12g;Carbs: 42g.

# Turkish Canned Pinto Bean Salad

Servings:4
Cooking Time: 3 Minutes
**Ingredients:**
- ¼ cup extra-virgin olive oil, divided
- 3 garlic cloves, lightly crushed and peeled
- 2 cans pinto beans, rinsed
- 2 cups plus 1 tablespoon water
- Salt and pepper, to taste
- ¼ cup tahini

- 3 tablespoons lemon juice
- 1 tablespoon ground dried Aleppo pepper, plus extra for serving
- 8 ounces cherry tomatoes, halved
- ¼ red onion, sliced thinly
- ½ cup fresh parsley leaves
- 2 hard-cooked large eggs, quartered
- 1 tablespoon toasted sesame seeds

**Directions:**
1. Add 1 tablespoon of the olive oil and garlic to a medium saucepan over medium heat. Cook for about 3 minutes, stirring constantly, or until the garlic turns golden but not brown.
2. Add the beans, 2 cups of the water and 1 teaspoon salt and bring to a simmer. Remove from the heat, cover and let sit for 20 minutes. Drain the beans and discard the garlic.
3. In a large bowl, whisk together the remaining 3 tablespoons of the oil, tahini, lemon juice, Aleppo, the remaining 1 tablespoon of the water and ¼ teaspoon salt. Stir in the beans, tomatoes, onion and parsley. Season with salt and pepper to taste.
4. Transfer to a serving platter and top with the eggs. Sprinkle with the sesame seeds and extra Aleppo before serving.

**Nutrition Info:**
- Info Per Serving: Calories: 402;Fat: 18.9g;Protein: 16.2g;Carbs: 44.4g.

# Italian Sautéd Cannellini Beans

Servings:6
Cooking Time: 15 Minutes
**Ingredients:**
- 2 teaspoons extra-virgin olive oil
- ½ cup minced onion
- ¼ cup red wine vinegar
- 1 can no-salt-added tomato paste
- 2 tablespoons raw honey
- ½ cup water
- ¼ teaspoon ground cinnamon
- 2 cans cannellini beans

**Directions:**
1. Heat the olive oil in a saucepan over medium heat until shimmering.
2. Add the onion and sauté for 5 minutes or until translucent.
3. Pour in the red wine vinegar, tomato paste, honey, and water. Sprinkle with cinnamon. Stir to mix well.
4. Reduce the heat to low, then pour all the beans into the saucepan. Cook for 10 more minutes. Stir constantly.
5. Serve immediately.

**Nutrition Info:**
- Info Per Serving: Calories: 435;Fat: 2.1g;Protein: 26.2g;Carbs: 80.3g.

# Green Bean & Pork Fettuccine

Servings:4
Cooking Time:40 Minutes
**Ingredients:**
- 1 tbsp olive oil
- 16 oz fettuccine
- 4 pork loin, cut into strips
- Salt and black pepper to taste
- ½ cup green beans, chopped
- 1 lemon, zested and juiced
- ¼ cup chicken broth
- 1 cup crème fraiche
- 6 basil leaves, chopped
- 1 cup shaved Parmesan cheese

**Directions:**
1. In a pot of boiling water, cook the fettuccine pasta for 8-10 minutes until al dente. Drain and set aside.
2. Heat olive oil in a skillet, season the pork with salt, pepper, and cook for 10 minutes. Mix in green beans and cook for 5 minutes. Stir in lemon zest, lemon juice, and chicken broth. Cook for 5 more minutes or until the liquid reduces by a quarter. Add crème fraiche and mix well. Pour in pasta and basil and cook for 1 minute. Top with Parmesan cheese.

**Nutrition Info:**
- Info Per Serving: Calories: 586;Fat: 32g;Protein: 59g;Carbs: 9g.

# Spinach & Salmon Fettuccine In White Sauce

Servings:4
Cooking Time:35 Minutes
**Ingredients:**
- 5 tbsp butter
- 16 oz fettuccine
- 4 salmon fillets, cubed
- Salt and black pepper to taste
- 3 garlic cloves, minced
- 1 ¼ cups heavy cream
- ½ cup dry white wine
- 1 tsp grated lemon zest
- 1 cup baby spinach
- Lemon wedges for garnishing

**Directions:**
1. In a pot of boiling water, cook the fettuccine pasta for 8-10 minutes until al dente. Drain and set aside.
2. Melt half of the butter in a large skillet; season the salmon with salt, black pepper, and cook in the butter until golden brown on all sides and flaky within, 8 minutes. Transfer to a plate and set aside.
3. Add the remaining butter to the skillet to melt and stir in the garlic. Cook until fragrant, 1 minute. Mix in heavy cream, white wine, lemon zest, salt, and pepper. Allow boiling over low heat for 5 minutes. Stir in spinach, allow wilting for 2 minutes and stir in fettuccine and salmon until well-coated in the sauce. Garnish with lemon wedges.

**Nutrition Info:**
- Info Per Serving: Calories: 795;Fat: 46g;Protein: 72g;Carbs: 20g.

# Tomato Sauce And Basil Pesto Fettuccine

Servings:4
Cooking Time: 15 Minutes
**Ingredients:**
- 4 Roma tomatoes, diced
- 2 teaspoons no-salt-added tomato paste
- 1 tablespoon chopped fresh oregano
- 2 garlic cloves, minced
- 1 cup low-sodium vegetable soup
- ½ teaspoon sea salt
- 1 packed cup fresh basil leaves
- ¼ cup pine nuts
- ¼ cup grated Parmesan cheese
- 2 tablespoons extra-virgin olive oil
- 1 pound cooked whole-grain fettuccine

**Directions:**
1. Put the tomatoes, tomato paste, oregano, garlic, vegetable soup, and salt in a skillet. Stir to mix well.
2. Cook over medium heat for 10 minutes or until lightly thickened.
3. Put the remaining ingredients, except for the fettuccine, in a food processor and pulse to combine until smooth.
4. Pour the puréed basil mixture into the tomato mixture, then add the fettuccine. Cook for a few minutes or until heated through and the fettuccine is well coated.
5. Serve immediately.

**Nutrition Info:**
- Info Per Serving: Calories: 389;Fat: 22.7g;Protein: 9.7g;Carbs: 40.2g.

# Pasta In Dilly Walnut Sauce

Servings:4
Cooking Time:10 Minutes
**Ingredients:**
- 3 tbsp extra-virgin olive oil
- 8 oz whole-wheat pasta
- ¼ cup walnuts, chopped
- 3 garlic cloves, finely minced
- ½ cup fresh dill, chopped
- ¼ cup grated Parmesan cheese

**Directions:**
1. Cook the whole-wheat pasta according to pack instructions, drain and let it cool. Place the olive oil, dill, garlic, Parmesan cheese, and walnuts in a food processor and blend for 15 seconds or until paste forms. Pour over the cooled pasta and toss to combine. Serve immediately.

**Nutrition Info:**

- Info Per Serving: Calories: 559;Fat: 17g;Protein: 21g;Carbs: 91g.

# Black Bean & Chickpea Burgers

Servings:4
Cooking Time:35 Minutes
**Ingredients:**
- 1 tsp olive oil
- 1 can black beans
- 1 can chickpeas
- ½ white onion, chopped
- 2 garlic cloves, minced
- 2 free-range eggs
- 1 tsp ground cumin
- Salt and black pepper to taste
- 1 cup panko breadcrumbs
- ½ cup old-fashioned rolled oats
- 6 hamburger buns, halved
- 2 avocados
- 2 tbsp lemon juice
- 6 large lettuce leaves

**Directions:**
1. Preheat oven to 380° F. Blitz the black beans, chickpeas, eggs, cumin, salt, and pepper in a food processor until smooth. Transfer the mixture to a bowl and add the onion and garlic and mix well. Stir in the bread crumbs and oats. Shape the mixture into 6 balls, flatten them with your hands to make patties. Brush both sides of the burgers with oil. Arrange them on a parchment-lined baking sheet. Bake for 30 minutes, flippingonce until slightly crispy on the edges.
2. Meanwhile, mash the avocado with the lemon juice and a pinch of salt with a fork until smooth; set aside. Toast the buns for 2-3 minutes. Spread the avocado mixture onto the base of each bun, then top with the burgers and lettuce leaves. Finish with the bun tops. Serve and enjoy!

**Nutrition Info:**
- Info Per Serving: Calories: 867;Fat: 22g;Protein: 39g;Carbs: 133g.

# Moroccan Rice Pilaf

Servings:4
Cooking Time:40 Minutes
**Ingredients:**
- 2 tbsp olive oil
- ¼ cup pine nuts
- 1 ¼ cups brown rice
- 1 onion, diced
- 2 cups chicken stock
- 1 cinnamon stick
- ¼ cup dried apricots, chopped
- Salt and black pepper to taste

**Directions:**
1. Warm the olive oil in a large saucepan over medium heat.

2. Sauté the onions and pine nuts for 5-7 minutes, or until the pine nuts are golden and the onion is translucent. Add the rice and sauté for 2 minutes until lightly browned. Pour the stock and bring it to a boil. Add the cinnamon and apricots.
3. Lower the heat, cover the pan, and simmer for 17-20 minutes or until the rice is tender and the liquid is mostly absorbed. When ready, remove from the heat and fluff with a fork. Season to taste and serve warm.

**Nutrition Info:**
- Info Per Serving: Calories: 510;Fat: 24g;Protein: 13g;Carbs: 62g.

# Carrot & Barley Risotto

Servings:6
Cooking Time:1 Hour 20 Minutes
**Ingredients:**
- 2 tbsp olive oil
- 4 cups vegetable broth
- 4 cups water
- 1 onion, chopped fine
- 1 carrot, chopped
- 1 ½ cups pearl barley
- 1 cup dry white wine
- ¼ tsp dried oregano
- 2 oz Parmesan cheese, grated
- Salt and black pepper to taste

**Directions:**
1. Bring broth and water to a simmer in a saucepan. Reduce heat to low and cover to keep warm.
2. Heat 1 tbsp of oil in a pot over medium heat until sizzling. Stir-fry onion and carrot until softened, 6-7 minutes. Add barley and cook, stirring often, until lightly toasted and aromatic, 4 minutes. Add wine and cook, stirring frequently for 2 minutes. Stir in 3 cups of water and oregano, bring to a simmer, and cook, stirring occasionally until liquid is absorbed, 25 minutes. Stir in 2 cups of broth, bring to a simmer, and cook until the liquid is absorbed, 15 minutes.
3. Continue cooking, stirring often and adding warm broth as needed to prevent the pot bottom from becoming dry until barley is cooked through but still somewhat firm in the center, 15-20 minutes. Off heat, adjust consistency with the remaining warm broth as needed. Stir in Parmesan and the remaining oil and season with salt and pepper to taste. Serve.

**Nutrition Info:**
- Info Per Serving: Calories: 355;Fat: 21g;Protein: 16g;Carbs: 35g.

## Ziti Marinara Bake

Servings:4
Cooking Time:60 Minutes
**Ingredients:**
- For the Marinara Sauce:
- 2 tbsp olive oil
- ¼ onion, diced
- 3 cloves garlic, chopped
- 1 can tomatoes, diced
- Sprig of fresh thyme
- ½ bunch fresh basil
- Salt and pepper to taste
- For the Ziti:
- 1 lb ziti
- 3 ½ cups marinara sauce
- 1 cup cottage cheese
- 1 cup grated Mozzarella
- ¾ cup grated Pecorino cheese

**Directions:**
1. In a saucepan, warm the olive oil over medium heat. Stir-fry onion and garlic until lightly browned, 3 minutes. Add the tomatoes and herbs, and bring to a boil, then simmer for 7 minutes, covered. Set aside. Discard the herb sprigs and stir in sea salt and black pepper to taste.
2. Preheat the oven to 375°F. Prepare the pasta according to package directions. Drain and mix the pasta in a bowl along with 2 cups of marinara sauce, cottage cheese, and half the Mozzarella and Pecorino cheeses. Transfer the mixture to a baking dish, and top with the remaining marinara sauce and cheese. Bake for 25 to 35 minutes, or until bubbly and golden brown. Serve warm.

**Nutrition Info:**
- Info Per Serving: Calories: 455;Fat: 17g;Protein: 19g;Carbs: 62g.

# Sides , Salads, And Soups Recipes

## Eggplant Stew With Almonds

Servings:4
Cooking Time:30 Minutes
**Ingredients:**
- 3 eggplants, halved
- 2 tomatoes, chopped
- 2 red bell peppers, chopped,
- ¼ tbsp tomato paste
- 2 tbsp fresh parsley, chopped
- 3 oz toasted almonds, chopped
- 2 tbsp capers
- ¼ cup extra virgin olive oil
- Salt to taste

**Directions:**
1. Grease the instant pot with 2 tbsp of olive oil. Make the first layer with halved eggplants tucking the ends Gently to fit in. Make the second layer with tomatoes and red bell peppers. Spread the tomato paste evenly over the vegetables, sprinkle with almonds and salted capers. Add the remaining olive oil, salt, and pepper. Pour 1 ½ cups of water and seal the lid. Cook on High Pressure for 13 minutes. Do a quick release.

**Nutrition Info:**
- Info Per Serving: Calories: 248;Fat: 13.7g;Protein: 6g;Carbs: 32g.

## Cherry, Plum, Artichoke, And Cheese Board

Servings:4
Cooking Time: 0 Minutes
**Ingredients:**
- 2 cups rinsed cherries
- 2 cups rinsed and sliced plums
- 2 cups rinsed carrots, cut into sticks
- 1 cup canned low-sodium artichoke hearts, rinsed and drained
- 1 cup cubed feta cheese

**Directions:**
1. Arrange all the ingredients in separated portions on a clean board or a large tray, then serve with spoons, knife, and forks.

**Nutrition Info:**
- Info Per Serving: Calories: 417;Fat: 13.8g;Protein: 20.1g;Carbs: 56.2g.

## Arugula And Fig Salad

Servings:2
Cooking Time: 0 Minutes
**Ingredients:**
- 3 cups arugula
- 4 fresh, ripe figs, stemmed and sliced
- 2 tablespoons olive oil
- ¼ cup lightly toasted pecan halves
- 2 tablespoons crumbled blue cheese

- 1 to 2 tablespoons balsamic glaze

**Directions:**

1. Toss the arugula and figs with the olive oil in a large bowl until evenly coated.

2. Add the pecans and blue cheese to the bowl. Toss the salad lightly.

3. Drizzle with the balsamic glaze and serve immediately.

**Nutrition Info:**

- Info Per Serving: Calories: 517;Fat: 36.2g;Protein: 18.9g;Carbs: 30.2g.

## Zoodles With Tomato-mushroom Sauce

Servings:4

Cooking Time:25 Minutes

**Ingredients:**

- 1 lb oyster mushrooms, chopped
- 2 tbsp olive oil
- 1 cup chicken broth
- 1 tsp Mediterranean sauce
- 1 yellow onion, minced
- 1 cup pureed tomatoes
- 2 garlic cloves, minced
- 2 zucchinis, spiralized

**Directions:**

1. Warm the olive oil in a saucepan over medium heat and sauté the zoodles for 1-2 minutes; reserve. Sauté the onion and garlic in the same saucepan for 2-3 minutes. Add in the mushrooms and continue to cook for 2 to 3 minutes until they release liquid. Add in the remaining ingredients and cover the pan; let it simmer for 10 minutes longer until everything is cooked through. Top the zoodles with the prepared mushroom sauce and serve.

**Nutrition Info:**

- Info Per Serving: Calories: 95;Fat: 6.4g;Protein: 6g;Carbs: 5g.

## Gorgonzola, Fig & Prosciutto Salad

Servings:2

Cooking Time:15 Minutes

**Ingredients:**

- 2 tbsp crumbled Gorgonzola cheese
- 2 tbsp olive oil
- 3 cups Romaine lettuce, torn
- 4 figs, sliced
- 3 thin prosciutto slices
- ¼ cup pecan halves, toasted
- 1 tbsp balsamic vinegar

**Directions:**

1. Toss lettuce and figs in a large bowl. Drizzle with olive oil. Slice the prosciutto lengthwise into 1-inch strips. Add the prosciutto, pecans, and Gorgonzola cheese to the bowl. Toss the salad lightly. Drizzle with balsamic vinegar.

**Nutrition Info:**

- Info Per Serving: Calories: 519;Fat: 38g;Protein: 20g;Carbs: 29g.

## Carrot & Celery Bean Soup

Servings:6

Cooking Time:35 Minutes

**Ingredients:**

- 3 tbsp olive oil
- 1 onion, finely chopped
- 3 garlic cloves, minced
- 2 cups carrots, diced
- 2 cups celery, diced
- 1 medium potato, cubed
- 2 oz cubed pancetta
- 2 cans white beans, rinsed
- 6 cups vegetable broth
- Salt and black pepper to taste

**Directions:**

1. Heat the olive oil in a stockpot over medium heat. Add the pancetta, onion, and garlic and cook for 3-4 minutes, stirring often. Add the carrots and celery and cook for another 3-5 minutes until tender. Add the beans, potato, broth, salt, and pepper. Stir and simmer for about 20 minutes, stirring occasionally. Serve warm.

**Nutrition Info:**

- Info Per Serving: Calories: 244;Fat: 7.2g;Protein: 9g;Carbs: 36.4g.

## Classic Potato Salad With Green Onions

Servings:4

Cooking Time:25 Minutes

**Ingredients:**

- 2 ½ lb baby potatoes, halved
- Salt and black pepper to taste
- 1 cup light mayonnaise
- Juice of 1 lemon
- 2 green onions, chopped
- ¼ cup parsley, chopped

**Directions:**

1. Place potatoes and enough water in a pot over medium heat and bring to a boil. Cook for 12 minutes and drain; set aside.

2. In a bowl, mix mayonnaise, salt, pepper, lemon juice, and green onions. Add in the baby potatoes and toss to coat. Top with parsley and serve immediately.

**Nutrition Info:**

- Info Per Serving: Calories: 360;Fat: 20g;Protein: 11g;Carbs: 25g.

# Green Bean & Rice Chicken Soup

Servings:4
Cooking Time:45 Minutes
**Ingredients:**
- 2 tbsp olive oil
- 4 cups chicken stock
- ½ lb chicken breasts strips
- 1 celery stalk, chopped
- 2 garlic cloves, minced
- 1 yellow onion, chopped
- ½ cup white rice
- 1 egg, whisked
- ½ lemon, juiced
- 1 cup green beans, chopped
- 1 cup carrots, chopped
- ½ cup dill, chopped
- Salt and black pepper to taste

**Directions:**
1. Warm the olive oil in a pot over medium heat and sauté onion, garlic, celery, carrots, and chicken for 6-7 minutes.
2. Pour in stock and rice. Bring to a boil and simmer for 10 minutes. Stir in green beans, salt, and pepper and cook for 15 minutes. Whisk the egg and lemon juice and pour into the pot. Stir and cook for 2 minutes. Serve topped with dill.

**Nutrition Info:**
- Info Per Serving: Calories: 270;Fat: 19g;Protein: 15g;Carbs: 20g.

# Quick Za´atar Spice

Servings:4
Cooking Time:5 Minutes
**Ingredients:**
- 1 tsp ground cumin
- 1 tsp ground coriander
- ½ cup dried thyme
- 2 tbsp sesame seeds, toasted
- 1 ½ tbsp ground sumac
- ¼ tsp Aleppo chili flakes

**Directions:**
1. Mix all the ingredients in a bowl. Store in a glass jar at room temperature for up to 7-9 months.

**Nutrition Info:**
- Info Per Serving: Calories: 175;Fat: 13.9g;Protein: 5g;Carbs: 12g.

# Carrot & Tomato Salad With Cilantro

Servings:4
Cooking Time:10 Minutes
**Ingredients:**
- 2 tbsp olive oil
- 4 tomatoes, chopped
- 1 carrot, grated
- ¼ cup lime juice
- 1 garlic clove, minced
- Salt and black pepper to taste
- 1 lettuce head, chopped
- 2 green onions, chopped
- ½ cup cilantro, chopped

**Directions:**
1. Toss lime juice, garlic, salt, pepper, olive oil, carrot, lettuce, onions, tomatoes, cilantro in a bowl. Serve cold.

**Nutrition Info:**
- Info Per Serving: Calories: 120;Fat: 4g;Protein: 3g;Carbs: 4g.

# Spanish Lentil Soup With Rice

Servings:4
Cooking Time:30 Minutes
**Ingredients:**
- 2 tbsp olive oil
- ½ cup red lentils, rinsed
- ½ cup Spanish rice
- 4 cups vegetable stock
- Salt to taste
- 1 onion, finely chopped
- 2 garlic cloves, sliced
- 1 carrot, finely diced
- 1 tsp turmeric
- 4 sage leaves, chopped

**Directions:**
1. Heat the olive oil in a stockpot over medium heat. Sauté the onion, carrot, and garlic for 5 minutes until the onion and garlic are golden brown. Stir in the turmeric for 1 minute. Pour in stock, lentils, rice, and salt. Simmer for 15-20 minutes, stirring occasionally. Serve the soup garnished with chopped sage leaves.

**Nutrition Info:**
- Info Per Serving: Calories: 230;Fat: 7.2g;Protein: 9g;Carbs: 36.8g.

# Pecorino Zucchini Strips

Servings:4
Cooking Time:30 Minutes
**Ingredients:**
- 4 zucchini, quartered lengthwise
- 2 tbsp olive oil
- ½ cup grated Pecorino cheese
- 1 tbsp dried dill
- ¼ tsp garlic powder
- Salt and black pepper to taste

**Directions:**
1. Preheat oven to 350° F. Combine zucchini and olive oil in a bowl. Mix cheese, salt, garlic powder, dill, and pepper in a bowl. Add in zucchini and toss to combine. Arrange the zucchini fingers on a lined baking sheet and bake for about 20 minutes until golden. Set oven to broil and broil for 2 minutes until crispy. Serve and enjoy!

**Nutrition Info:**

- Info Per Serving: Calories: 103;Fat: 8.2g;Protein: 3.5g;Carbs: 6g.

# Kalamata Olive & Lentil Salad

Servings:4

Cooking Time:25 Min + Chilling Time

**Ingredients:**

- 1 cup red lentils, rinsed
- 1 tsp yellow mustard
- ½ lemon, juiced
- 2 tbsp tamari sauce
- 2 scallion stalks, chopped
- ¼ cup extra-virgin olive oil
- 2 garlic cloves, minced
- 1 cup butterhead lettuce, torn
- 2 tbsp fresh parsley, chopped
- 2 tbsp fresh cilantro, chopped
- 1 tsp fresh basil
- 1 tsp fresh oregano
- 12 cherry tomatoes, halved
- 6 Kalamata olives, halved

**Directions:**

1. Pour 5 cups of salted water and lentils in a large pot over high heat and bring to a boil. Reduce the heat to medium-low and simmer for 15-18 minutes until the lentils are tender. Drain and let it cool completely. Transfer them to a salad bowl and add in the remaining ingredients, except for the olives; toss until well combined. Top with olives and serve.

**Nutrition Info:**

- Info Per Serving: Calories: 348;Fat: 16g;Protein: 16g;Carbs: 41g.

# Spinach & Bean Salad With Goat Cheese

Servings:4

Cooking Time:35 Minutes

**Ingredients:**

- 4 tbsp olive oil
- 1 garlic clove, minced
- ½ tsp cumin
- ½ tsp chili flakes
- 2 tbsp red wine vinegar
- 1 tbsp fresh lemon juice
- 1 tbsp fresh dill
- Salt to taste
- 1 can black beans
- 2 cups fresh baby spinach
- ¼ lb goat cheese, crumbled
- ½ cup spring onions, sliced
- 1 jalapeño pepper, chopped
- 2 bell peppers, chopped

**Directions:**

1. In a small bowl, combine the garlic, cumin, chili flakes, olive oil, vinegar, lemon juice, dill, and salt. Put in the fridge.
2. Mix the black beans, baby spinach, spring onions, jalapeño pepper, and bell pepper in another bowl. Remove the dressing from the fridge and pour over the salad; toss to coat. Top with the goat cheese and serve.

**Nutrition Info:**

- Info Per Serving: Calories: 633;Fat: 25g;Protein: 32g;Carbs: 72g.

# Bell Pepper & Lentil Salad With Tomatoes

Servings:4

Cooking Time:10 Minutes

**Ingredients:**

- 2 tomatoes, chopped
- 1 green bell pepper, chopped
- 14 oz canned lentils, drained
- 2 spring onions, chopped
- 1 red bell pepper, chopped
- 2 tbsp cilantro, chopped
- 2 tsp balsamic vinegar

**Directions:**

1. Mix lentils, spring onions, tomatoes, bell peppers, cilantro, and vinegar in a bowl. Serve immediately.

**Nutrition Info:**

- Info Per Serving: Calories: 210;Fat: 3g;Protein: 7g;Carbs: 12g.

# Baby Potato And Olive Salad

Servings:6

Cooking Time: 20 Minutes

**Ingredients:**

- 2 pounds baby potatoes, cut into 1-inch cubes
- 1 tablespoon low-sodium olive brine
- 3 tablespoons freshly squeezed lemon juice
- ¼ teaspoon kosher salt
- 3 tablespoons extra-virgin olive oil
- ½ cup sliced olives
- 2 tablespoons torn fresh mint
- 1 cup sliced celery
- 2 tablespoons chopped fresh oregano

**Directions:**

1. Put the tomatoes in a saucepan, then pour in enough water to submerge the tomatoes about 1 inch.
2. Bring to a boil over high heat, then reduce the heat to medium-low. Simmer for 14 minutes or until the potatoes are soft.
3. Meanwhile, combine the olive brine, lemon juice, salt, and olive oil in a small bow. Stir to mix well.
4. Transfer the cooked tomatoes in a colander, then rinse with running cold water. Pat dry with paper towels.
5. Transfer the tomatoes in a large salad bowl, then drizzle with olive brine mixture. Spread with remaining ingredients and toss to combine well.

6. Serve immediately.
**Nutrition Info:**
- Info Per Serving: Calories: 220;Fat: 6.1g;Protein: 4.3g;Carbs: 39.2g.

# Tomato & Apple Salad With Walnuts

Servings:4
Cooking Time:5 Minutes
**Ingredients:**
- 2 tbsp olive oil
- 1 apple, peeled and chopped
- 1 head Iceberg lettuce, torn
- 1 tbsp apple cider vinegar
- 2 tbsp walnuts, chopped
- 1 tomato, sliced
- 8 anchovy stuffed olives
- Salt to taste

**Directions:**
1. Combine lettuce, apple cider vinegar, salt, olive oil, apple, and walnuts in a salad bowl. Toss to coat. Top with tomato and olives and serve right away.
**Nutrition Info:**
- Info Per Serving: Calories: 160;Fat: 2g;Protein: 3g;Carbs: 4g.

# Roasted Root Vegetable Soup

Servings:6
Cooking Time: 35 Minutes
**Ingredients:**
- 2 parsnips, peeled and sliced
- 2 carrots, peeled and sliced
- 2 sweet potatoes, peeled and sliced
- 1 teaspoon chopped fresh rosemary
- 1 teaspoon chopped fresh thyme
- 1 teaspoon sea salt
- ½ teaspoon freshly ground black pepper
- 2 tablespoons extra-virgin olive oil
- 4 cups low-sodium vegetable soup
- ½ cup grated Parmesan cheese, for garnish (optional)

**Directions:**
1. Preheat the oven to 400ºF. Line a baking sheet with aluminum foil.
2. Combine the parsnips, carrots, and sweet potatoes in a large bowl, then sprinkle with rosemary, thyme, salt, and pepper, and drizzle with olive oil. Toss to coat the vegetables well.
3. Arrange the vegetables on the baking sheet, then roast in the preheated oven for 30 minutes or until lightly browned and soft. Flip the vegetables halfway through the roasting.
4. Pour the roasted vegetables with vegetable broth in a food processor, then pulse until creamy and smooth.
5. Pour the puréed vegetables in a saucepan, then warm over low heat until heated through.

6. Spoon the soup in a large serving bowl, then scatter with Parmesan cheese. Serve immediately.
**Nutrition Info:**
- Info Per Serving: Calories: 192;Fat: 5.7g;Protein: 4.8g;Carbs: 31.5g.

# Cucumber & Tomato Salad With Anchovies

Servings:4
Cooking Time:10 Minutes
**Ingredients:**
- 2 tbsp extra virgin olive oil
- 1 tbsp lemon juice
- 4 canned anchovy fillets
- 6 black olives
- ½ head Romaine lettuce, torn
- Salt and black pepper to taste
- 1 cucumber, cubed
- 3 tomatoes, cubed
- 2 spring onions, chopped

**Directions:**
1. Whisk the olive oil, lemon juice, salt, and pepper in a bowl. Add the cucumber, tomatoes, and spring onions and toss to coat. Top with anchovies and black olives and serve.
**Nutrition Info:**
- Info Per Serving: Calories: 113;Fat: 8.5g;Protein: 2.9g;Carbs: 9g.

# Chickpea Tuna Salad

Servings:4
Cooking Time:15 Minutes
**Ingredients:**
- 1 can solid white albacore tuna, drained
- ¼ cup olive oil
- ¼ cup balsamic vinegar
- ½ tsp minced garlic
- ¼ tsp dried oregano
- Salt and black pepper to taste
- 2 tbsp capers, drained
- 4 cups baby greens
- 1 cup canned chickpeas
- ¼ cup olives, sliced
- 2 Roma tomatoes, chopped
- ¼ cup feta cheese, crumbled

**Directions:**
1. In a bowl, whisk together the olive oil, balsamic vinegar, garlic, oregano, salt, and pepper until emulsified. Stir in capers. Place the baby greens in a salad bowl and top with tuna, chickpeas, olives, and tomatoes. Drizzle the vinaigrette overall and sprinkle with feta cheese. Serve immediately.
**Nutrition Info:**
- Info Per Serving: Calories: 226;Fat: 13g;Protein: 5g;Carbs: 29g.

# Basil Zucchini Marinara

Servings:4
Cooking Time:25 Minutes
**Ingredients:**
- 2 tbsp olive oil
- 1 shallot, chopped
- 1 garlic clove, minced
- 1 zucchini, sliced into rounds
- Salt and black pepper to taste
- 1 cup marinara sauce
- ¼ cup mozzarella, shredded
- 2 tbsp fresh basil, chopped

**Directions:**
1. Warm the olive oil in a skillet over medium heat. Sauté the shallot and garlic for 3 minutes until just tender and fragrant. Add in the zucchini and season with salt and pepper; cook for 4 minutes until lightly browned. Add marinara sauce and bring to a simmer; cook until zucchini is tender, 5-8 minutes. Scatter the mozzarella cheese on top of the zucchini layer and cover; heat for about 3 minutes until the cheese is melted. Sprinkle with basil and serve immediately.

**Nutrition Info:**
- Info Per Serving: Calories: 93;Fat: 7g;Protein: 3g;Carbs: 5g.

# Mushroom-barley Soup

Servings:6
Cooking Time:10 Minutes
**Ingredients:**
- 3 tbsp olive oil
- 1 onion, chopped
- 1 cup carrots, chopped
- ½ cup celery, chopped
- 1 cup mushrooms, chopped
- 6 cups vegetable broth
- 1 cup pearl barley
- 2 tbsp tomato paste
- ½ tsp dried thyme
- ½ cup Parmesan cheese

**Directions:**
1. Warm the olive oil in a large stockpot over medium heat. Add the onion, celery, and carrots and cook for 5 minutes, stirring frequently. Add the mushrooms and cook for 3 minutes until tender. Pour in the broth, barley, tomato paste, and thyme. Bring the soup to a boil. Simmer for another 15-18 minutes until the barley is cooked through. Top with cheese and serve.

**Nutrition Info:**
- Info Per Serving: Calories: 195;Fat: 4.2g;Protein: 7g;Carbs: 33.8g.

# Bell Pepper & Chickpea Salad

Servings:4
Cooking Time:40 Min + Chilling Time
**Ingredients:**
- 1 cup chickpeas, soaked
- 1 cucumber, sliced
- 10 cherry tomatoes, halved
- 1 red bell peppers, sliced
- 1 green bell pepper, sliced
- 1 tsp yellow mustard
- 1 tsp coriander seeds
- ½ hot banana pepper, minced
- 1 tbsp fresh lemon juice
- 1 tbsp balsamic vinegar
- 2 tbsp olive oil
- Salt and black pepper to taste
- 2 tbsp fresh cilantro, chopped
- 2 tbsp capers

**Directions:**
1. Cover the chickpeas with water by 2 inches in a pot over medium heat. Bring it to a boil. Turn the heat to a simmer and continue to cook for about 40 minutes or until tender. Drain, let cool and transfer to a salad bowl. Add in the remaining ingredients and toss to combine well. Serve.

**Nutrition Info:**
- Info Per Serving: Calories: 470;Fat: 13g;Protein: 22g;Carbs: 73g.

# Feta & Olive Salad

Servings:4
Cooking Time:10 Minutes
**Ingredients:**
- ½ cup extra-virgin olive oil
- 1 head iceberg lettuce, torn
- 2 tomatoes, sliced
- 1 cucumber, sliced
- 1 red onion, thinly sliced
- ¼ cup lemon juice
- Salt to taste
- 1 clove garlic, minced
- 1 cup Kalamata olives, pitted
- 6 oz feta cheese, crumbled
- 2 tbsp dill, chopped

**Directions:**
1. Place the lettuce in a large salad bowl. Add the tomatoes, cucumber, onion, and dill. In another small bowl, whisk together the olive oil, lemon juice, salt, and garlic. Pour the dressing over the salad and gently toss to evenly coat. Sprinkle the salad with the Kalamata olives and feta cheese. Serve and enjoy!

**Nutrition Info:**
- Info Per Serving: Calories: 539;Fat: 50.2g;Protein: 9g;Carbs: 18g.

# Green Salad With Lentils & Feta Cheese

Servings:4
Cooking Time:25 Min + Cooling Time
**Ingredients:**
- 2 tbsp olive oil
- 1 head broccoli, cut into florets
- 1 lb baby spinach
- 2 green onions, sliced
- 1 garlic clove, minced
- 1 cup brown lentils
- Salt and black pepper to taste
- ½ tsp sweet paprika
- ½ tsp ginger, grated
- ¼ cup lemon juice
- ¾ cup feta cheese, crumbled

**Directions:**
1. Blanch the broccoli in salted water in a pot over medium heat for 3-4 minutes. Drain and set aside to cool.
2. Warm the olive oil in the pot and cook green onions and garlic for 3 minutes. Pour in lentils and cover with water. Simmer covered for 15-20 minutes. Drain and let it cool.
3. In a bowl, whisk lemon juice, salt, pepper, sweet paprika, and ginger. Divide the baby spinach between four salad plates, top with lentils and broccoli and drizzle with the prepared dressing. Sprinkle with feta cheese and serve topped.

**Nutrition Info:**
- Info Per Serving: Calories: 300;Fat: 4g;Protein: 22g;Carbs: 50g.

# Broccoli & Garlic Stir Fry

Servings:4
Cooking Time:15 Minutes
**Ingredients:**
- 1 red bell pepper, cut into chunks
- 3 tbsp olive oil
- 2 garlic cloves, minced
- ½ tsp red pepper flakes
- ½ lb broccoli florets
- Salt to taste
- 2 tsp lemon juice
- 1 tbsp anchovy paste

**Directions:**
1. Warm the olive oil in a skillet over medium heat. Add the broccoli, garlic, and red pepper flakes and stir briefly for 3-4 minutes until the florets turn bright green. Season with salt. Add 2 tbsp of water and let broccoli cook for another 2–3 minutes. Stir in the red bell pepper, lemon juice, and anchovy paste and cook for 1 more minute. Serve immediately.

**Nutrition Info:**
- Info Per Serving: Calories: 114;Fat: 11g;Protein: 3g;Carbs: 4g.

# Radicchio Salad With Sunflower Seeds

Servings:4
Cooking Time:10 Minutes
**Ingredients:**
- 3 tbsp olive oil
- 1 cup radicchio, shredded
- 1 lettuce head, torn
- 1 cup raisins
- 2 tbsp lemon juice
- ¼ cup chives, chopped
- Salt and black pepper to taste
- 1 tbsp sunflower seeds, toasted

**Directions:**
1. Mix olive oil, raisins, lemon juice, chives, radicchio, salt, pepper, lettuce, and sunflower seeds in a bowl. Serve.

**Nutrition Info:**
- Info Per Serving: Calories: 70;Fat: 3g;Protein: 1g;Carbs: 3g.

# Beef Stew With Veggies

Servings:6
Cooking Time:75 Minutes
**Ingredients:**
- ¼ cup flour
- 1 tsp paprika
- 1 tsp ground black pepper
- 2 lb beef chuck, cubed
- 2 tbsp olive oil
- 2 tbsp butter
- 1 onion, diced
- 3 garlic cloves, minced
- 1 cup dry red wine
- 2 cups beef stock
- 1 tbsp dried Italian Seasoning
- 2 tsp Worcestershire sauce
- 4 cups potatoes, diced
- 2 celery stalks, chopped
- 3 cups carrots, chopped
- 3 tomatoes, chopped
- 2 bell peppers, chopped
- Salt and black pepper to taste
- 2 tbsp fresh parsley, chopped

**Directions:**
1. Preheat your Instant Pot on Sauté mode. In a bowl, mix black pepper, beef, flour, paprika, and salt. Toss the ingredients and ensure the beef is well-coated.Warm the butter and oil in the pot, add in meat, and cook for 8- 10 minutes until browned. Set aside. To the same fat, add garlic, onion, and celery, bell peppers, and cook for 4-5 minutes until tender.
2. Deglaze with wine, scrape the bottom to get rid of any browned beef bits. Pour in beef stock, Worcestershire sauce, and Italian seasoning. Return beef to the pot; add carrots,

tomatoes, and potatoes. Seal the lid, press Meat/Stew and cook on High Pressure for 35 minutes. Release Pressure naturally for 10 minutes. Taste and adjust the seasonings as necessary. Serve on plates and scatter over the parsley.

**Nutrition Info:**
- Info Per Serving: Calories: 548;Fat: 19g;Protein: 51g;Carbs: 35g.

# Greek Salad With Dressing

Servings:4
Cooking Time: 0 Minutes
**Ingredients:**
- 1 head iceberg lettuce
- 2 cups cherry tomatoes
- 1 large cucumber
- 1 medium onion
- ¼ cup lemon juice
- ½ cup extra-virgin olive oil
- 1 teaspoon salt
- 1 clove garlic, minced
- 1 cup Kalamata olives, pitted
- 1 package feta cheese, crumbled

**Directions:**
1. Cut the lettuce into 1-inch pieces and put them in a large salad bowl.
2. Cut the tomatoes in half and add them to the salad bowl.
3. Slice the cucumber into bite-sized pieces and add them to the salad bowl.
4. Thinly slice the onion and add it to the salad bowl.
5. In a separate bowl, whisk together the olive oil, lemon juice, salt, and garlic. Pour the dressing over the salad and gently toss to evenly coat.
6. Top the salad with the Kalamata olives and feta cheese and serve.

**Nutrition Info:**
- Info Per Serving: Calories: 539;Fat: 50.0g;Protein: 9.0g;Carbs: 18.0g.

# Tomato & Roasted Eggplant Soup

Servings:6
Cooking Time:60 Minutes
**Ingredients:**
- 2 tbsp olive oil
- 3 eggplants, sliced lengthwise
- Salt to taste
- 1 red onion, chopped
- 2 tbsp garlic, minced
- 1 tsp dried thyme
- Salt and black pepper to taste
- 2 ripe tomatoes, halved
- 5 cups chicken broth
- ¼ cup heavy cream
- 2 tbsp fresh basil, chopped

**Directions:**

1. Preheat oven to 400° F. Place the eggplants on a greased sheet pan and drizzle with some olive oil. Roast for 45 minutes. Remove from oven and allow to cool. When cool, remove all of the insides, discarding the skins.
2. Warm the remaining olive oil in a large skillet over medium heat. Add the onions and garlic and cook for 5 minutes until soft and translucent. Add the thyme and season with salt and pepper. Put the eggplant, tomatoes, and onion in your food processor and process until smooth. Pour the chicken broth into a pot and bring to a boil. Reduce heat to a simmer and add the eggplant mixture. Stir until well combined and fold in the heavy cream. Adjust to taste. Serve topped with basil.

**Nutrition Info:**
- Info Per Serving: Calories: 124;Fat: 5.1g;Protein: 3.5g;Carbs: 19g.

# Summer Fruit & Cheese Salad

Servings:6
Cooking Time:10 Minutes
**Ingredients:**
- 1 cantaloupe, quartered and seeded
- 2 tbsp extra-virgin olive oil
- ½ small seedless watermelon
- 1 cup grape tomatoes
- 2 cups Goat cheese, crumbled
- ⅓ cup mint leaves, torn into small pieces
- 1 tbsp balsamic vinegar
- Salt and black pepper to taste

**Directions:**
1. Scoop balls out of the cantaloupe melon using a melon-baller. Put the balls in a shallow bowl. Repeat the process with the watermelon. Add the watermelon balls to the cantaloupe bowl. Add the tomatoes, Goat cheese, mint, olive oil, vinegar, pepper, and salt, and gently mix until everything is incorporated. Serve and enjoy!

**Nutrition Info:**
- Info Per Serving: Calories: 58;Fat: 2.2g;Protein: 1.1g;Carbs: 8.8g.

# Turkish Chickpeas

Servings:4
Cooking Time:40 Minutes
**Ingredients:**
- 3 tbsp olive oil
- 2 cans chickpeas
- 2 tsp smoked paprika
- ½ tsp ground coriander
- ½ tsp cumin
- ½ tsp dried oregano
- Salt and white pepper to taste

**Directions:**
1. Preheat the oven to 400° F. Spread the chickpeas onto a greased baking sheet. In a bowl, combine the olive oil, paprika, ground coriander, cumin, oregano, salt, and white pepper. Pour the mixture over the chickpeas and toss to

combine. Bake for 30 minutes or until the chickpeas turn golden brown, shaking once or twice the baking sheet.

**Nutrition Info:**
- Info Per Serving: Calories: 308;Fat: 13g;Protein: 11g;Carbs: 40g.

## Italian-style Chicken Stew

Servings:4
Cooking Time:20 Minutes
**Ingredients:**
- 2 fire-roasted tomatoes, peeled, chopped
- 2 lb chicken wings
- 2 potatoes, peeled and chopped
- 1 carrot, chopped
- 2 garlic cloves, chopped
- 2 tbsp olive oil
- 1 tsp smoked paprika, ground
- 4 cups chicken broth
- 2 tbsp fresh parsley, chopped
- Salt and black pepper to taste
- 1 cup spinach, chopped

**Directions:**
1. Preheat your Instant Pot on Sauté mode. Rub the chicken with salt, pepper, and paprika, and place in the pot. Stir in all remaining ingredients. Seal the lid and cook on High Pressure for 8 minutes. When ready, do a quick release.

**Nutrition Info:**
- Info Per Serving: Calories: 626;Fat: 26g;Protein: 74g;Carbs: 23g.

## Eggplant & Sweet Potato Salad

Servings:4
Cooking Time:25 Minutes
**Ingredients:**
- 1 tbsp olive oil
- 4 cups arugula
- 2 baby eggplants, cubed
- 2 sweet potatoes, cubed
- 1 red onion, cut into wedges
- 1 tsp hot paprika
- 2 tsp cumin, ground
- Salt and black pepper to taste
- ¼ cup lime juice

**Directions:**
1. Warm the olive oil in a skillet over medium heat and cook eggplants and potatoes for 5 minutes. Stir in onion, paprika, cumin, salt, pepper, and lime juice and cook for another 10 minutes. Mix in arugula and serve.

**Nutrition Info:**
- Info Per Serving: Calories: 210;Fat: 9g;Protein: 5g;Carbs: 13g.

## Spinach & Pea Salad With Rice

Servings:2
Cooking Time:30 Minutes
**Ingredients:**
- 1 tbsp olive oil
- Salt and black pepper to taste
- ½ cup baby spinach
- ½ cup green peas, blanched
- 1 garlic clove, minced
- ½ cup white rice, rinsed
- 6 cherry tomatoes, halved
- 1 tbsp parsley, chopped
- 2 tbsp Italian salad dressing

**Directions:**
1. Bring a large pot of salted water to a boil over medium heat. Pour in the rice, cover, and simmer on low heat for 15-18 minutes or until the rice is al dente. Drain and let cool.
2. In a bowl, whisk the olive oil, garlic, salt, and black pepper. Toss the green peas, baby spinach, and rice together. Pour the dressing all over and gently stir to combine. Decorate with cherry tomatoes and parsley and serve. Enjoy!

**Nutrition Info:**
- Info Per Serving: Calories: 160;Fat: 14g;Protein: 4g;Carbs: 9g.

## Andalusian Gazpacho

Servings:4
Cooking Time:15 Min + Chilling Time
**Ingredients:**
- 1 cucumber, peeled and chopped
- ¼ cup extra-virgin olive oil
- ¼ cup bread cubes, soaked
- 3 cups tomato juice
- 6 tomatoes, chopped
- 3 garlic cloves, minced
- 2 red bell peppers, chopped
- 1 red onion, chopped
- 1 green onion, sliced
- ½ red chili pepper, sliced
- ¼ cup red wine vinegar
- ¼ cup basil leaves, torn
- Salt and black pepper to taste

**Directions:**
1. In a food processor, blend cucumber, soaked bread, tomatoes, garlic, red onion, bell peppers, tomato juice, olive oil, vinegar, basil, salt, and pepper until smooth. Refrigerate for 1-2 hours. Serve topped with 7 chili pepper and green onion.

**Nutrition Info:**
- Info Per Serving: Calories: 226;Fat: 13.4g;Protein: 5g;Carbs: 27g.

# Lamb & Spinach Soup

Servings:4
Cooking Time:60 Minutes
**Ingredients:**
- ½ lb lamb shoulder, cut into bite-sized pieces
- 2 tbsp olive oil
- 1 onion, chopped
- 2 garlic cloves, minced
- 10 oz spinach, chopped
- 4 cups vegetable broth
- Salt and black pepper to taste

**Directions:**
1. Warm the olive oil on Sauté in your Instant Pot. Sauté the lamb, onion, and garlic for 6-8 minutes, stirring often. Pour in the broth and adjust the seasoning with salt and pepper. Seal the lid, press Soup/Broth, and cook for 30 minutes on High Pressure. Do a natural pressure release for 10 minutes. Press Sauté and add the spinach. Cook for 5 minutes. Serve.

**Nutrition Info:**
- Info Per Serving: Calories: 188;Fat: 12g;Protein: 14g;Carbs: 9g.

# Lebanese Crunchy Salad With Seeds

Servings:4
Cooking Time:15 Minutes
**Ingredients:**
- For the Salad
- 1 head Romaine lettuce, separated into leaves
- 1 cup sunflower seeds, toasted
- 1 Lebanese cucumber, sliced
- 1 tbsp cilantro, chopped
- 2 tbsp black olives, pitted
- 8 cherry tomatoes, halved
- For Dressing
- 1 lemon, juiced
- ½ tsp Mediterranean herb mix
- 2 tbsp onions, chopped
- ½ tsp paprika
- ½ tsp garlic, chopped
- Salt and black pepper to taste

**Directions:**
1. Toss all of the salad ingredients in a bowl. Whisk all of the dressing ingredients until creamy and smooth. Dress your salad and serve.

**Nutrition Info:**
- Info Per Serving: Calories: 210;Fat: 16g;Protein: 8g;Carbs: 7g.

# Cumin Cauli Mash

Servings:4
Cooking Time:25 Minutes
**Ingredients:**
- 2 tbsp butter
- ¼ cup grated Parmesan cheese
- 4 cups cauliflower florets
- ¼ cup milk
- 2 tbsp wholegrain mustard
- 1 tsp ground cumin
- 1 tsp crushed chilies
- Salt and black pepper to taste

**Directions:**
1. Boil the cauliflower in a pot of salted water for 10 minutes. Drain and place in a large bowl. Add in milk, butter, cheese, mustard, cumin, salt, and pepper. Mash until smooth with a potato masher. Top with crushed chilies and serve.

**Nutrition Info:**
- Info Per Serving: Calories: 117;Fat: 8g;Protein: 4.6g;Carbs: 8.3g.

# Artichoke And Arugula Salad

Servings:6
Cooking Time: 0 Minutes
**Ingredients:**
- Salad:
- 6 canned oil-packed artichoke hearts, sliced
- 6 cups baby arugula leaves
- 6 fresh olives, pitted and chopped
- 1 cup cherry tomatoes, sliced in half
- Dressing:
- 1 teaspoon Dijon mustard
- 2 tablespoons balsamic vinegar
- 1 clove garlic, minced
- 2 tablespoons extra-virgin olive oil
- For Garnish:
- 4 fresh basil leaves, thinly sliced

**Directions:**
1. Combine the ingredients for the salad in a large salad bowl, then toss to combine well.
2. Combine the ingredients for the dressing in a small bowl, then stir to mix well.
3. Dressing the salad, then serve with basil leaves on top.

**Nutrition Info:**
- Info Per Serving: Calories: 134;Fat: 12.1g;Protein: 1.6g;Carbs: 6.2g.

# Sumptuous Greek Vegetable Salad

Servings:6
Cooking Time: 0 Minutes
**Ingredients:**
- Salad:
- 1 can chickpeas, drained and rinsed
- 1 can artichoke hearts, drained and halved
- 1 head Bibb lettuce, chopped

- 1 cucumber, peeled deseeded, and chopped
- 1½ cups grape tomatoes, halved
- ¼ cup chopped basil leaves
- ½ cup sliced black olives
- ½ cup cubed feta cheese
- Dressing:
- 1 tablespoon freshly squeezed lemon juice (from about ½ small lemon)
- ¼ teaspoon freshly ground black pepper
- 1 tablespoon chopped fresh oregano
- 2 tablespoons extra-virgin olive oil
- 1 tablespoon red wine vinegar
- 1 teaspoon honey

**Directions:**
1. Combine the ingredients for the salad in a large salad bowl, then toss to combine well.
2. Combine the ingredients for the dressing in a small bowl, then stir to mix well.
3. Dressing the salad and serve immediately.

**Nutrition Info:**
- Info Per Serving: Calories: 165;Fat: 8.1g;Protein: 7.2g;Carbs: 17.9g.

# Beef Stew With Eggplant & Parmesan

Servings:6
Cooking Time:50 Minutes
**Ingredients:**
- 9 oz beef neck, cut into bite-sized pieces
- 1 eggplant, chopped
- 2 cups fire-roasted tomatoes
- ½ tbsp fresh green peas
- 1 tbsp beef broth
- 4 tbsp olive oil
- 2 tbsp tomato paste
- 1 tbsp ground chili pepper
- Salt to taste
- Parmesan cheese for garnish

**Directions:**
1. Preheat your Instant Pot on Sauté mode. Rub the meat with salt, cayenne, and chili pepper. Warm the olive oil in the pot and brown the meat for 5-7 minutes or until golden.
2. Add all the remaining ingredients and seal the lid. Cook on Meat/Stew mode for 40 minutes on High. When ready, do a natural release for 10 minutes. Sprinkle with freshly grated Parmesan cheese. Serve warm and enjoy!

**Nutrition Info:**
- Info Per Serving: Calories: 403;Fat: 11g;Protein: 15g;Carbs: 4.2g.

# Pesto Ravioli Salad

Servings:6
Cooking Time:15 Minutes
**Ingredients:**
- 1 cup smoked mozzarella cheese, cubed
- ¼ tsp lemon zest
- 1 cup basil pesto
- ½ cup mayonnaise
- 2 red bell peppers, chopped
- 18 oz cheese ravioli

**Directions:**
1. Bring to a boil salted water in a pot over high heat. Add the ravioli and cook, uncovered, for 4-5 minutes, stirring occasionally; drain and place them in a salad bowl to cool slightly. Blend the lemon zest, pesto, and mayonnaise in a large bowl and stir in mozzarella cheese and bell peppers. Pour the mixture over the ravioli and toss to coat. Serve.

**Nutrition Info:**
- Info Per Serving: Calories: 447;Fat: 32g;Protein: 18g;Carbs: 24g.

# Kale & Chicken Soup With Vermicelli

Servings:4
Cooking Time:25 Minutes
**Ingredients:**
- 2 tbsp olive oil
- 1 carrot, chopped
- 1 leek, chopped
- ½ cup vermicelli
- 4 cups chicken stock
- 2 cups kale, chopped
- 2 chicken breasts, cubed
- 1 cup orzo
- ¼ cup lemon juice
- 2 tbsp parsley, chopped
- Salt and black pepper to taste

**Directions:**
1. Warm the olive oil in a pot over medium heat and sauté leek and chicken for 6 minutes. Stir in carrot and chicken stock and bring to a boil. Cook for 10 minutes. Add in vermicelli, kale, orzo, and lemon juice and continue cooking for another 5 minutes. Adjust the seasoning with salt and pepper and sprinkle with parsley. Ladle into soup bowls and serve.

**Nutrition Info:**
- Info Per Serving: Calories: 310;Fat: 13g;Protein: 13g;Carbs: 17g.

# Endive & Tuna Salad With Pine Nuts

Servings:6
Cooking Time:10 Minutes
**Ingredients:**
- 1 can tuna in olive oil, drained and flaked
- 1 endive head, chopped
- 1 shallot, sliced
- 3 tbsp chives, chopped
- 3 tbsp mayonnaise
- 1 tsp Dijon mustard
- 1/2 lemon, juiced and zested
- Salt and black pepper to taste
- ¼ cup toasted pine nuts

**Directions:**
1. In a salad bowl, toss endive, tuna, shallot, and chives. Whisk the mayonnaise, mustard, lemon zest, lemon juice, salt, and pepper in a small bowl. Spoon the mayonnaise mixture over the tuna salad and top with pine nuts. Serve.

**Nutrition Info:**
- Info Per Serving: Calories: 128;Fat: 8g;Protein: 10g;Carbs: 5g.

# Corn & Cucumber Salad

Servings:4
Cooking Time:10 Minutes
**Ingredients:**
- 3 tbsp olive oil
- 3 tbsp pepitas, roasted
- 2 tbsp cilantro, chopped
- 1 cup corn
- 1 cup radishes, sliced
- 2 avocados, mashed
- 2 cucumbers, chopped
- 2 tbsp Greek yogurt
- 1 tsp balsamic vinegar
- 2 tbsp lime juice
- Salt and black pepper to taste

**Directions:**
1. In a bowl, whisk the olive oil, avocados, salt, pepper, lime juice, yogurt, and vinegar until smooth. Combine pepitas, cilantro, corn, radishes, and cucumbers in a salad bowl. Pour the avocado dressing over salad and toss to combine. Serve.

**Nutrition Info:**
- Info Per Serving: Calories: 410;Fat: 32g;Protein: 4g;Carbs: 25g.

# Horiatiki Salad (greek Salad)

Servings:4
Cooking Time:10 Minutes
**Ingredients:**
- 1 green bell pepper, cut into chunks
- 1 head romaine lettuce, torn
- ½ red onion, cut into rings
- 2 tomatoes, cut into wedges
- 1 cucumber, thinly sliced
- 3 tbsp extra-virgin olive oil
- 2 tbsp lemon juice
- Garlic salt and pepper to taste
- ¼ tsp dried Greek oregano
- 1 cup feta cheese, cubed
- 1 handful of Kalamata olives

**Directions:**
1. In a salad bowl, whisk the olive oil, lemon juice, pepper, garlic salt, and oregano. Add in the lettuce, red onion, tomatoes, cucumber, and bell pepper and mix with your hands to coat. Top with feta and olives and serve immediately.

**Nutrition Info:**
- Info Per Serving: Calories: 226;Fat: 19g;Protein: 8g;Carbs: 9g.

# Creamy Tomato Hummus Soup

Servings:4
Cooking Time:10 Minutes
**Ingredients:**
- 1 can diced tomatoes
- 1 cup traditional hummus
- 4 cups chicken stock
- ¼ cup basil leaves, sliced
- 1 cup garlic croutons

**Directions:**
1. Place the tomatoes, hummus, and chicken stock in your blender and blend until smooth. Pour the mixture into a saucepan over medium heat and bring it to a boil. Pour the soup into bowls. Sprinkle with basil and serve with croutons.

**Nutrition Info:**
- Info Per Serving: Calories: 148;Fat: 6.2g;Protein: 5g;Carbs: 18.8g.

# Bean & Zucchini Soup

Servings:4
Cooking Time:40 Minutes
**Ingredients:**
- 1 tbsp olive oil
- 1 onion, chopped
- 2 cloves garlic, minced
- 5 cups vegetable broth
- 1 cup dried chickpeas
- ½ cup pinto beans, soaked
- ½ cup navy beans, soaked
- 3 carrots, chopped
- 1 large celery stalk, chopped
- 1 tsp dried thyme
- 16 oz zucchini noodles
- Salt and black pepper to taste

**Directions:**
1. Warm the olive oil on Sauté in your Instant Pot. Stir in garlic and onion and cook for 5 minutes until golden brown. Mix in pepper, broth, carrots, salt, pepper, celery, beans, chickpeas, and thyme. Seal the lid and cook for 15 minutes on High Pressure. Release the pressure naturally for 10 minutes. Mix zucchini noodles into the soup and stir until wilted. Serve.

**Nutrition Info:**
- Info Per Serving: Calories: 481;Fat: 8g;Protein: 23g;Carbs: 83g.

# Mushroom & Spinach Orzo Soup

Servings:4
Cooking Time:20 Minutes
**Ingredients:**
- 2 tbsp butter
- 3 cups spinach
- ½ cup orzo
- 4 cups chicken broth
- 1 cup feta cheese, crumbled
- Salt and black pepper to taste
- ½ tsp dried oregano
- 1 onion, chopped
- 2 garlic cloves, minced
- 1 cup mushrooms, sliced

**Directions:**
1. Melt butter in a pot over medium heat and sauté onion, garlic, and mushrooms for 5 minutes until tender. Add in chicken broth, orzo, salt, pepper, and oregano. Bring to a boil and reduce the heat to a low. Continue simmering for 10 minutes, partially covered. Stir in spinach and continue to cook until the spinach wilts, about 3-4 minutes. Ladle into individual bowls and serve garnished with feta cheese.

**Nutrition Info:**
- Info Per Serving: Calories: 370;Fat: 11g;Protein: 23g;Carbs: 44g.

# Fish And Seafood Recipes

## Simple Fried Cod Fillets

Servings:4
Cooking Time: 10 Minutes
**Ingredients:**
- ½ cup all-purpose flour
- 1 teaspoon garlic powder
- 1 teaspoon salt
- 4 cod fillets
- 1 tablespoon extra-virgin olive oil

**Directions:**
1. Mix together the flour, garlic powder, and salt in a shallow dish.
2. Dredge each piece of fish in the seasoned flour until they are evenly coated.
3. Heat the olive oil in a medium skillet over medium-high heat.
4. Once hot, add the cod fillets and fry for 6 to 8 minutes, flipping the fish halfway through, or until the fish is opaque and flakes easily.
5. Remove from the heat and serve on plates.

**Nutrition Info:**
- Info Per Serving: Calories: 333;Fat: 18.8g;Protein: 21.2g;Carbs: 20.0g.

## Garlic Skillet Salmon

Servings:4
Cooking Time: 14 To 16 Minutes
**Ingredients:**
- 1 tablespoon extra-virgin olive oil
- 2 garlic cloves, minced
- 1 teaspoon smoked paprika
- 1½ cups grape or cherry tomatoes, quartered
- 1 jar roasted red peppers, drained and chopped
- 1 tablespoon water
- ¼ teaspoon freshly ground black pepper
- ¼ teaspoon kosher or sea salt
- 1 pound salmon fillets, skin removed and cut into 8 pieces
- 1 tablespoon freshly squeezed lemon juice

**Directions:**
1. In a large skillet over medium heat, heat the oil. Add the garlic and smoked paprika and cook for 1 minute, stirring often. Add the tomatoes, roasted peppers, water, black pepper, and salt. Turn up the heat to medium-high, bring to a simmer, and cook for 3 minutes, stirring occasionally and smashing the tomatoes with a wooden spoon toward the end of the cooking time.
2. Add the salmon to the skillet, and spoon some of the sauce over the top. Cover and cook for 10 to 12 minutes, or until the salmon is cooked through and just starts to flake.

3. Remove the skillet from the heat, and drizzle lemon juice over the top of the fish. Stir the sauce, then break up the salmon into chunks with a fork. Serve hot.

**Nutrition Info:**
- Info Per Serving: Calories: 255;Fat: 11.7g;Protein: 24.2g;Carbs: 5.9g.

## Easy Tomato Tuna Melts

Servings:2
Cooking Time: 3 To 4 Minutes
**Ingredients:**
- 1 can chunk light tuna packed in water, drained
- 2 tablespoons plain Greek yogurt
- 2 tablespoons finely chopped celery
- 1 tablespoon finely chopped red onion
- 2 teaspoons freshly squeezed lemon juice
- Pinch cayenne pepper
- 1 large tomato, cut into ¾-inch-thick rounds
- ½ cup shredded Cheddar cheese

**Directions:**
1. Preheat the broiler to High.
2. Stir together the tuna, yogurt, celery, red onion, lemon juice, and cayenne pepper in a medium bowl.
3. Place the tomato rounds on a baking sheet. Top each with some tuna salad and Cheddar cheese.
4. Broil for 3 to 4 minutes until the cheese is melted and bubbly. Cool for 5 minutes before serving.

**Nutrition Info:**
- Info Per Serving: Calories: 244;Fat: 10.0g;Protein: 30.1g;Carbs: 6.9g.

## Spicy Grilled Shrimp With Lemon Wedges

Servings:6
Cooking Time: 6 Minutes
**Ingredients:**
- 1 large clove garlic, crushed
- 1 teaspoon coarse salt
- 1 teaspoon paprika
- ½ teaspoon cayenne pepper
- 2 teaspoons lemon juice
- 2 tablespoons plus 1 teaspoon olive oil, divided
- 2 pounds large shrimp, peeled and deveined
- 8 wedges lemon, for garnish

**Directions:**
1. Preheat the grill to medium heat.
2. Stir together the garlic, salt, paprika, cayenne pepper, lemon juice, and 2 tablespoons of olive oil in a small bowl until a paste forms. Add the shrimp and toss until well coated.
3. Grease the grill grates lightly with remaining 1 teaspoon of olive oil.

4. Grill the shrimp for 4 to 6 minutes, flipping the shrimp halfway through, or until the shrimp is totally pink and opaque.

5. Garnish the shrimp with lemon wedges and serve hot.

**Nutrition Info:**

- Info Per Serving: Calories: 163;Fat: 5.8g;Protein: 25.2g;Carbs: 2.8g.

# Parsley Salmon Bake

Servings:4
Cooking Time:20 Minutes
**Ingredients:**

- 2 tbsp olive oil
- 1 lb salmon fillets
- ¼ fresh parsley, chopped
- 1 garlic clove, minced
- ¼ tsp dried dill
- ¼ tsp chili powder
- ¼ tsp garlic powder
- 1 lemon, grated
- Salt and black pepper to taste

**Directions:**

1. Preheat oven to 350 °F. Sprinkle the salmon with dill, chili powder, garlic powder, salt, and pepper.

2. Warm olive oil in a pan over medium heat and sear salmon skin-side down for 5 minutes. Transfer to the oven and bake for another 4-5 minutes. Combine parsley, lemon zest, garlic, and salt in a bowl. Serve salmon topped with the mixture.

**Nutrition Info:**

- Info Per Serving: Calories: 212;Fat: 14g;Protein: 22g;Carbs: 0.5g.

# One-pot Shrimp With White Beans

Servings:4
Cooking Time:23 Minutes
**Ingredients:**

- 1 lb large shrimp, peeled and deveined
- 3 tbsp olive oil
- Salt and black pepper to taste
- 1 red bell pepper, chopped
- 1 small red onion, chopped
- 2 garlic cloves, minced
- ¼ tsp red pepper flakes
- 2 cans cannellini beans
- 2 tbsp lemon zest

**Directions:**

1. Warm the olive oil in a skillet over medium heat. Add the shrimp and cook, without stirring, until spotty brown and edges turn pink, about 2 minutes. Remove the skillet from the heat, turn over the shrimp, and let sit until opaque throughout, about 30 seconds. Transfer shrimp to a bowl and cover with foil to keep warm.

2. Return the skillet to heat and reheat the olive oil. Sauté the bell pepper, garlic, and onion until softened, about 5 minutes. Stir in pepper flakes and salt for about 30 seconds.

Pour in the beans and cook until heated through, 5 minutes. Add the shrimp with any accumulated juices back to the skillet cook for about 1 minute. Stir in lemon zest and serve.

**Nutrition Info:**

- Info Per Serving: Calories: 300;Fat: 18g;Protein: 25g;Carbs: 11g.

# Shrimp & Gnocchi With Feta Cheese

Servings:4
Cooking Time:30 Minutes
**Ingredients:**

- 1 lb shrimp, shells and tails removed
- 1 jar roasted red peppers, chopped
- 2 tbsp olive oil
- 1 cup chopped fresh tomato
- 2 garlic cloves, minced
- ½ tsp dried oregano
- Black pepper to taste
- ¼ tsp crushed red peppers
- 1 lb potato gnocchi
- ½ cup cubed feta cheese
- ⅓ cup fresh basil leaves, torn

**Directions:**

1. Preheat oven to 425 °F. In a baking dish, mix the tomatoes, olive oil, garlic, oregano, black pepper, and crushed red peppers. Roast in the oven for 10 minutes. Stir in the roasted peppers and shrimp. Roast for 10 minutes until the shrimp turn pink. Bring a saucepan of salted water to the boil and cook the gnocchi for 1-2 mins, until floating. Drain. Remove the dish from the oven. Mix in the cooked gnocchi, sprinkle with feta and basil and serve.

**Nutrition Info:**

- Info Per Serving: Calories: 146;Fat: 5g;Protein: 23g;Carbs: 1g.

# Herby Cod Stew

Servings:4
Cooking Time:35 Minutes
**Ingredients:**

- 4 cod fillets, boneless, skinless, cubed
- 2 tbsp olive oil
- 2 tbsp parsley, chopped
- 2 tomatoes, chopped
- 2 tbsp cilantro, chopped
- 2 garlic cloves, minced
- ½ tsp paprika
- 2 cups chicken stock
- Salt and black pepper to taste
- 1 carrot, sliced
- 1 red bell pepper, chopped
- ½ cup black olives, pitted and halved
- 1 red onion, sliced

**Directions:**

1. Warm olive oil in a saucepan over medium heat and cook garlic, carrot, bell pepper, and onion for 5 minutes. Stir

in cod fillets, parsley, tomatoes, and paprika for 3-4 minutes. Pour in chicken stock and olives and bring to a boil. Cook for 15 minutes. Adjust the seasoning and sprinkle with cilantro.

**Nutrition Info:**

- Info Per Serving: Calories: 280;Fat: 16g;Protein: 3g;Carbs: 15g.

## Saucy Cod With Calamari Rings

Servings:4

Cooking Time:20 Minutes

**Ingredients:**

- 1 lb cod, skinless and cubed
- 2 tbsp olive oil
- 1 mango, peeled and cubed
- ½ lb calamari rings
- 1 tbsp garlic chili sauce
- ¼ cup lime juice
- ½ tsp smoked paprika
- ½ tsp cumin, ground
- 2 garlic cloves, minced
- Salt and black pepper to taste

**Directions:**

1. Warm the olive oil in a skillet over medium heat and cook chili sauce, lime juice, paprika, cumin, garlic, salt, pepper, and mango for 3 minutes. Stir in cod and calamari and cook for another 7 minutes. Serve warm.

**Nutrition Info:**

- Info Per Serving: Calories: 290;Fat: 13g;Protein: 16g;Carbs: 12g.

## Crunchy Pollock Fillets

Servings:4

Cooking Time:25 Minutes

**Ingredients:**

- 4 pollock fillets, boneless
- 2 cups potato chips, crushed
- 2 tbsp mayonnaise

**Directions:**

1. Preheat the oven to 380°F. Line a baking sheet with parchment paper. Rub each fillet with mayonnaise and dip them in the potato chips. Place fillets on the sheet and bake for 12 minutes. Serve with salad.

**Nutrition Info:**

- Info Per Serving: Calories: 240;Fat: 9g;Protein: 26g;Carbs: 10g.

## Roasted Salmon With Tomatoes & Capers

Servings:4

Cooking Time:25 Minutes

**Ingredients:**

- 1 tbsp olive oil
- 4 salmon steaks
- Salt and black pepper to taste
- ¼ mustard powder
- ½ tsp garlic powder
- 2 Roma tomatoes, chopped
- ¼ cup green olives, chopped
- 1 tsp capers
- ½ cup breadcrumbs
- 1 lemon, cut into wedges

**Directions:**

1. Preheat oven to 375 °F. Arrange the salmon fillets on a greased baking dish. Season with salt, pepper, garlic powder, and mustard powder and coat with the breadcrumbs. Drizzle with olive oil. Scatter the tomatoes, green olives, garlic, and capers around the fish fillets. Bake for 15 minutes until the salmon steaks flake easily with a fork. Serve with lemon wedges.

**Nutrition Info:**

- Info Per Serving: Calories: 504;Fat: 18g;Protein: 68g;Carbs: 14g.

## Chili Flounder Parcels

Servings:4

Cooking Time:20 Minutes

**Ingredients:**

- 2 tbsp olive oil
- 4 flounder fillets
- ¼ tsp red pepper flakes
- 4 fresh rosemary sprigs
- 2 garlic cloves, thinly sliced
- 1 cup cherry tomatoes, halved
- ½ chopped onion
- 2 tbsp capers
- 8 black olives, sliced
- 2 tbsp dry white wine
- Salt and black pepper to taste

**Directions:**

1. Preheat oven to 420ºF. Drizzle the flounder with olive oil and season with salt, pepper, and red pepper flakes. Divide fillets between 4 pieces of aluminium foil. Top each one with garlic, cherry tomatoes, capers, onion, and olives. Fold the edges to form packets with opened tops. Add in a rosemary sprig in each one and drizzle with the white wine. Seal the packets and arrange them on a baking sheet. Bake for 10 minutes or until the fish is cooked. Serve warm.

**Nutrition Info:**

- Info Per Serving: Calories: 242;Fat: 10g;Protein: 31.5g;Carbs: 4g.

# Dill Smoked Salmon & Eggplant Rolls

Servings:4
Cooking Time:20 Minutes
**Ingredients:**
- 2 eggplants, lengthwise cut into thin slices
- 2 tbsp olive oil
- 1 cup ricotta cheese, soft
- 4 oz smoked salmon, chopped
- 2 tsp lemon zest, grated
- 1 small red onion, sliced
- Salt and pepper to the taste

**Directions:**
1. Mix salmon, cheese, lemon zest, onion, salt, and pepper in a bowl. Grease the eggplant with olive oil and grill them on a preheated grill pan for 3-4 minutes per side. Set aside to cool. Spread the cooled eggplant slices with the salmon mixture. Roll out and secure with toothpicks and serve.

**Nutrition Info:**
- Info Per Serving: Calories: 310;Fat: 25g;Protein: 12g;Carbs: 16g.

# Anchovy Spread With Avocado

Servings:2
Cooking Time:5 Minutes
**Ingredients:**
- 1 avocado, peeled and pitted
- 1 tsp lemon juice
- ¼ celery stalk, chopped
- ¼ cup chopped shallots
- 2 anchovy fillets in olive oil
- Salt and black pepper to taste

**Directions:**
1. Combine lemon juice, avocado, celery, shallots, and anchovy fillets (with their olive oil) in a food processor. Blitz until smooth. Season with salt and black pepper. Serve.

**Nutrition Info:**
- Info Per Serving: Calories: 271;Fat: 20g;Protein: 15g;Carbs: 12g.

# Seafood Stew

Servings:4
Cooking Time:25 Minutes
**Ingredients:**
- ½ lb skinless trout, cubed
- 2 tbsp olive oil
- ½ lb clams
- ½ lb cod, cubed
- 1 onion, chopped
- ½ fennel bulb, chopped
- 2 garlic cloves, minced
- ¼ cup dry white wine
- 2 tbsp chopped fresh parsley
- 1 can tomato sauce

- 1 cup fish broth
- 1 tbsp Italian seasoning
- ⅛ tsp red pepper flakes
- Salt and black pepper to taste

**Directions:**
1. Warm olive oil in a pot over medium heat and sauté onion and fennel for 5 minutes. Add in garlic and cook for 30 seconds. Pour in the wine and cook for 1 minute. Stir in tomato sauce, clams, broth, cod, trout, salt, Italian seasoning, red pepper flakes, and pepper. Bring just a boil and simmer for 5 minutes. Discard any unopened clams. Top with parsley.

**Nutrition Info:**
- Info Per Serving: Calories: 372;Fat: 15g;Protein: 34g;Carbs: 25g.

# Crispy Sole Fillets

Servings:4
Cooking Time:10 Minutes
**Ingredients:**
- ¼ cup olive oil
- ½ cup flour
- ½ tsp paprika
- 8 skinless sole fillets
- Salt and black pepper to taste
- 4 lemon wedges

**Directions:**
1. Warm the olive oil in a skillet over medium heat. Mix the flour with paprika in a shallow dish. Coat the fish with the flour, shaking off any excess. Sear the sole fillets for 2-3 minutes per side until lightly browned. Serve with lemon wedges.

**Nutrition Info:**
- Info Per Serving: Calories: 219;Fat: 15g;Protein: 8.7g;Carbs: 13g.

# Baked Haddock With Rosemary Gremolata

Servings:6
Cooking Time:35 Min + Marinating Time
**Ingredients:**
- 1 cup milk
- Salt and black pepper to taste
- 2 tbsp rosemary, chopped
- 1 garlic clove, minced
- 1 lemon, zested
- 1 ½ lb haddock fillets

**Directions:**
1. In a large bowl, coat the fish with milk, salt, pepper, and 1 tablespoon of rosemary. Refrigerate for 2 hours.
2. Preheat oven to 380ºF. Carefully remove the haddock from the marinade, drain thoroughly, and place in a greased baking dish. Cover and bake 15–20 minutes until the fish is flaky. Remove fish from the oven and let it rest 5 minutes. To make the gremolata, mix the remaining rosemary, lemon zest, and garlic. Sprinkle the fish with gremolata and serve.

**Nutrition Info:**
- Info Per Serving: Calories: 112;Fat: 2g;Protein: 20g;Carbs: 3g.

# Grilled Lemon Pesto Salmon

Servings:2
Cooking Time: 6 To 10 Minutes
**Ingredients:**
- 10 ounces salmon fillet
- Salt and freshly ground black pepper, to taste
- 2 tablespoons prepared pesto sauce
- 1 large fresh lemon, sliced
- Cooking spray

**Directions:**
1. Preheat the grill to medium-high heat. Spray the grill grates with cooking spray.
2. Season the salmon with salt and black pepper. Spread the pesto sauce on top.
3. Make a bed of fresh lemon slices about the same size as the salmon fillet on the hot grill, and place the salmon on top of the lemon slices. Put any additional lemon slices on top of the salmon.
4. Grill the salmon for 6 to 10 minutes, or until the fish is opaque and flakes apart easily.
5. Serve hot.

**Nutrition Info:**
- Info Per Serving: Calories: 316;Fat: 21.1g;Protein: 29.0g;Carbs: 1.0g.

# Oil–poached Cod

Servings:4
Cooking Time:20 Minutes
**Ingredients:**
- 4 cod fillets, skins removed
- 3 cups olive oil
- Salt and black pepper to taste
- 1 lemon, zested and juiced
- 3 fresh thyme sprigs

**Directions:**
1. Heat the olive oil with thyme sprigs in a pot over low heat. Gently add the cod fillets and poach them for about 6 minutes or until the fish is completely opaque. Using a slotted spoon, carefully remove the fish to a plate lined with paper towels. Sprinkle with lemon zest, salt, and pepper. Drizzle with lemon juice and serve immediately.

**Nutrition Info:**
- Info Per Serving: Calories: 292;Fat: 34g;Protein: 18g;Carbs: 1g.

# Seared Halibut With Moroccan Chermoula

Servings:4
Cooking Time:30 Min + Marinating Time
**Ingredients:**
- 2 tbsp olive oil
- 1 tsp dry thyme
- 1 tsp dry rosemary
- 4 halibut steaks
- Salt and black pepper to taste
- Chermoula
- 2 tbsp olive oil
- ¾ cup fresh cilantro
- 2 tbsp lemon juice
- 4 garlic cloves, minced
- ½ tsp ground cumin
- ½ tsp paprika
- ¼ tsp salt
- ½ tsp cayenne pepper

**Directions:**
1. In a large bowl, coat the fish with 2 tbsp olive oil, rosemary, thyme, salt, and pepper. Let it marinate for 15 minutes. Process cilantro, lemon juice, olive oil, garlic, cumin, paprika, salt, and cayenne pepper in your food processor until smooth, about 1 minute, scraping down sides of the bowl as needed. Set aside the chermoula until ready to serve.
2. Preheat oven to 325 °F. Place the halibut in a baking tray. Bake for 10-12 minutes until halibut flakes apart when gently prodded with a paring knife. Serve with chermoula.

**Nutrition Info:**
- Info Per Serving: Calories: 187;Fat: 11g;Protein: 19g;Carbs: 1.1g.

# Garlic Shrimp With Mushrooms

Servings:4
Cooking Time: 15 Minutes
**Ingredients:**
- 1 pound fresh shrimp, peeled, deveined, and patted dry
- 1 teaspoon salt
- 1 cup extra-virgin olive oil
- 8 large garlic cloves, thinly sliced
- 4 ounces sliced mushrooms (shiitake, baby bella, or button)
- ½ teaspoon red pepper flakes
- ¼ cup chopped fresh flat-leaf Italian parsley

**Directions:**
1. In a bowl, season the shrimp with salt. Set aside.
2. Heat the olive oil in a large skillet over medium-low heat.
3. Add the garlic and cook for 3 to 4 minutes until fragrant, stirring occasionally.
4. Sauté the mushrooms for 5 minutes, or until they start to exude their juices.

5. Stir in the shrimp and sprinkle with red pepper flakes and sauté for 3 to 4 minutes more, or until the shrimp start to turn pink.

6. Remove the skillet from the heat and add the parsley. Stir to combine and serve warm.

**Nutrition Info:**

- Info Per Serving: Calories: 619;Fat: 55.5g;Protein: 24.1g;Carbs: 3.7g.

# Lime-orange Squid Meal

Servings:4
Cooking Time:30 Minutes
**Ingredients:**

- 1 lb baby squid, cleaned, body and tentacles chopped
- 3 tbsp olive oil
- ½ cup green olives, chopped
- ½ tsp lime zest, grated
- 1 tbsp lime juice
- ½ tsp orange zest, grated
- 1 tsp red pepper flakes
- 1 tbsp parsley, chopped
- 4 garlic cloves, minced
- 1 shallot, chopped
- 1 cup vegetable stock
- 2 tbsp red wine vinegar
- Salt and black pepper to taste

**Directions:**

1. Warm the olive oil in a skillet over medium heat and stir in lime zest, lime juice, orange zest, red pepper flakes, garlic, shallot, olives, stock, vinegar, salt, and pepper. Bring to a boil and simmer for 10 minutes. Mix in squid and parsley and cook for another 10 minutes. Serve hot.

**Nutrition Info:**

- Info Per Serving: Calories: 310;Fat: 10g;Protein: 12g;Carbs: 23g.

# Tuna Gyros With Tzatziki

Servings:4
Cooking Time:15 Minutes
**Ingredients:**

- 4 oz tzatziki
- ½ lb canned tuna, drained
- ½ cup tahini
- 4 sundried tomatoes, diced
- 2 tbsp warm water
- 2 garlic cloves, minced
- 1 tbsp lemon juice
- 4 pita wraps
- 5 black olives, chopped
- Salt and black pepper to taste

**Directions:**

1. In a bowl, combine the tahini, water, garlic, lemon juice, salt, and black pepper. Warm the pita wraps in a grilled pan for a few minutes, turning once. Spread the tahini and tzatziki sauces over the warmed pitas and top with tuna, sundried tomatoes, and olives. Fold in half and serve immediately.

**Nutrition Info:**

- Info Per Serving: Calories: 334;Fat: 24g;Protein: 21.3g;Carbs: 9g.

# Thyme Hake With Potatoes

Servings:4
Cooking Time:40 Minutes
**Ingredients:**

- 1 ½ lb russet potatoes, unpeeled
- ¼ cup olive oil
- ½ tsp garlic powder
- ½ tsp paprika
- Salt and black pepper to taste
- 4 skinless hake fillets
- 4 fresh thyme sprigs
- 1 lemon, sliced

**Directions:**

1. Preheat oven to 425 °F. Slice the potatoes and toss them with some olive oil, salt, pepper, paprika, and garlic powder in a bowl. Microwave for 12-14 minutes until potatoes are just tender, stirring halfway through microwaving.

2. Transfer the potatoes to a baking dish and press gently into an even layer. Season the hake with salt and pepper, and arrange it skinned side down over the potatoes. Drizzle with the remaining olive oil, then place thyme sprigs and lemon slices on top. Bake for 15-18 minutes until hake flakes apart when gently prodded with a paring knife. Serve and enjoy!

**Nutrition Info:**

- Info Per Serving: Calories: 410;Fat: 16g;Protein: 34g;Carbs: 33g.

# Asian-inspired Tuna Lettuce Wraps

Servings:2
Cooking Time: 0 Minutes
**Ingredients:**

- ⅓ cup almond butter
- 1 tablespoon freshly squeezed lemon juice
- 1 teaspoon low-sodium soy sauce
- 1 teaspoon curry powder
- ½ teaspoon sriracha, or to taste
- ½ cup canned water chestnuts, drained and chopped
- 2 package tuna packed in water, drained
- 2 large butter lettuce leaves

**Directions:**

1. Stir together the almond butter, lemon juice, soy sauce, curry powder, sriracha in a medium bowl until well mixed. Add the water chestnuts and tuna and stir until well incorporated.

2. Place 2 butter lettuce leaves on a flat work surface, spoon half of the tuna mixture onto each leaf and roll up into a wrap. Serve immediately.

**Nutrition Info:**

- Info Per Serving: Calories: 270;Fat: 13.9g;Protein: 19.1g;Carbs: 18.5g.

## Sicilian-style Squid With Zucchini

Servings:4
Cooking Time:25 Minutes
**Ingredients:**
- 2 tbsp olive oil
- 10 oz squid, cut into pieces
- 2 zucchinis, chopped
- 2 tbsp cilantro, chopped
- 1 jalapeno pepper, chopped
- 3 tbsp balsamic vinegar
- Salt and black pepper to taste
- 1 tbsp dill, chopped

**Directions:**
1. Warm the olive oil in a skillet over medium heat and sauté squid for 5 minutes. Stir in zucchini, cilantro, jalapeño pepper, vinegar, salt, pepper, and dill and cook for another 10 minutes. Serve right away.

**Nutrition Info:**
- Info Per Serving: Calories: 240;Fat: 16g;Protein: 12g;Carbs: 24g.

## Herby Tuna Gratin

Servings:4
Cooking Time:20 Minutes
**Ingredients:**
- 10 oz canned tuna, flaked
- 4 eggs, whisked
- ½ cup mozzarella, shredded
- 1 tbsp chives, chopped
- 1 tbsp parsley, chopped
- Salt and black pepper to taste

**Directions:**
1. Preheat the oven to 360°F. Mix tuna, eggs, chives, parsley, salt, and pepper in a bowl. Transfer to a greased baking dish and bake for 15 minutes. Scatter cheese on top and let sit for 5 minutes. Cut before serving.

**Nutrition Info:**
- Info Per Serving: Calories: 300;Fat: 15g;Protein: 7g;Carbs: 13g.

## Seafood Paella

Servings:4
Cooking Time:22 Minutes
**Ingredients:**
- 2 tbsp olive oil
- 1 onion, finely chopped
- 3 garlic cloves, minced
- 1 red bell pepper, chopped
- ½ lb squid rings
- 1 tsp saffron
- 1 tsp paprika
- 1 cup Spanish rice
- 1 cup peeled shrimp
- 1 lb mussels, cleaned
- ½ cup green peas
- 2 tbsp parsley, chopped
- 1 lemon, cut into wedges
- Salt and black pepper to taste

**Directions:**
1. Warm the olive oil in a saucepan over medium heat. Sauté the onion, bell pepper, and garlic for 3 minutes. Add squid and fry for 5-6 minutes until golden. Stir in paprika, rice, saffron, and 2 cups of water. Bring to a boil and simmer for 15-18 minutes. Stir in shrimp, mussels, and green peas for 5-8 minutes. Season with salt and pepper. Sprinkle with parsley and serve with lemon wedges.

**Nutrition Info:**
- Info Per Serving: Calories: 507;Fat: 11g;Protein: 49g;Carbs: 51g.

## Crispy Fish Sticks

Servings:4
Cooking Time:15 Minutes
**Ingredients:**
- 2 eggs, lightly beaten
- 1 tbsp milk
- 1 lb skinned tilapia fillet strips
- ½ cup yellow cornmeal
- ½ cup panko bread crumbs
- ¼ tsp smoked paprika
- 1 Spanish Padrón pepper, sliced
- Salt and black pepper to taste

**Directions:**
1. Put a large, rimmed baking sheet in your oven. Preheat the oven to 400 °F with the pan inside. In a large bowl, mix the eggs and milk. Add the fish strips to the egg mixture and stir gently to coat. Put the cornmeal, bread crumbs, smoked paprika, salt, and black pepper in a zip-top plastic bag. Transfer the fish to the bag, letting the excess egg wash drip off into the bowl before transferring. Seal the bag and shake gently to completely coat each fish stick.
2. Carefully remove the hot baking sheet with oven mitts from the oven and spray it with nonstick cooking spray. Remove the fish sticks from the bag and arrange them on the hot baking sheet. Top with Padrón pepper and bake for 6-8 minutes until gentle pressure with a fork causes the fish to flake.

**Nutrition Info:**
- Info Per Serving: Calories: 238;Fat: 3g;Protein: 22g;Carbs: 28g.

## Glazed Broiled Salmon

Servings:4
Cooking Time: 5 To 10 Minutes
**Ingredients:**
- 4 salmon fillets
- 3 tablespoons miso paste
- 2 tablespoons raw honey
- 1 teaspoon coconut aminos
- 1 teaspoon rice vinegar

**Directions:**

1. Preheat the broiler to High. Line a baking dish with aluminum foil and add the salmon fillets.
2. Whisk together the miso paste, honey, coconut aminos, and vinegar in a small bowl. Pour the glaze over the fillets and spread it evenly with a brush.
3. Broil for about 5 minutes, or until the salmon is browned on top and opaque. Brush any remaining glaze over the salmon and broil for an additional 5 minutes if needed. The cooking time depends on the thickness of the salmon.
4. Let the salmon cool for 5 minutes before serving.
**Nutrition Info:**
- Info Per Serving: Calories: 263;Fat: 8.9g;Protein: 30.2g;Carbs: 12.8g.

## Italian Canned Tuna & Bean Bowl
Servings:6
Cooking Time:30 Minutes
**Ingredients:**
- 3 tbsp olive oil
- 1 lb kale, chopped
- 1 onion, chopped
- 3 garlic cloves, minced
- 1 can sliced olives
- ¼ cup capers
- ¼ tsp red pepper flakes
- 2 cans tuna in olive oil
- 1 can cannellini beans
- ½ cup chicken broth
- Salt and black pepper to taste
**Directions:**
1. Steam the kale for approximately 4 minutes or until crisp-tender and set aside. Warm the olive oil in a saucepan over medium heat. Sauté the onion and garlic for 4 minutes, stirring often. Add the chicken broth, olives, capers, and crushed red pepper flakes and cook for 4-5 minutes, stirring often. Add the kale and stir. Remove to a bowl and mix in the tuna, beans, pepper, and salt. Serve and enjoy!
**Nutrition Info:**
- Info Per Serving: Calories: 636;Fat: 60g;Protein: 8g;Carbs: 22g.

## Shrimp & Spinach A La Puttanesca
Servings:4
Cooking Time:20 Minutes
**Ingredients:**
- 1 lb fresh shrimp, shells and tails removed
- 1 cup baby spinach
- 16 oz cooked spaghetti
- 2 tbsp olive oil
- 3 anchovy fillets, chopped
- 3 garlic cloves, minced
- ½ tsp crushed red pepper
- 1 can tomatoes, diced
- 12 black olives, sliced
- 2 tbsp capers

- 1 tsp dried oregano
**Directions:**
1. Warm the olive oil in a large skillet over medium heat. Add in the anchovies, garlic, and crushed red peppers and cook for 3 minutes, stirring frequently and mashing up the anchovies with a wooden spoon until they have melted into the oil. Pour in the tomatoes with their juices, olives, capers, and oregano. Simmer until the sauce is lightly bubbling, about 3-4 minutes. Stir in the shrimp. Cook for 6-8 minutes or until they turn pink and white, stirring occasionally. Add the baby spinach and spaghetti and stir for 2 minutes until the spinach wilts. Serve and enjoy!
**Nutrition Info:**
- Info Per Serving: Calories: 362;Fat: 13g;Protein: 30g;Carbs: 31g.

## Shrimp & Salmon In Tomato Sauce
Servings:4
Cooking Time:30 Minutes
**Ingredients:**
- 1 lb shrimp, peeled and deveined
- 2 tbsp olive oil
- 1 lb salmon fillets
- Salt and black pepper to taste
- 1 cups tomatoes, chopped
- 1 onion, chopped
- 2 garlic cloves, minced
- ¼ tsp red pepper flakes
- 1 cup fish stock
- 1 tbsp cilantro, chopped
**Directions:**
1. Preheat the oven to 360°F. Line a baking sheet with parchment paper. Season the salmon with salt and pepper, drizzle with some olive oil, and arrange them on the sheet. Bake for 15 minutes. Remove to a serving plate.
2. Warm the remaining olive oil in a skillet over medium heat and sauté onion and garlic for 3 minutes until tender. Pour in tomatoes, fish stock, salt, pepper, and red pepper flakes and bring to a boil. Simmer for 10 minutes. Stir in shrimp and cook for another 8 minutes. Pour the sauce over the salmon and serve sprinkled with cilantro.
**Nutrition Info:**
- Info Per Serving: Calories: 240;Fat: 16g;Protein: 18g;Carbs: 22g.

## Bell Pepper & Scallop Skillet
Servings:4
Cooking Time:25 Minutes
**Ingredients:**
- 3 tbsp olive oil
- 2 celery stalks, sliced
- 2 lb sea scallops, halved
- 3 garlic cloves, minced
- Juice of 1 lime
- 1 red bell pepper, chopped
- 1 tbsp capers, chopped

- 1 tbsp mayonnaise
- 1 tbsp rosemary, chopped
- 1 cup chicken stock

**Directions:**

1. Warm olive oil in a skillet over medium heat and cook celery and garlic for 2 minutes. Stir in bell pepper, lime juice, capers, rosemary, and stock and bring to a boil. Simmer for 8 minutes. Mix in scallops and mayonnaise and cook for 5 minutes.

**Nutrition Info:**

- Info Per Serving: Calories: 310;Fat: 16g;Protein: 9g;Carbs: 33g.

## Shrimp And Pea Paella

Servings:2
Cooking Time: 60 Minutes

**Ingredients:**

- 2 tablespoons olive oil
- 1 garlic clove, minced
- ½ large onion, minced
- 1 cup diced tomato
- ½ cup short-grain rice
- ½ teaspoon sweet paprika
- ½ cup dry white wine
- 1¼ cups low-sodium chicken stock
- 8 ounces large raw shrimp
- 1 cup frozen peas
- ¼ cup jarred roasted red peppers, cut into strips
- Salt, to taste

**Directions:**

1. Heat the olive oil in a large skillet over medium-high heat.
2. Add the garlic and onion and sauté for 3 minutes, or until the onion is softened.
3. Add the tomato, rice, and paprika and stir for 3 minutes to toast the rice.
4. Add the wine and chicken stock and stir to combine. Bring the mixture to a boil.
5. Cover and reduce the heat to medium-low, and simmer for 45 minutes, or until the rice is just about tender and most of the liquid has been absorbed.
6. Add the shrimp, peas, and roasted red peppers. Cover and cook for an additional 5 minutes. Season with salt to taste and serve.

**Nutrition Info:**

- Info Per Serving: Calories: 646;Fat: 27.1g;Protein: 42.0g;Carbs: 59.7g.

## Farro & Trout Bowls With Avocado

Servings:4
Cooking Time:50 Minutes

**Ingredients:**

- 4 tbsp olive oil
- 8 trout fillets, boneless
- 1 cup farro
- Juice of 2 lemons

- Salt and black pepper to taste
- 1 avocado, chopped
- ¼ cup balsamic vinegar
- 1 garlic cloves, minced
- ¼ cup parsley, chopped
- ¼ cup mint, chopped
- 2 tbsp yellow mustard

**Directions:**

1. Boil salted water in a pot over medium heat and stir in farro. Simmer for 30 minutes and drain. Remove to a bowl and combine with lemon juice, mustard, garlic, salt, pepper, and half olive oil. Set aside. Mash the avocado with a fork in a bowl and mix with vinegar, salt, pepper, parsley, and mint.
2. Warm the remaining oil in a skillet over medium heat and brown trout fillets skin-side down for 10 minutes on both sides. Let cool and cut into pieces. Put over farro and stir in avocado dressing. Serve immediately.

**Nutrition Info:**

- Info Per Serving: Calories: 290;Fat: 13g;Protein: 37g;Carbs: 6g.

## Halibut Confit With Sautéed Leeks

Servings:4
Cooking Time:45 Minutes

**Ingredients:**

- 1 tsp fresh lemon zest
- ¼ cup olive oil
- 4 skinless halibut fillets
- Salt and black pepper to taste
- 1 lb leeks, sliced
- 1 tsp Dijon mustard
- ¾ cup dry white wine
- 1 tbsp fresh cilantro, chopped
- 4 lemon wedges

**Directions:**

1. Warm the olive oil in a skillet over medium heat. Season the halibut with salt and pepper. Sear in the skillet for 6-7 minutes until cooked all the way through. Carefully transfer the halibut to a large plate. Add leeks, mustard, salt, and pepper to the skillet and sauté for 10-12 minutes, stirring frequently, until softened. Pour in the wine and lemon zest and bring to a simmer. Top with halibut. Reduce the heat to low, cover, and simmer for 6-10 minutes. Carefully transfer halibut to a serving platter, tent loosely with aluminum foil, and let rest while finishing leeks. Increase the heat and cook the leeks for 2-4 minutes until the sauce is slightly thickened. Adjust the seasoning with salt and pepper. Pour the leek mixture around the halibut, sprinkle with cilantro, and serve with lemon wedges.

**Nutrition Info:**

- Info Per Serving: Calories: 566;Fat: 19g;Protein: 78g;Carbs: 17g.

# Lemon Shrimp With Black Olives

Servings:4
Cooking Time:25 Minutes
**Ingredients:**
- 1 lb shrimp, peeled and deveined
- 3 tbsp olive oil
- 1 lemon, juiced
- 1 tbsp flour
- 1 cup fish stock
- Salt and black pepper to taste
- 1 cup black olives, halved
- 1 tbsp rosemary, chopped

**Directions:**
1. Warm the olive oil in a skillet over medium heat and sear shrimp for 4 minutes on both sides; set aside. In the same skillet over low heat, stir in the flour for 2-3 minutes.
2. Gradually pour in the fish stock and lemon juice while stirring and simmer for 3-4 minutes until the sauce thickens. Adjust the seasoning with salt and pepper and mix in shrimp, olives, and rosemary. Serve immediately.

**Nutrition Info:**
- Info Per Serving: Calories: 240;Fat: 16g;Protein: 9g;Carbs: 16g.

# Salmon Baked In Foil

Servings:4
Cooking Time: 25 Minutes
**Ingredients:**
- 2 cups cherry tomatoes
- 3 tablespoons extra-virgin olive oil
- 3 tablespoons lemon juice
- 3 tablespoons almond butter
- 1 teaspoon oregano
- ½ teaspoon salt
- 4 salmon fillets

**Directions:**
1. Preheat the oven to 400ºF.
2. Cut the tomatoes in half and put them in a bowl.
3. Add the olive oil, lemon juice, butter, oregano, and salt to the tomatoes and gently toss to combine.
4. Cut 4 pieces of foil, about 12-by-12 inches each.
5. Place the salmon fillets in the middle of each piece of foil.
6. Divide the tomato mixture evenly over the 4 pieces of salmon. Bring the ends of the foil together and seal to form a closed pocket.
7. Place the 4 pockets on a baking sheet. Bake in the preheated oven for 25 minutes.
8. Remove from the oven and serve on a plate.

**Nutrition Info:**
- Info Per Serving: Calories: 410;Fat: 32.0g;Protein: 30.0g;Carbs: 4.0g.

# Hot Tomato & Caper Squid Stew

Servings:4
Cooking Time:50 Minutes
**Ingredients:**
- 1 cans whole peeled tomatoes, diced
- ¼ cup olive oil
- 1 onion, chopped
- 1 celery rib, sliced
- 3 garlic cloves, minced
- ¼ tsp red pepper flakes
- 1 red chili, minced
- ½ cup dry white wine
- 2 lb squid, sliced into rings
- Salt and black pepper to taste
- ⅓ cup green olives, chopped
- 1 tbsp capers
- 2 tbsp fresh parsley, chopped

**Directions:**
1. Warm the olive oil in a pot over medium heat. Sauté the onion, garlic, red chili, and celery until softened, about 5 minutes. Stir in pepper flakes and cook for about 30 seconds. Stir in wine, scraping up any browned bits, and cook until nearly evaporated, about 1 minute. Add 1 cup of water and season with salt and pepper. Stir the squid in the pot. Reduce heat to low, cover, and simmer until squid has released its liquid, about 15 minutes. Pour in tomatoes, olives, and capers, and continue to cook until squid is very tender, 30-35 minutes. Top with parsley. Serve and enjoy!

**Nutrition Info:**
- Info Per Serving: Calories: 334;Fat: 12g;Protein: 28g;Carbs: 30g.

# Baked Lemon Salmon

Servings:4
Cooking Time: 20 Minutes
**Ingredients:**
- ¼ teaspoon dried thyme
- Zest and juice of ½ lemon
- ¼ teaspoon salt
- ½ teaspoon freshly ground black pepper
- 1 pound salmon fillet
- Nonstick cooking spray

**Directions:**
1. Preheat the oven to 425ºF. Coat a baking sheet with nonstick cooking spray.
2. Mix together the thyme, lemon zest and juice, salt, and pepper in a small bowl and stir to incorporate.
3. Arrange the salmon, skin-side down, on the coated baking sheet. Spoon the thyme mixture over the salmon and spread it all over.
4. Bake in the preheated oven for about 15 to 20 minutes, or until the fish flakes apart easily. Serve warm.

**Nutrition Info:**
- Info Per Serving: Calories: 162;Fat: 7.0g;Protein: 23.1g;Carbs: 1.0g.

# Grilled Sardines With Herby Sauce

Servings:4
Cooking Time:15 Min + Marinating Time
**Ingredients:**
- 12 sardines, gutted and cleaned
- 1 lemon, cut into wedges
- 2 garlic cloves, minced
- 2 tbsp capers, finely chopped
- 1 tbsp whole capers
- 1 shallot, diced
- 1 tsp anchovy paste
- 1 lemon, zested and juiced
- 2 tbsp olive oil
- 1 tbsp parsley, finely chopped
- 1 tbsp basil, finely chopped

**Directions:**
1. In a bowl, blend garlic, chopped capers, shallot, anchovy paste, lemon zest, and olive oil. Add the sardines and toss to coat; let them sit to marinate for about 30 minutes.
2. Preheat your grill to high. Place the sardines on the grill. Cook for 3-4 minutes per side until the skin is browned and beginning to blister. Pour the marinade in a saucepan over medium heat and add the whole capers, parsley, basil, and lemon juice. Cook for 2-3 minutes until thickens. Pour the sauce over grilled sardines. Serve with lemon wedges.

**Nutrition Info:**
- Info Per Serving: Calories: 395;Fat: 21g;Protein: 46g;Carbs: 2.1g.

# Dilly Haddock In Tomato Sauce

Servings:4
Cooking Time:20 Minutes
**Ingredients:**
- 4 haddock fillets, boneless
- 1 cup vegetable stock
- 2 garlic cloves, minced
- 2 cups cherry tomatoes, halved
- Salt and black pepper to taste
- 2 tbsp dill, chopped

**Directions:**
1. In a skillet over medium heat, cook cherry tomatoes, garlic, salt, and pepper for 5 minutes. Stir in haddock fillets and vegetable stock and bring to a simmer. Cook covered for 10-12 minutes. Serve topped with dill.

**Nutrition Info:**
- Info Per Serving: Calories: 190;Fat: 2g;Protein: 35g;Carbs: 6g.

# Lemon-garlic Sea Bass

Servings:2
Cooking Time:25 Minutes
**Ingredients:**
- 2 tbsp olive oil
- 2 sea bass fillets
- 1 lemon, juiced
- 4 garlic cloves, minced
- Salt and black pepper to taste

**Directions:**
1. Preheat the oven to 380°F. Line a baking sheet with parchment paper. Brush sea bass fillets with lemon juice, olive oil, garlic, salt, and pepper and arrange them on the sheet. Bake for 15 minutes. Serve with salad.

**Nutrition Info:**
- Info Per Serving: Calories: 530;Fat: 30g;Protein: 54g;Carbs: 15g.

# Garlic Shrimp With Arugula Pesto

Servings:2
Cooking Time: 5 Minutes
**Ingredients:**
- 3 cups lightly packed arugula
- ½ cup lightly packed basil leaves
- ¼ cup walnuts
- 3 tablespoons olive oil
- 3 medium garlic cloves
- 2 tablespoons grated Parmesan cheese
- 1 tablespoon freshly squeezed lemon juice
- Salt and freshly ground black pepper, to taste
- 1 package zucchini noodles
- 8 ounces cooked, shelled shrimp
- 2 Roma tomatoes, diced

**Directions:**
1. Process the arugula, basil, walnuts, olive oil, garlic, Parmesan cheese, and lemon juice in a food processor until smooth, scraping down the sides as needed. Season with salt and pepper to taste.
2. Heat a skillet over medium heat. Add the pesto, zucchini noodles, and cooked shrimp. Toss to combine the sauce over the noodles and shrimp, and cook until heated through.
3. Taste and season with more salt and pepper as needed. Serve topped with the diced tomatoes.

**Nutrition Info:**
- Info Per Serving: Calories: 435;Fat: 30.2g;Protein: 33.0g;Carbs: 15.1g.

# Salmon Stuffed Peppers

Servings:4
Cooking Time:25 Minutes
**Ingredients:**
- 4 bell peppers
- 10 oz canned salmon, drained
- 12 black olives, chopped
- 1 red onion, finely chopped

- ½ tsp garlic, minced
- 1/3 cup mayonnaise
- 1 cup cream cheese
- 1 tsp Mediterranean seasoning
- Salt and pepper flakes to taste

**Directions:**
1. Preheat oven to 390 °F. Cut the peppers into halves and remove the seeds. In a mixing bowl, combine the salmon, onion, garlic, mayonnaise, olives, salt, red pepper, Mediterranean spice mix, and cream cheese. Divide the mixture between the peppers and bake them in the oven for 10-12 minutes or until cooked through. Serve and enjoy!

**Nutrition Info:**
- Info Per Serving: Calories: 272;Fat: 14g;Protein: 29g;Carbs: 5g.

# Balsamic Asparagus & Salmon Roast

Servings:4
Cooking Time:20 Minutes
**Ingredients:**
- 2 tbsp olive oil
- 4 salmon fillets, skinless
- 2 tbsp balsamic vinegar
- 1 lb asparagus, trimmed
- Salt and black pepper to taste

**Directions:**
1. Preheat the oven to 380ºF. In a roasting pan, arrange the salmon fillets and asparagus spears. Season with salt and pepper and drizzle with olive oil and balsamic vinegar; roast for 12-15 minutes. Serve warm.

**Nutrition Info:**
- Info Per Serving: Calories: 310;Fat: 16g;Protein: 21g;Carbs: 19g.

# Andalusian Prawns With Capers

Servings:4
Cooking Time:25 Minutes
**Ingredients:**
- 1 lb prawns, peeled, deveined
- 2 tbsp olive oil
- 1 lemon, zested and juiced
- 2 tomatoes, chopped
- 1 cup spring onions, chopped
- 2 tbsp capers, chopped
- 2 tbsp dill, chopped
- Salt and black pepper to taste

**Directions:**
1. Warm the olive oil in a skillet over medium heat and cook onions and capers for 2-3 minutes. Stir in prawns, lemon zest, tomatoes, dill, salt, and pepper and cook for another 6 minutes. Serve drizzled with lemon juice.

**Nutrition Info:**

- Info Per Serving: Calories: 230;Fat: 14g;Protein: 6g;Carbs: 23g.

# Mackerel And Green Bean Salad

Servings:2
Cooking Time: 10 Minutes
**Ingredients:**
- 2 cups green beans
- 1 tablespoon avocado oil
- 2 mackerel fillets
- 4 cups mixed salad greens
- 2 hard-boiled eggs, sliced
- 1 avocado, sliced
- 2 tablespoons lemon juice
- 2 tablespoons olive oil
- 1 teaspoon Dijon mustard
- Salt and black pepper, to taste

**Directions:**
1. Cook the green beans in a medium saucepan of boiling water for about 3 minutes until crisp-tender. Drain and set aside.
2. Melt the avocado oil in a pan over medium heat. Add the mackerel fillets and cook each side for 4 minutes.
3. Divide the greens between two salad bowls. Top with the mackerel, sliced egg, and avocado slices.
4. In another bowl, whisk together the lemon juice, olive oil, mustard, salt, and pepper, and drizzle over the salad. Add the cooked green beans and toss to combine, then serve.

**Nutrition Info:**
- Info Per Serving: Calories: 737;Fat: 57.3g;Protein: 34.2g;Carbs: 22.1g.

# Fennel & Bell Pepper Salmon

Servings:4
Cooking Time:30 Minutes
**Ingredients:**
- 2 tbsp olive oil
- 4 salmon fillets, boneless
- 1 fennel bulb, sliced
- Salt and black pepper to taste
- ½ tsp chili powder
- 1 yellow bell pepper, diced
- 1 red bell pepper, chopped
- 1 green bell pepper, chopped

**Directions:**
1. Warm olive oil in a skillet over medium heat. Season the salmon with chili powder, salt, and pepper and cook for 6-8 minutes, turning once. Remove to a serving plate. Add fennel and peppers to the skillet and cook for another 10 minutes until tender. Top the salmon with the mixture.

**Nutrition Info:**
- Info Per Serving: Calories: 580;Fat: 19g;Protein: 35g;Carbs: 73g.

# Poultry And Meats Recipes

## Bell Pepper & Onion Pork Chops

Servings:4
Cooking Time:30 Minutes
**Ingredients:**
- 2 tbsp olive oil
- 4 pork chops
- Salt and black pepper to taste
- 1 tsp fennel seeds
- 1 red bell pepper, sliced
- 1 green bell pepper, sliced
- 1 yellow onion, thinly sliced
- 2 tsp Italian seasoning
- 2 garlic cloves, minced
- 1 tbsp balsamic vinegar

**Directions:**
1. Warm the olive oil in a large skillet over medium heat. Season the pork chops with salt and pepper and add them to the skillet. Cook for 6-8 minutes on both sides or until golden brown; reserve. Sauté the garlic, sliced bell peppers, onions, fennel seeds, and herbs in the skillet for 6-8 minutes until tender, stirring occasionally. Return the pork, cover, and lower the heat to low. Cook for another 3 minutes or until the pork is cooked through. Transfer the pork and vegetables to a serving platter. Add the vinegar to the skillet and stir to combine for 1-2 minutes. Drizzle the sauce over the pork.

**Nutrition Info:**
- Info Per Serving: Calories: 508;Fat: 40g;Protein: 31g;Carbs: 8g.

## Chili Beef Stew

Servings:4
Cooking Time:35 Minutes
**Ingredients:**
- 2 tbsp olive oil
- 1 lb beef stew, ground
- Salt and black pepper to taste
- 1 onion, chopped
- 2 garlic cloves, minced
- 1 tbsp chili paste
- 2 tbsp balsamic vinegar
- ¼ cup chicken stock
- ¼ cup mint, chopped

**Directions:**
1. Warm the olive oil in a skillet over medium heat and cook onion for 3 minutes. Put in beef stew and cook for another 3 minutes. Stir in salt, pepper, garlic, chili paste, vinegar, stock, and mint and cook for an additional 20-25 minutes.

**Nutrition Info:**
- Info Per Serving: Calories: 310;Fat: 14g;Protein: 20g;Carbs: 16g.

## Rosemary Pork Chops With Cabbage Mix

Servings:4
Cooking Time:35 Minutes
**Ingredients:**
- ½ green cabbage head, shredded
- 2 tsp olive oil
- 4 pork chops
- 4 bell peppers, chopped
- 1 tsp rosemary
- 2 tbsp wine vinegar
- 2 spring onions, chopped
- Salt and black pepper to taste

**Directions:**
1. Warm half of oil in a skillet over medium heat. Cook spring onions for 3 minutes. Stir in vinegar, cabbage, bell peppers, salt, and pepper and simmer for 10 minutes. Heat off.
2. Preheat the grill over medium heat. Sprinkle pork chops with remaining oil, salt, pepper, and rosemary and grill for 10 minutes on both sides. Share chops into plates with cabbage mixture on the side. Serve immediately.

**Nutrition Info:**
- Info Per Serving: Calories: 230;Fat: 19g;Protein: 13g;Carbs: 18g.

## Mushroom Chicken Piccata

Servings:4
Cooking Time:25 Minutes
**Ingredients:**
- 3 tbsp olive oil
- 2 tbsp butter
- 1 lb chicken breasts, sliced
- Salt and black pepper to taste
- ¼ cup ground flaxseed
- 2 tbsp almond flour
- 2 cups mushrooms, sliced
- ½ cup white wine
- ¼ cup lemon juice
- ¼ cup capers, chopped
- ¼ cup parsley, chopped
- 16 oz cooked spaghetti

**Directions:**
1. Combine the ground flaxseed, almond flour, salt, and pepper in a bowl. Coat the chicken with the mixture.
2. Warm the olive oil in a large skillet over medium heat. Sear the chicken for 3-4 minutes per side until golden; reserve. Add the butter to the skillet and sauté the mushrooms and for 5-7 minutes. Pour in the white wine, lemon juice, capers, and salt and bring to a boil, whisking to incorporate any little browned bits that have stuck to the bottom of the skillet. Lower the heat to low and return the

browned chicken. Cover and simmer 5-6 more minutes until the sauce thickens. Place the spaghetti in a serving platter and spoon the chicken and mushrooms on top. Garnish with parsley.

**Nutrition Info:**

- Info Per Serving: Calories: 538;Fat: 44g;Protein: 30g;Carbs: 8g.

# Beef, Tomato, And Lentils Stew

Servings:4
Cooking Time: 10 Minutes
**Ingredients:**

- 1 tablespoon extra-virgin olive oil
- 1 pound extra-lean ground beef
- 1 onion, chopped
- 1 can chopped tomatoes with garlic and basil, drained
- 1 can lentils, drained
- ½ teaspoon sea salt
- ⅛ teaspoon freshly ground black pepper

**Directions:**

1. Heat the olive oil in a pot over medium-high heat until shimmering.
2. Add the beef and onion to the pot and sauté for 5 minutes or until the beef is lightly browned.
3. Add the remaining ingredients. Bring to a boil. Reduce the heat to medium and cook for 4 more minutes or until the lentils are tender. Keep stirring during the cooking.
4. Pour them in a large serving bowl and serve immediately.

**Nutrition Info:**

- Info Per Serving: Calories: 460;Fat: 14.8g;Protein: 44.2g;Carbs: 36.9g.

# Provençal Flank Steak Au Pistou

Servings:4
Cooking Time:25 Minutes
**Ingredients:**

- 8 tbsp olive oil
- 1 lb flank steak
- Salt and black pepper to taste
- ½ cup parsley, chopped
- ¼ cup fresh basil, chopped
- 2 garlic cloves, minced
- ½ tsp celery seeds
- 1 orange, zested and juiced
- 1 tsp red pepper flakes
- 1 tbsp red wine vinegar

**Directions:**

1. Place the parsley, basil, garlic, orange zest and juice, celery seeds, salt, pepper, and red pepper flakes, and pulse until finely chopped in your food processor. With the processor running, stream in the red wine vinegar and 6 tbsp of olive oil until well combined. Set aside until ready to serve.
2. Preheat your grill. Rub the steak with the remaining olive oil, salt, and pepper. Place the steak on the grill and cook for 6-8 minutes on each side. Remove and leave to sit for 10 minutes. Slice the steak and drizzle with pistou. Serve.

**Nutrition Info:**

- Info Per Serving: Calories: 441;Fat: 36g;Protein: 25g;Carbs: 3g.

# Parsley Eggplant Lamb

Servings:4
Cooking Time:70 Minutes
**Ingredients:**

- 2 tbsp olive oil
- 1 cup chicken stock
- 1 ½ lb lamb meat, cubed
- 2 eggplants, cubed
- 2 onions, chopped
- 2 tbsp tomato paste
- 2 tbsp parsley, chopped
- 4 garlic cloves, minced

**Directions:**

1. Warm the olive oil in a skillet over medium heat and cook onions and garlic for 4 minutes. Put in lamb and cook for 6 minutes. Stir in eggplants and tomato paste for 5 minutes. Pour in the stock and bring to a boil. Cook for another 50 minutes, stirring often. Serve garnished with parsley.

**Nutrition Info:**

- Info Per Serving: Calories: 310;Fat: 19g;Protein: 15g;Carbs: 23g.

# Greek Beef Kebabs

Servings:2
Cooking Time: 20 Minutes
**Ingredients:**

- 6 ounces beef sirloin tip, trimmed of fat and cut into 2-inch pieces
- 3 cups of any mixture of vegetables: mushrooms, summer squash, zucchini, onions, red peppers, cherry tomatoes
- ½ cup olive oil
- ¼ cup freshly squeezed lemon juice
- 2 tablespoons balsamic vinegar
- 2 teaspoons dried oregano
- 1 teaspoon garlic powder
- 1 teaspoon salt
- 1 teaspoon minced fresh rosemary
- Cooking spray

**Directions:**

1. Put the beef in a plastic freezer bag.
2. Slice the vegetables into similar-size pieces and put them in a second freezer bag.
3. Make the marinade: Mix the olive oil, lemon juice, balsamic vinegar, oregano, garlic powder, salt, and rosemary in a measuring cup. Whisk well to combine. Pour half of the marinade over the beef, and the other half over the vegetables.

4. Put the beef and vegetables in the refrigerator to marinate for 4 hours.

5. When ready, preheat the grill to medium-high heat and spray the grill grates with cooking spray.

6. Thread the meat onto skewers and the vegetables onto separate skewers.

7. Grill the meat for 3 minutes per side. They should only take 10 to 12 minutes to cook, depending on the thickness of the meat.

8. Grill the vegetables for about 3 minutes per side, or until they have grill marks and are softened. Serve hot.

**Nutrition Info:**
- Info Per Serving: Calories: 284;Fat: 18.2g;Protein: 21.0g;Carbs: 9.0g.

## Fennel Beef Ribs

Servings:4
Cooking Time:2 Hours 10 Minutes
**Ingredients:**
- 2 tbsp olive oil
- 2 lb beef ribs
- 2 garlic cloves, minced
- 1 onion, chopped
- ½ cup chicken stock
- 1 tbsp ground fennel seeds

**Directions:**
1. Preheat oven to 360° F. Mix garlic, onion, stock, olive oil, fennel seeds, and beef ribs in a roasting pan and bake for 2 hours. Serve hot with salad.

**Nutrition Info:**
- Info Per Serving: Calories: 300;Fat: 10g;Protein: 25g;Carbs: 18g.

## Eggplant & Turkey Moussaka

Servings:4
Cooking Time:55 Minutes
**Ingredients:**
- 5 tbsp olive oil
- 1 lb ground turkey
- 1 can diced tomatoes
- 1 cup Greek yogurt
- 2 small eggplants, sliced
- 2 shallots, chopped
- 2 garlic cloves, minced
- 2 tbsp tomato paste
- 1 tsp dried oregano
- 1 egg, beaten
- Salt and black pepper to taste
- ¼ tsp ground coriander
- 2 oz grated Halloumi cheese
- 2 tbsp chopped fresh parsley

**Directions:**
1. Preheat oven to 400° F. Warm olive oil in a pan over medium heat and cook the eggplant slices for 6-8 minutes on both sides. Remove to paper towels. In the same pan, sauté shallots and garlic for 3 minutes, stirring often. Add in ground turkey and cook for 5 minutes until no longer pink. Stir in tomato paste, tomatoes, oregano, ground coriander, salt, and pepper; cook for 4-5 minutes.

2. Combine yogurt, egg, salt, and pepper in a bowl. Spread half of the turkey mixture on a baking dish, add a layer of eggplant, then remaining meat, and finally remaining eggplants. Bake for 15 minutes. Remove and top with the yogurt mixture. Sprinkle with the cheese and return in the oven for 5-8 minutes until the cheese melts. Top with parsley.

**Nutrition Info:**
- Info Per Serving: Calories: 521;Fat: 33g;Protein: 42g;Carbs: 23g.

## Spinach-ricotta Chicken Rolls

Servings:4
Cooking Time:55 Minutes
**Ingredients:**
- 2 tbsp olive oil
- 4 chicken breast halves
- 1 lb baby spinach
- 2 garlic cloves, minced
- 1 lemon, zested
- ½ cup crumbled ricotta cheese
- 1 tbsp pine nuts, toasted
- Salt and black pepper to taste

**Directions:**
1. Preheat oven to 350° F. Pound the chicken breasts to ½-inch thickness with a meat mallet and season with salt and pepper.

2. Warm olive oil in a pan over medium heat and sauté spinach for 4-5 minutes until it wilts. Stir in garlic, salt, lemon zest, and pepper for 20-30 seconds. Let cool slightly and add in ricotta cheese and pine nuts; mix well. Spoon the mixture over the chicken breasts, wrap around the filling, and secure the ends with toothpicks. Arrange the breasts on a greased baking dish and bake for 35-40 minutes. Let sit for a few minutes and slice. Serve immediately.

**Nutrition Info:**
- Info Per Serving: Calories: 260;Fat: 14g;Protein: 28g;Carbs: 6.5g.

## Greek-style Chicken & Vegetable Stir-fry

Servings:4
Cooking Time:30 Minutes
**Ingredients:**
- 2 tbsp olive oil
- 1 lb chicken breasts, chopped
- Salt and black pepper to taste
- 2 cloves garlic, minced
- 2 red bell pepper, chopped
- 1 onion, chopped
- ½ lemon, juiced and zested
- ½ cup feta cheese, crumbled

- 2 tbsp fresh dill, chopped

**Directions:**

1. Warm the olive oil in a skillet over medium heat. Season the chicken with salt and pepper. Add the chicken and sear for about 4 minutes; reserve. Add the onion, garlic, and bell pepper to the same skillet and stir-fry for 6-8 minutes until crisp-tender. Return the chicken to the skillet and sprinkle with lemon zest and juice. Cook for 1 more minute. Sprinkle with feta cheese and dill and remove from the heat. Cover and allow to sit for 2–3 minutes until the cheese melts. Serve.

**Nutrition Info:**

- Info Per Serving: Calories: 347;Fat: 22g;Protein: 28g;Carbs: 10g.

# Drunken Lamb Bake

Servings:4
Cooking Time:90 Minutes

**Ingredients:**

- 3 tbsp butter
- 2 lb leg of lamb, sliced
- 3 garlic cloves, chopped
- 2 onions, chopped
- 3 cups vegetable stock
- 2 cups dry red wine
- 2 tbsp tomato pastes
- 1 tsp thyme, chopped
- Salt and black pepper to taste

**Directions:**

1. Preheat the oven to 360° F. Melt butter in a skillet over medium heat. Sear lamb for 10 minutes on both sides. Remove to a roasting pan. In the same skillet, add and cook onions and garlic for 5 minutes. Stir in stock, red wine, tomato paste, thyme, salt, and pepper and bring to a boil. Cook for 10 minutes and pour over lamb. Bake for 1 hour.

**Nutrition Info:**

- Info Per Serving: Calories: 290;Fat: 22g;Protein: 19g;Carbs: 17g.

# Creamy Beef Stew

Servings:4
Cooking Time:35 Minutes

**Ingredients:**

- 2 tbsp olive oil
- 2 pears, peeled and cubed
- 1 lb beef stew meat, cubed
- 2 tbsp dill, chopped
- 2 oz heavy cream
- Salt and black pepper to taste

**Directions:**

1. Warm the olive oil in a skillet over medium heat and sear beef for 5 minutes. Stir in pears, dill, heavy cream, salt, and pepper and bring to a boil. Simmer for 20 minutes.

**Nutrition Into:**

- Info Per Serving: Calories: 340;Fat: 18g;Protein: 16g;Carbs: 23g.

# Chicken & Vegetable Skewers

Servings:6
Cooking Time:20 Minutes

**Ingredients:**

- 2 tbsp olive oil
- 1 ½ lb chicken breasts, cubed
- 1 tbsp fresh chives, chopped
- 1 zucchini, sliced thick
- 1 tbsp Italian seasoning
- 1 cup bell peppers, sliced
- 1 red onion, cut into wedges
- 1 ½ cups cherry tomatoes

**Directions:**

1. Preheat grill to high. Toss the chicken cubes with olive oil and Italian seasoning. Thread them onto skewers, alternating with the vegetables. Grill the skewers for 10 minutes, turning them occasionally to ensure even cooking. Top with chives.

**Nutrition Info:**

- Info Per Serving: Calories: 295;Fat: 14g;Protein: 36g;Carbs: 6g.

# Chicken Tagine With Vegetables

Servings:6
Cooking Time:67 Minutes

**Ingredients:**

- 1 ½ lb boneless skinless chicken thighs, cut into chunks
- 2 zucchini, sliced into half-moons
- 4 tbsp olive oil
- Salt and black pepper to taste
- 1 small red onion, chopped
- 2 cloves garlic, minced
- 1 red bell pepper, chopped
- 2 tomatoes, chopped
- 1 tbsp harissa paste
- 1 cup water
- 1 cup black olives, halved
- ¼ cup fresh cilantro, chopped

**Directions:**

1. Warm the olive oil in a large skillet over medium heat. Season the chicken with salt and pepper and brown for 6-8 minutes on all sides. Add the onion, garlic, and bell pepper and sauté for 5 minutes until tender. Stir in harissa paste and tomatoes for 1 minute and pour in 1 cup of water. Bring to a boil and lower the heat to low. Cover and simmer for 35-45 minutes until the chicken is tender and cooked through. Stir in zucchini and olives and continue to cook for 10 minutes until the zucchini is tender. Serve topped with cilantro.

**Nutrition Info:**

- Info Per Serving: Calories: 358;Fat: 25g;Protein: 25g;Carbs: 8g.

# French Chicken Cassoulet

Servings:4
Cooking Time:40 Minutes
**Ingredients:**
- 1 tbsp olive oil
- ½ cup heavy cream
- 4 chicken breasts, halved
- 1/3 cup yellow mustard
- Salt and black pepper to taste
- 1 onion, chopped
- 1 ½ cups chicken stock
- ¼ tsp dried oregano

**Directions:**
1. Warm stock in a saucepan over medium heat and stir in mustard, onion, salt, pepper, and oregano. Bring to a boil and cook for 8 minutes. Warm olive oil in a skillet over medium heat. Sear chicken for 6 minutes on both sides. Transfer to the saucepan and simmer for another 12 minutes. Stir in heavy cream for 2 minutes. Serve warm.

**Nutrition Info:**
- Info Per Serving: Calories: 260;Fat: 12g;Protein: 27g;Carbs: 18g.

# Spiced Roast Chicken

Servings:6
Cooking Time: 35 Minutes
**Ingredients:**
- 1 teaspoon garlic powder
- 1 teaspoon ground paprika
- ½ teaspoon ground cumin
- ½ teaspoon ground coriander
- ½ teaspoon salt
- ¼ teaspoon ground cayenne pepper
- 6 chicken legs
- 1 teaspoon extra-virgin olive oil

**Directions:**
1. Preheat the oven to 400ºF.
2. Combine the garlic powder, paprika, cumin, coriander, salt, and cayenne pepper in a small bowl.
3. On a clean work surface, rub the spices all over the chicken legs until completely coated.
4. Heat the olive oil in an ovenproof skillet over medium heat.
5. Add the chicken thighs and sear each side for 8 to 10 minutes, or until the skin is crispy and browned.
6. Transfer the skillet to the preheated oven and continue cooking for 10 to 15 minutes, or until the juices run clear and it registers an internal temperature of 165ºF.
7. Remove from the heat and serve on plates.

**Nutrition Info:**
- Info Per Serving: Calories: 275;Fat: 15.6g;Protein: 30.3g;Carbs: 0.9g.

# Grilled Beef With Mint-jalapeño Vinaigrette

Servings:4
Cooking Time:25 Minutes
**Ingredients:**
- 2 tbsp olive oil
- 1 lb beef steaks
- 3 jalapeños, chopped
- 2 tbsp balsamic vinegar
- 1 cup mint leaves, chopped
- Salt and black pepper to taste
- 1 tbsp sweet paprika

**Directions:**
1. Warm half of oil in a skillet over medium heat and sauté jalapeños, balsamic vinegar, mint, salt, pepper, and paprika for 5 minutes. Preheat the grill to high. Rub beef steaks with the remaining oil, salt, and pepper and grill for 6 minutes on both sides. Top with mint vinaigrette and serve.

**Nutrition Info:**
- Info Per Serving: Calories: 320;Fat: 13g;Protein: 18g;Carbs: 19g.

# One-pan Sicilian Chicken

Servings:4
Cooking Time:25 Minutes
**Ingredients:**
- 1 lb chicken breasts, halved
- Salt and black pepper to taste
- 2 tbsp olive oil
- 1 red onion, thinly sliced
- ½ cup mixed bell pepper strips
- 2 garlic cloves, minced
- 1 tbsp capers, rinsed
- 3 tbsp fresh basil, chopped
- 2 tbsp balsamic vinegar
- ½ tsp red pepper flakes

**Directions:**
1. Warm the olive oil in a skillet over medium heat. Season the chicken with salt and pepper. Sear chicken for 4-5 minutes on each side until golden brown; remove to a plate. Sauté the onion, garlic, and peppers in the same skillet for 3-4 minutes until soft, stirring often. Stir in vinegar and red pepper flakes. Return the chicken and add the capers. Cover and reduce the heat. Simmer for about 6 minutes until the chicken is cooked through. Serve hot topped with basil.

**Nutrition Info:**
- Info Per Serving: Calories: 272;Fat: 17g;Protein: 24g;Carbs: 3g.

# Rich Pork In Cilantro Sauce

Servings:4
Cooking Time:30 Minutes
**Ingredients:**
- ½ cup olive oil
- 1 lb pork stew meat, cubed
- 1 tbsp walnuts, chopped
- 2 tbsp cilantro, chopped
- 2 tbsp basil, chopped
- 2 garlic cloves, minced
- Salt and black pepper to taste
- 2 cups Greek yogurt

**Directions:**
1. In a food processor, blend cilantro, basil, garlic, walnuts, yogurt, salt, pepper, and half of the oil until smooth.
2. Warm the remaining oil in a skillet over medium heat. Brown pork meat for 5 minutes. Pour sauce over meat and bring to a boil. Cook for another 15 minutes. Serve.

**Nutrition Info:**
- Info Per Serving: Calories: 280;Fat: 12g;Protein: 19g;Carbs: 21g.

# Greek-style Chicken & Egg Bake

Servings:4
Cooking Time:45 Minutes
**Ingredients:**
- ½ lb Halloumi cheese, grated
- 1 tbsp olive oil
- 1 lb chicken breasts, cubed
- 4 eggs, beaten
- 1 tsp dry mustard
- 2 cloves garlic, crushed
- 2 red bell peppers, sliced
- 1 red onion, sliced
- 2 tomatoes, chopped
- 1 tsp sweet paprika
- ½ tsp dried basil
- Salt to taste

**Directions:**
1. Preheat oven to 360° F. Warm the olive oil in a skillet over medium heat. Add the bell peppers, garlic, onion, and salt and cook for 3 minutes. Stir in tomatoes for an additional 5 minutes. Put in chicken breasts, paprika, dry mustard, and basil. Cook for another 6-8 minutes. Transfer the mixture to a greased baking pan and pour over the beaten eggs; season with salt. Bake for 15-18 minutes. Remove and spread the cheese over the top. Let cool for a few minutes. Serve sliced.

**Nutrition Info:**
- Info Per Serving: Calories: 480;Fat: 31g;Protein: 39g;Carbs: 12g.

# Lamb Kebabs With Lemon-yogurt Sauce

Servings:4
Cooking Time:25 Minutes
**Ingredients:**
- 2 tbsp olive oil
- 1 lb ground lamb
- 2 tbsp chopped fresh mint
- ¼ cup flour
- ¼ cup chopped red onions
- ¼ cup toasted pine nuts
- 2 tsp ground cumin
- Salt to taste
- 1 tsp ground cinnamon
- ½ tsp ground nutmeg
- ½ tsp black pepper
- 1 cup Greek yogurt
- 1 lemon, zested and juiced

**Directions:**
1. In a small bowl, whisk the yogurt, olive oil, salt, and lemon zest, and lemon juice. Keep in the refrigerator until ready to serve. Warm the olive oil in a pot over low heat. In a large bowl, combine the lamb, mint, flour, red onions, pine nuts, cumin, salt, cinnamon, ginger, nutmeg, and pepper and mix well with your hands. Shape the mixture into 12 patties. Thread the patties onto skewers and place them on a lined cookie sheet. Set under your preheated broiler for about 12 minutes, flipping once halfway through cooking. Serve the skewers with yogurt sauce.

**Nutrition Info:**
- Info Per Serving: Calories: 500;Fat: 42g;Protein: 23g;Carbs: 9g.

# Tomato & Basil Chicken Breasts

Servings:4
Cooking Time:30 Minutes
**Ingredients:**
- 2 tbsp olive oil
- 1 lb chicken breasts
- ½ tsp garlic powder
- ¼ tsp chili powder
- Salt and black pepper to taste
- 1 large tomato, sliced thinly
- 1 cup mozzarella, shredded
- 1 can diced tomatoes
- 2 tbsp fresh basil leaves, torn
- 4 tsp balsamic vinegar

**Directions:**
1. Preheat oven to 450° F. Flatten the chicken breasts with a rolling pin. Add the chicken, olive oil, garlic powder, chili powder, black pepper, and salt to a resealable bag. Seal the bag and massage the ingredients into the chicken. Take the chicken out of the bag and place it on a greased baking sheet.

2. Bake the chicken for 15-18 minutes or until the meat reaches an internal temperature of 160° F and the juices run clear. Layer the tomato slices on each chicken breast and top with mozzarella cheese. Broil the chicken for another 2-3 minutes or until the cheese melts. Remove the chicken from the oven. Microwave the crushed tomatoes for 1 minute. Divide the tomatoes between plates and top with chicken breasts. Scatter with basil and a drizzle of balsamic vinegar.

**Nutrition Info:**

- Info Per Serving: Calories: 258;Fat: 10g;Protein: 14g;Carbs: 28g.

## Baked Turkey With Veggies

Servings:4
Cooking Time:70 Minutes
**Ingredients:**

- 2 tbsp olive oil
- 1 lb turkey breasts, sliced
- ¼ cup chicken stock
- 1 carrot, chopped
- 1 red onion, chopped
- 2 mixed bell peppers, chopped
- Salt and black pepper to taste
- 1 tbsp cilantro, chopped

**Directions:**

1. Preheat oven to 380° F. Grease a roasting pan with olive oil. Combine turkey, stock, carrots, bell peppers, onion, salt, and pepper in the pan and bake for 1 hour. Top with cilantro.

**Nutrition Info:**

- Info Per Serving: Calories: 510;Fat: 15g;Protein: 11g;Carbs: 16g.

## Picante Green Pea & Chicken

Servings:4
Cooking Time:35 Minutes
**Ingredients:**

- 2 tbsp olive oil
- 1 lb chicken breasts, halved
- 1 tsp chili powder
- Salt and black pepper to taste
- 1 tsp garlic powder
- 1 tbsp smoked paprika
- ½ cup chicken stock
- 2 tsp sherry vinegar
- 3 tsp hot sauce
- 2 tsp cumin, ground
- 1 cup green peas
- 1 carrot, chopped

**Directions:**

1. Warm the olive oil in a skillet over medium heat and cook chicken for 6 minutes on both sides. Sprinkle with chili powder, salt, pepper, garlic powder, and paprika. Pour in the chicken stock, vinegar, hot sauce, cumin, carrot, and green peas and bring to a boil; cook for an additional 15 minutes.

**Nutrition Info:**

- Info Per Serving: Calories: 240;Fat: 19g;Protein: 14g;Carbs: 16g.

## Slow Cooker Brussel Sprout & Chicken

Servings:4
Cooking Time:8 Hours 20 Minutes
**Ingredients:**

- 2 tbsp olive oil
- 1 lb Brussels sprouts, halved
- 2 lb chicken breasts, cubed
- 1 ½ cups veggie stock
- 2 red onions, sliced
- 2 garlic cloves, minced
- 1 tbsp sweet paprika
- ½ cup tomato sauce
- Salt and black pepper to taste

**Directions:**

1. Warm the olive oil in a skillet over medium heat and sear the chicken for 10 minutes on all sides. Remove to your slow cooker. Add in onions, stock, garlic, paprika, Brussels sprouts, tomato sauce, salt, pepper, and dill. Cover the lid and cook for 8 hours on Low. Serve immediately.

**Nutrition Info:**

- Info Per Serving: Calories: 302;Fat: 15g;Protein: 16g;Carbs: 17g.

## Beef Keftedes (greek Meatballs)

Servings:6
Cooking Time:20 Min + Chilling Time
**Ingredients:**

- 2 bread slices, soaked in water, squeezed, and crumbled
- 4 tbsp olive oil
- 2 lb ground beef
- 2 medium onions, grated
- 1 tbsp minced garlic
- 2 large eggs, beaten
- 2 tsp dried Greek oregano
- 2 tbsp fresh parsley, chopped
- 1 tsp fresh mint, chopped
- 1/8 tsp ground cumin
- Salt and black pepper to taste

**Directions:**

1. Mix well all the ingredients, except for the olive oil, in a large bowl. Shape the mixture into balls and place them on a tray. Cover with plastic wrap and place in the fridge for at least 2 hours. Warm the olive oil in a skillet over medium heat and sear the keftedes 6-8 minutes until they are browned on all sides. Work in batches as needed. Serve immediately.

**Nutrition Info:**

- Info Per Serving: Calories: 567;Fat: 46g;Protein: 28g;Carbs: 8g.

# Valencian Arroz Con Pollo

Servings:4
Cooking Time:40 Minutes
**Ingredients:**
- 2 tbsp olive oil
- 3 cups chicken stock
- 1 cup brown rice
- 1 tbsp balsamic vinegar
- 1 lb chicken breasts, cubed
- 6 scallions, chopped
- Salt and black pepper to taste
- 1 tbsp sweet paprika
- 1 red bell pepper, chopped
- 1 green bell pepper, chopped

**Directions:**
1. Warm the olive oil in a skillet over medium heat and cook chicken for 5 minutes, stirring occasionally. Put in scallions and bell peppers and cook for another 5 minutes. Stir in rice, stock, vinegar, salt, pepper, and paprika and bring to a boil. Cook for 20 minutes. Serve immediately.

**Nutrition Info:**
- Info Per Serving: Calories: 310;Fat: 10g;Protein: 25g;Carbs: 19g.

# Chicken Caprese

Servings:4
Cooking Time:50 Minutes
**Ingredients:**
- 1 tsp garlic powder
- ½ cup basil pesto
- 4 chicken breast halves
- 3 tomatoes, sliced
- 1 cup mozzarella, shredded
- Salt and black pepper to taste

**Directions:**
1. Preheat the oven to 390° F. Line a baking dish with parchment paper and grease with cooking spray. Combine chicken, garlic powder, salt, pepper, and pesto in a bowl and arrange them on the sheet. Top with tomatoes and mozzarella and bake for 40 minutes. Serve hot.

**Nutrition Info:**
- Info Per Serving: Calories: 350;Fat: 21g;Protein: 33g;Carbs: 5g.

# Chicken Souvlaki

Servings:4
Cooking Time:20 Min + Cooling Time
**Ingredients:**
- 1 red bell pepper, cut into chunks
- 2 chicken breasts, cubed
- 2 tbsp olive oil
- 2 cloves garlic, minced
- 8 oz cipollini onions
- ½ cup lemon juice
- Salt and black pepper to taste

- 1 tsp rosemary, chopped
- 1 cup tzatziki sauce

**Directions:**
1. In a bowl, mix oil, garlic, salt, pepper, and lemon juice and add the chicken, cipollini, rosemary, and bell pepper. Refrigerate for 2 hours. Preheat your grill to high heat. Thread chicken, bell pepper, and cipollini onto skewers and grill them for 6 minutes per side. Serve with tzatziki sauce.

**Nutrition Info:**
- Info Per Serving: Calories: 363;Fat: 14.1g;Protein: 32g;Carbs: 8g.

# Wine Chicken Breasts With Capers

Servings:4
Cooking Time:25 Minutes
**Ingredients:**
- 2 tbsp butter
- 1 lb chicken breasts
- ½ cup flour
- ½ tsp ground nutmeg
- ½ cup chicken broth
- ½ cup dry white wine
- 1 lemon, juiced and zested
- 1 tbsp capers
- 2 tbsp chopped fresh cilantro
- Salt and black pepper to taste

**Directions:**
1. Cut the chicken into 4 pieces and pound them to ¼-inch thickness using a meat mallet. Combine flour, nutmeg, salt, and pepper in a bowl. Roll the chicken in the mixture and shake off the excess flour. Warm butter in a skillet over medium heat and brown the chicken for 6-8 minutes on both sides; set aside. Scrape the bottom of the pot with white wine. Add in broth, lemon juice, lemon zest, and capers. Simmer for 3-4 minutes until thickens. Pour the sauce over the chicken and sprinkle with cilantro to serve.

**Nutrition Info:**
- Info Per Serving: Calories: 355;Fat: 15g;Protein: 33g;Carbs: 13g.

# Mushroom & Pork Stew

Servings:4
Cooking Time:8 Hours 10 Minutes
**Ingredients:**
- 2 tbsp olive oil
- 2 lb pork stew meat, cubed
- 1 lb mushrooms, chopped
- Salt and black pepper to taste
- 2 cups chicken stock
- 1 carrot, chopped
- 1 yellow onion, chopped
- 2 garlic cloves, minced
- 2 cups tomatoes, chopped
- ½ cup parsley, chopped

**Directions:**

1. Place pork meat, salt, pepper, stock, olive oil, onion, carrot, garlic, mushrooms, and tomatoes in your slow cooker. Cover with the lid and cook for 8 hours on Low. Top with parsley.

**Nutrition Info:**
- Info Per Serving: Calories: 340;Fat: 18g;Protein: 17g;Carbs: 13g.

# Macadamia Pork

Servings:4
Cooking Time: 10 Minutes
**Ingredients:**
- 1 pork tenderloin, cut into ½-inch slices and pounded thin
- 1 teaspoon sea salt, divided
- ¼ teaspoon freshly ground black pepper, divided
- ½ cup macadamia nuts
- 1 cup unsweetened coconut milk
- 1 tablespoon extra-virgin olive oil

**Directions:**
1. Preheat the oven to 400ºF.
2. On a clean work surface, rub the pork with ½ teaspoon of the salt and ⅛ teaspoon of the ground black pepper. Set aside.
3. Ground the macadamia nuts in a food processor, then combine with remaining salt and black pepper in a bowl. Stir to mix well and set aside.
4. Combine the coconut milk and olive oil in a separate bowl. Stir to mix well.
5. Dredge the pork chops into the bowl of coconut milk mixture, then dunk into the bowl of macadamia nut mixture to coat well. Shake the excess off.
6. Put the well-coated pork chops on a baking sheet, then bake for 10 minutes or until the internal temperature of the pork reaches at least 165ºF.
7. Transfer the pork chops to a serving plate and serve immediately.

**Nutrition Info:**
- Info Per Serving: Calories: 436;Fat: 32.8g;Protein: 33.1g;Carbs: 5.9g.

# Exotic Pork Chops

Servings:4
Cooking Time:35 Minutes
**Ingredients:**
- 2 tbsp olive oil
- 2 cups chicken stock
- 2 garlic cloves, minced
- 4 pork loin chops, boneless
- 2 spring onions, chopped
- 2 mangos, peeled and cubed
- 1 tsp sweet paprika
- Salt and black pepper to taste
- ½ tsp dried oregano

**Directions:**

1. Warm the olive oil in a skillet over medium heat and sear pork chops for 4 minutes on both sides. Put in onions and garlic and cook for another 3 minutes. Stir in mangos, paprika, salt, pepper, oregano, and chicken stock and cook for 15 minutes, stirring often. Serve immediately.

**Nutrition Info:**
- Info Per Serving: Calories: 310;Fat: 15g;Protein: 25g;Carbs: 13g.

# Crispy Pesto Chicken

Servings:2
Cooking Time: 50 Minutes
**Ingredients:**
- 12 ounces small red potatoes, scrubbed and diced into 1-inch pieces
- 1 tablespoon olive oil
- ½ teaspoon garlic powder
- ¼ teaspoon salt
- 1 boneless, skinless chicken breast
- 3 tablespoons prepared pesto

**Directions:**
1. Preheat the oven to 425ºF. Line a baking sheet with parchment paper.
2. Combine the potatoes, olive oil, garlic powder, and salt in a medium bowl. Toss well to coat.
3. Arrange the potatoes on the parchment paper and roast for 10 minutes. Flip the potatoes and roast for an additional 10 minutes.
4. Meanwhile, put the chicken in the same bowl and toss with the pesto, coating the chicken evenly.
5. Check the potatoes to make sure they are golden brown on the top and bottom. Toss them again and add the chicken breast to the pan.
6. Turn the heat down to 350ºF and roast the chicken and potatoes for 30 minutes. Check to make sure the chicken reaches an internal temperature of 165ºF and the potatoes are fork-tender.
7. Let cool for 5 minutes before serving.

**Nutrition Info:**
- Info Per Serving: Calories: 378;Fat: 16.0g;Protein: 29.8g;Carbs: 30.1g.

# Chermoula Roasted Pork Tenderloin

Servings:2
Cooking Time: 20 Minutes
**Ingredients:**
- ½ cup fresh cilantro
- ½ cup fresh parsley
- 6 small garlic cloves
- 3 tablespoons olive oil, divided
- 3 tablespoons freshly squeezed lemon juice
- 2 teaspoons cumin
- 1 teaspoon smoked paprika
- ½ teaspoon salt, divided
- Pinch freshly ground black pepper
- 1 pork tenderloin

**Directions:**

1. Preheat the oven to 425ºF.

2. In a food processor, combine the cilantro, parsley, garlic, 2 tablespoons of olive oil, lemon juice, cumin, paprika, and ¼ teaspoon of salt. Pulse 15 to 20 times, or until the mixture is fairly smooth. Scrape the sides down as needed to incorporate all the ingredients. Transfer the sauce to a small bowl and set aside.

3. Season the pork tenderloin on all sides with the remaining ¼ teaspoon of salt and a generous pinch of black pepper.

4. Heat the remaining 1 tablespoon of olive oil in a sauté pan.

5. Sear the pork for 3 minutes, turning often, until golden brown on all sides.

6. Transfer the pork to a baking dish and roast in the preheated oven for 15 minutes, or until the internal temperature registers 145ºF.

7. Cool for 5 minutes before serving.

**Nutrition Info:**

• Info Per Serving: Calories: 169;Fat: 13.1g;Protein: 11.0g;Carbs: 2.9g.

# Parmesan Chicken Breasts

Servings:4
Cooking Time:35 Minutes
**Ingredients:**

• 1 tbsp olive oil
• 1 ½ lb chicken breasts, cubed
• 1 tsp ground coriander
• 1 tsp parsley flakes
• 2 garlic cloves, minced
• 1 cup heavy cream
• Salt and black pepper to taste
• ¼ cup Parmesan cheese, grated
• 1 tbsp basil, chopped

**Directions:**

1. Warm the olive oil in a skillet over medium heat and brown chicken, salt, and pepper for 6 minutes on all sides. Add in garlic and cook for another minute. Stir in coriander, parsley, and cream and cook for an additional 20 minutes. Serve scattered with basil and Parmesan cheese.

**Nutrition Info:**

• Info Per Serving: Calories: 260;Fat: 18g;Protein: 27g;Carbs: 26g.

# Savory Tomato Chicken

Servings:4
Cooking Time:90 Minutes
**Ingredients:**

• 3 tbsp olive oil
• 1 can diced tomatoes,
• 4 chicken breast halves
• 2 whole cloves
• ¼ cup chicken broth
• 2 tbsp tomato paste

• ¼ tsp chili flakes
• 1 tsp ground allspice
• ½ tsp dried mint
• 1 cinnamon stick
• Salt and black pepper to taste

**Directions:**

1. Place tomatoes, chicken broth, olive oil, tomato paste, chili flakes, mint, allspice, cloves, cinnamon stick, salt, and pepper in a pot over medium heat and bring just to a boil. Then, lower the heat and simmer for 30 minutes. Strain the sauce through a fine-mesh sieve and discard the cloves and cinnamon stick. Let it cool completely.

2. Preheat oven to 350° F. Lay the chicken on a baking dish and pour the sauce over. Bake covered with aluminum foil for 40-45 minutes. Uncover and continue baking for 5 more minutes.

**Nutrition Info:**

• Info Per Serving: Calories: 259;Fat: 14g;Protein: 24g;Carbs: 11g.

# Cocktail Meatballs In Almond Sauce

Servings:4
Cooking Time:30 Minutes
**Ingredients:**

• 3 tbsp olive oil
• 8 oz ground pork
• 8 oz ground beef
• ½ cup finely minced onions
• 1 large egg, beaten
• 1 potato, shredded
• Salt and black pepper to taste
• 1 tsp garlic powder
• ½ tsp oregano
• 2 tbsp chopped parsley
• ¼ cup ground almonds
• 1 cup chicken broth
• ¼ cup butter

**Directions:**

1. Place the ground meat, onions, egg, potato, salt, garlic powder, pepper, and oregano in a large bowl. Shape the mixture into small meatballs, about 1 inch in diameter, and place on a plate. Let sit for 10 minutes at room temperature.

2. Warm the olive oil in a skillet over medium heat. Add the meatballs and brown them for 6-8 minutes on all sides; reserve. In the hot skillet, melt the butter and add the almonds and broth. Cook for 3-5 minutes. Add the meatballs to the skillet, cover, and cook for 8-10 minutes. Top with parsley.

**Nutrition Info:**

• Info Per Serving: Calories: 449;Fat: 42g;Protein: 16g;Carbs: 3g.

# Rich Beef Meal

Servings:4
Cooking Time:40 Minutes
**Ingredients:**
- 1 tbsp olive oil
- 1 lb beef meat, cubed
- 1 red onion, chopped
- 1 garlic clove, minced
- 1 celery stalk, chopped
- Salt and black pepper to taste
- 14 oz canned tomatoes, diced
- 1 cup vegetable stock
- ½ tsp ground nutmeg
- 2 tsp dill, chopped

**Directions:**
1. Warm the olive oil in a skillet over medium heat and cook onion and garlic for 5 minutes. Put in beef and cook for 5 more minutes. Stir in celery, salt, pepper, tomatoes, stock, nutmeg, and dill and bring to a boil. Cook for 20 minutes.

**Nutrition Info:**
- Info Per Serving: Calories: 300;Fat: 14g;Protein: 19g;Carbs: 16g.

# Gyro Burgers With Tahini Sauce

Servings:4
Cooking Time: 10 Minutes
**Ingredients:**
- 2 tablespoons extra-virgin olive oil
- 1 tablespoon dried oregano
- 1¼ teaspoons garlic powder, divided
- 1 teaspoon ground cumin
- ½ teaspoon freshly ground black pepper
- ¼ teaspoon kosher or sea salt
- 1 pound beef flank steak, top round steak, or lamb leg steak, center cut, about 1 inch thick
- 1 medium green bell pepper, halved and seeded
- 2 tablespoons tahini or peanut butter
- 1 tablespoon hot water (optional)
- ½ cup plain Greek yogurt
- 1 tablespoon freshly squeezed lemon juice
- 1 cup thinly sliced red onion
- 4 whole-wheat pita breads, warmed
- Nonstick cooking spray

**Directions:**
1. Set an oven rack about 4 inches below the broiler element. Preheat the oven broiler to high. Line a large, rimmed baking sheet with aluminum foil. Place a wire cooling rack on the foil, and spray the rack with nonstick cooking spray. Set aside.
2. In a small bowl, whisk together the olive oil, oregano, 1 teaspoon of garlic powder, cumin, pepper, and salt. Rub the oil mixture on all sides of the steak, reserving 1 teaspoon of the mixture. Place the steak on the prepared rack. Rub the remaining oil mixture on the bell pepper, and place on the rack, cut-side down. Press the pepper with the heel of your hand to flatten.
3. Broil for 5 minutes. Flip the steak and the pepper pieces, and broil for 2 to 5 minutes more, until the pepper is charred and the internal temperature of the meat measures 145ºF on a meat thermometer. Put the pepper and steak on a cutting board to rest for 5 minutes.
4. Meanwhile, in a small bowl, whisk the tahini until smooth. Add the remaining ¼ teaspoon of garlic powder and the yogurt and lemon juice, and whisk thoroughly.
5. Slice the steak crosswise into ¼-inch-thick strips. Slice the bell pepper into strips. Divide the steak, bell pepper, and onion among the warm pita breads. Drizzle with tahini sauce and serve.

**Nutrition Info:**
- Info Per Serving: Calories: 348;Fat: 15.0g;Protein: 33.0g;Carbs: 20.0g.

# Herby Chicken With Asparagus Sauce

Servings:4
Cooking Time:40 Minutes
**Ingredients:**
- 1 chicken legs
- 4 garlic cloves, minced
- 4 fresh thyme, minced
- 3 fresh rosemary, minced
- Salt and black pepper to taste
- 2 tbsp olive oil
- 8 oz asparagus, chopped
- 1 onion, chopped
- 1 cup chicken stock
- 1 tbsp soy sauce
- 1 fresh thyme sprig
- 1 tbsp flour
- 2 tbsp parsley, chopped

**Directions:**
1. Warm the olive oil on Sauté in your Instant Pot. Add in onion and asparagus and sauté for 5 minutes until softened. Pour in chicken stock, 1 thyme sprig, black pepper, soy sauce, and salt, and stir. Insert a trivet over the asparagus mixture. Rub all sides of the chicken with garlic, rosemary, black pepper, lemon zest, thyme, and salt. Arrange the chicken legs on the trivet. Seal the lid, select Manual, and cook for 20 minutes on High Pressure. Do a quick release. Remove the chicken to a serving platter. In the inner pot, sprinkle flour over the asparagus mixture and blend the sauce with an immersion blender until desired consistency. Top the chicken with asparagus sauce and garnish with parsley. Serve and enjoy!

**Nutrition Info:**
- Info Per Serving: Calories: 193;Fat: 11g;Protein: 16g;Carbs: 10g.

# Pork Butt With Leeks

Servings:4
Cooking Time:1 Hour 40 Minutes
**Ingredients:**

- 2 lb boneless pork butt roast, cubed
- 3 tbsp olive oil
- Salt and black pepper to taste
- 2 lb leeks, sliced
- 2 garlic cloves, minced
- 1 can diced tomatoes
- 1 cup dry white wine
- ½ cup chicken broth
- 1 bay leaf
- 2 tsp chopped fresh parsley

**Directions:**

1. Season the pork with salt and pepper. Warm the oil in a saucepan over medium heat. Brown the pork on all sides, about 8 minutes; transfer to a bowl. Add the leeks, salt, and pepper to fat left in saucepan and sauté for 5-7 minutes, stirring occasionally, until softened and lightly browned. Stir in garlic and cook until fragrant, about 30 seconds. Pour in tomatoes and their juice, scraping up any browned bits, and cook until tomato liquid is nearly evaporated, 10-12 minutes.
2. Preheat oven to 325° F. Add the wine, broth, and bay leaf to the saucepan and return the pork with any accumulated juices; bring to a simmer. Cover, transfer to the oven and cook for about 60 minutes until the pork is tender and falls apart when prodded with a fork. Remove and discard the bay leaf. Sprinkle with parsley. Serve and enjoy!

**Nutrition Info:**

- Info Per Serving: Calories: 369;Fat: 14g;Protein: 37g;Carbs: 25g.

# Asparagus & Chicken Skillet

Servings:4
Cooking Time:30 Minutes
**Ingredients:**

- 2 tbsp olive oil
- 1 lb chicken breasts, sliced
- Salt and black pepper to taste
- 1 lb asparagus, chopped
- 6 sundried tomatoes, diced
- 3 tbsp capers, drained
- 2 tbsp lemon juice

**Directions:**

1. Warm the olive oil in a skillet over medium heat. Cook asparagus, tomatoes, salt, pepper, capers, and lemon juice for 10 minutes. Remove to a bowl. Brown chicken in the same skillet for 8 minutes on both sides. Put veggies back to skillet and cook for another 2-3 minutes. Serve and enjoy!

**Nutrition Info:**

- Info Per Serving: Calories: 560;Fat: 29g;Protein: 45g;Carbs: 34g.

# Pork Chops In Wine Sauce

Servings:4
Cooking Time:30 Minutes
**Ingredients:**

- 2 tbsp olive oil
- 4 pork chops
- 1 cup red onion, sliced
- 10 black peppercorns, crushed
- ¼ cup vegetable stock
- ¼ cup dry white wine
- 2 garlic cloves, minced
- Salt to taste

**Directions:**

1. Warm the olive oil in a skillet over medium heat and sear pork chops for 8 minutes on both sides. Put in onion and garlic and cook for another 2 minutes. Mix in stock, wine, salt, and peppercorns and cook for 10 minutes, stirring often.

**Nutrition Info:**

- Info Per Serving: Calories: 240;Fat: 10g;Protein: 25g;Carbs: 14g.

# Peppery Chicken Bake

Servings:4
Cooking Time:70 Minutes
**Ingredients:**

- 3 tbsp olive oil
- 1 lb chicken breasts, sliced
- 2 lb cherry tomatoes, halved
- 1 onion, chopped
- 3 garlic cloves, minced
- 3 red chili peppers, chopped
- ½ lemon, zested
- Salt and black pepper to taste

**Directions:**

1. Warm the olive oil in a skillet over medium heat and brown chicken for 8 minutes on both sides. Remove to a roasting pan. In the same skillet, add onion, garlic, and chili peppers and cook for 2 minutes. Pour the mixture over the chicken and toss to coat. Add in tomatoes, lemon zest, 1 cup of water, salt, and pepper. Bake for 45 minutes. Serve and enjoy!

**Nutrition Info:**

- Info Per Serving: Calories: 280;Fat: 14g;Protein: 34g;Carbs: 25g.

# Cardamon Chicken Breasts

Servings:4
Cooking Time:8 Hours 10 Minutes
**Ingredients:**

- 2 tbsp olive oil
- 2 chicken breasts, halved
- Juice of ½ lemon
- Zest of ½ lemon, grated
- 2 tsp cardamom, ground

- Salt and black pepper to taste
- 2 spring onions, chopped
- 2 tbsp tomato paste
- 2 garlic cloves, minced
- 1 cup pineapple juice
- ½ cup chicken stock
- ¼ cup cilantro, chopped

**Directions:**

1. Place chicken, lemon juice, lemon zest, cardamom, salt, pepper, olive oil, spring onions, tomato paste, garlic, pineapple juice, and stock in your slow cooker. Cover with the lid and cook for 8 hours on Low. Garnish with cilantro.

**Nutrition Info:**

- Info Per Serving: Calories: 340;Fat: 13g;Protein: 18g;Carbs: 25g.

## Saucy Green Pea & Chicken

Servings:4
Cooking Time:40 Minutes

**Ingredients:**

- 2 tbsp olive oil
- 1 tsp dried thyme
- 1 lb chicken breasts, cubed
- Salt and black pepper to taste
- 1 cup chicken stock
- ½ cup tomato sauce
- 1 cup green peas
- 2 tbsp chives, chopped

**Directions:**

1. Warm the olive oil in a pot over medium heat and sauté the chicken for 8 minutes, stirring occasionally. Season with thyme, salt, and pepper. Pour in chicken stock and tomato sauce and bring to a boil. Simmer for 20 minutes. Add in green peas and cook for 4-5 minutes. Top with chives.

**Nutrition Info:**

- Info Per Serving: Calories: 316;Fat: 16g;Protein: 35g;Carbs: 7g.

## Creamy Chicken Balls With Almonds

Servings:4
Cooking Time:30 Minutes

**Ingredients:**

- 2 tbsp olive oil
- 1 lb ground chicken
- 2 tsp toasted chopped almonds
- 1 egg, whisked
- 2 tsp turmeric powder
- 2 garlic cloves, minced
- Salt and black pepper to taste
- 1 ¼ cups heavy cream
- ¼ cup parsley, chopped
- 1 tbsp chives, chopped

**Directions:**

1. Place chicken, almonds, egg, turmeric powder, garlic, salt, pepper, parsley, and chives in a bowl and toss to combine. Form meatballs out of the mixture. Warm olive oil in a skillet over medium heat. Brown meatballs for 8 minutes on all sides. Stir in cream and cook for another 10 minutes.

**Nutrition Info:**

- Info Per Serving: Calories: 290;Fat: 10g;Protein: 36g;Carbs: 26g.

# Fruits, Desserts And Snacks Recipes

## Honeyed Pistachio Dumplings

Servings:4
Cooking Time:25 Minutes
**Ingredients:**
- 1 cup vegetable oil
- ½ cup warm milk
- 2 cups flour
- 2 eggs, beaten
- 1 tsp sugar
- 1 ½ oz active dry yeast
- 1 cup warm water
- ½ tsp vanilla extract
- 1 tsp cinnamon
- 1 orange, zested
- 4 tbsp honey
- 2 tbsp pistachios, chopped

**Directions:**
1. In a bowl, sift the flour and combine it with the cinnamon and orange zest. In another bowl, mix the sugar, yeast, and ½ cup of warm water. Leave to stand until the yeast dissolves. Stir in milk, eggs, vanilla, and flour mixture. Beat with an electric mixer until smooth. Cover the bowl with plastic wrap and let sit to rise in a warm place for at least 1 hour.
2. Pour the vegetable oil into a deep pan or wok to come halfway up the sides and heat the oil. Add some more oil if necessary. Using a teaspoon, form balls, one by one, and drop in the hot oil one after another. Fry the balls on all sides, until golden brown. Remove them with a slotted spoon to paper towels to soak the excess fat. Repeat the process until the dough is exhausted. Drizzle with honey and sprinkle with pistachios.

**Nutrition Info:**
- Info Per Serving: Calories: 890;Fat: 59g;Protein: 15g;Carbs: 78g.

## Honey Baked Cinnamon Apples

Servings:2
Cooking Time: 20 Minutes
**Ingredients:**
- 1 teaspoon extra-virgin olive oil
- 4 firm apples, peeled, cored, and sliced
- ½ teaspoon salt
- 1½ teaspoons ground cinnamon, divided
- 2 tablespoons unsweetened almond milk
- 2 tablespoons honey

**Directions:**
1. Preheat the oven to 375ºF. Coat a small casserole dish with the olive oil.
2. Toss the apple slices with the salt and ½ teaspoon of the cinnamon in a medium bowl. Spread the apples in the prepared casserole dish and bake in the preheated oven for 20 minutes.
3. Meanwhile, in a small saucepan, heat the milk, honey, and remaining 1 teaspoon of cinnamon over medium heat, stirring frequently.
4. When it reaches a simmer, remove the pan from the heat and cover to keep warm.
5. Divide the apple slices between 2 plates and pour the sauce over the apples. Serve warm.

**Nutrition Info:**
- Info Per Serving: Calories: 310;Fat: 3.4g;Protein: 1.7g;Carbs: 68.5g.

## Bruschetta With Tomato & Basil

Servings:4
Cooking Time:20 Minutes
**Ingredients:**
- 1 ciabatta loaf, halved lengthwise
- 2 tbsp olive oil
- 3 tbsp basil, chopped
- 4 tomatoes, cubed
- 1 shallot, sliced
- 2 garlic cloves, minced
- Salt and black pepper to taste
- 1 tbsp balsamic vinegar
- ½ tsp garlic powder

**Directions:**
1. Preheat the oven to 380 °F. Line a baking sheet with parchment paper. Cut in half each half of the ciabatta loaf. Place them on the sheet and sprinkle with some olive oil. Bake for 10 minutes. Mix tomatoes, shallot, basil, garlic, salt, pepper, olive oil, vinegar, and garlic powder in a bowl and let sit for 10 minutes. Apportion the mixture among bread pieces.

**Nutrition Info:**
- Info Per Serving: Calories: 170;Fat: 5g;Protein: 5g;Carbs: 30g.

## Dark Chocolate Barks

Servings:6
Cooking Time:20 Min + Freezing Time
**Ingredients:**
- ½ cup quinoa
- ½ tsp sea salt
- 1 cup dark chocolate chips
- ½ tsp mint extract
- ½ cup pomegranate seeds

**Directions:**
1. Toast the quinoa in a greased saucepan for 2-3 minutes, stirring frequently. Remove the pan from the stove and mix in the salt. Set aside 2 tablespoons of the toasted quinoa.
2. Microwave the chocolate for 1 minute. Stir until the chocolate is completely melted. Mix the toasted quinoa and

mint extract into the melted chocolate. Line a large, rimmed baking sheet with parchment paper. Spread the chocolate mixture onto the sheet. Sprinkle the remaining 2 tablespoons of quinoa and pomegranate seeds, pressing with a spatula. Freeze the mixture for 10-15 minutes or until set. Remove and break into about 2-inch jagged pieces. Store in the refrigerator until ready to serve.

**Nutrition Info:**
- Info Per Serving: Calories: 268;Fat: 12g;Protein: 4g;Carbs: 37g.

# Banana, Cranberry, And Oat Bars

Servings:16
Cooking Time: 40 Minutes
**Ingredients:**
- 2 tablespoon extra-virgin olive oil
- 2 medium ripe bananas, mashed
- ½ cup almond butter
- ½ cup maple syrup
- ⅓ cup dried cranberries
- 1½ cups old-fashioned rolled oats
- ¼ cup oat flour
- ¼ cup ground flaxseed
- ¼ teaspoon ground cloves
- ½ cup shredded coconut
- ½ teaspoon ground cinnamon
- 1 teaspoon vanilla extract

**Directions:**
1. Preheat the oven to 400ºF. Line a 8-inch square pan with parchment paper, then grease with olive oil.
2. Combine the mashed bananas, almond butter, and maple syrup in a bowl. Stir to mix well.
3. Mix in the remaining ingredients and stir to mix well until thick and sticky.
4. Spread the mixture evenly on the square pan with a spatula, then bake in the preheated oven for 40 minutes or until a toothpick inserted in the center comes out clean.
5. Remove them from the oven and slice into 16 bars to serve.

**Nutrition Info:**
- Info Per Serving: Calories: 145;Fat: 7.2g;Protein: 3.1g;Carbs: 18.9g.

# Lamb Ragu Tagliatelle

Servings:4
Cooking Time:25 Minutes
**Ingredients:**
- 2 tbsp olive oil
- 16 oz tagliatelle
- 1 tsp paprika
- 1 tsp cumin
- Salt and black pepper to taste
- 1 lb ground lamb
- 1 cup onions, chopped
- ¼ cup parsley, chopped

- 2 garlic cloves, minced

**Directions:**
1. Boil the tagliatelle in a pot over medium heat for 9-11 minutes or until "al dente". Drain and set aside.
2. Warm the olive oil in a skillet over medium heat and sauté lamb, onions, and garlic until the meat is browned, about 10-15 minutes. Stir in cumin, paprika, salt, and pepper for 1-2 minutes. Spoon tagliatelle on a platter and scatter lamb over. Top with parsley and serve.

**Nutrition Info:**
- Info Per Serving: Calories: 140;Fat: 10g;Protein: 6g;Carbs: 7g.

# Mascarpone Baked Pears

Servings:2
Cooking Time: 20 Minutes
**Ingredients:**
- 2 ripe pears, peeled
- 1 tablespoon plus 2 teaspoons honey, divided
- 1 teaspoon vanilla, divided
- ¼ teaspoon ground coriander
- ¼ teaspoon ginger
- ¼ cup minced walnuts
- ¼ cup mascarpone cheese
- Pinch salt
- Cooking spray

**Directions:**
1. Preheat the oven to 350ºF. Spray a small baking dish with cooking spray.
2. Slice the pears in half lengthwise. Using a spoon, scoop out the core from each piece. Put the pears, cut side up, in the baking dish.
3. Whisk together 1 tablespoon of honey, ½ teaspoon of vanilla, ginger, and coriander in a small bowl. Pour this mixture evenly over the pear halves.
4. Scatter the walnuts over the pear halves.
5. Bake in the preheated oven for 20 minutes, or until the pears are golden and you're able to pierce them easily with a knife.
6. Meanwhile, combine the mascarpone cheese with the remaining 2 teaspoons of honey, ½ teaspoon of vanilla, and a pinch of salt. Stir to combine well.
7. Divide the mascarpone among the warm pear halves and serve.

**Nutrition Info:**
- Info Per Serving: Calories: 308;Fat: 16.0g;Protein: 4.1g;Carbs: 42.7g.

# Goat Cheese Dip With Scallions & Lemon

Servings:4
Cooking Time:10 Minutes
**Ingredients:**
- 2 tbsp extra virgin olive oil
- 2 oz goat cheese, crumbled
- ¾ cup sour cream
- 2 tbsp scallions, chopped
- 1 tbsp lemon juice
- Salt and black pepper to taste

**Directions:**
1. Combine goat cheese, sour cream, scallions, lemon juice, salt, pepper, and olive oil in a bowl and transfer to the fridge for 10 minutes before serving.

**Nutrition Info:**
- Info Per Serving: Calories: 230;Fat: 12g;Protein: 6g;Carbs: 9g.

# Kid´s Marzipan Balls

Servings:6
Cooking Time:10 Minutes
**Ingredients:**
- ½ cup avocado oil
- 1 ½ cup almond flour
- ½ cup sugar
- 2 tsp almond extract

**Directions:**
1. Add the almond flour and sugar and pulse to your food processor until the mixture is ground. Add the almond extract and pulse until combined. With the processor running, stream in oil until the mixture starts to form a large ball. Turn off the food processor. With hands, form the marzipan into six 1-inch diameter balls. Press to hold the mixture together. Store in an airtight container in the refrigerator for up to 14 days.

**Nutrition Info:**
- Info Per Serving: Calories: 157;Fat: 17g;Protein: 2g;Carbs: 0g.

# Garlic-yogurt Dip With Walnuts

Servings:4
Cooking Time:5 Minutes
**Ingredients:**
- 2 cups Greek yogurt
- 3 garlic cloves, minced
- ¼ cup dill, chopped
- 1 green onion, chopped
- ¼ cup walnuts, chopped
- Salt and black pepper to taste

**Directions:**
1. Combine garlic, yogurt, dill, walnuts, salt, and pepper in a bowl. Serve topped with green onion.

**Nutrition Info:**
- Info Per Serving: Calories: 210;Fat: 7g;Protein: 9g;Carbs: 16g.

# Festive Pumpkin Cheesecake

Servings:6
Cooking Time:50 Min + Chilling Time
**Ingredients:**
- ½ cup butter, melted
- 1 cup flour
- 1 can pumpkin purée
- 1 ½ cups mascarpone cheese
- ½ cup sugar
- 4 large eggs
- 2 tsp vanilla extract
- 2 tsp pumpkin pie spice

**Directions:**
1. Preheat oven to 350 °F. In a small bowl, combine the flour and melted butter with a fork until well combined. Press the mixture into the bottom of a greased baking pan. In a large bowl, beat together the pumpkin purée, mascarpone cheese, and sugar using an electric mixer.
2. Add the eggs, one at a time, beating after each addition. Stir in the vanilla and pumpkin pie spice until just combined. Pour the mixture over the crust and bake until set, 40-45 minutes. Allow to cool to room temperature. Refrigerate for at least 6 hours before serving. Serve chilled.

**Nutrition Info:**
- Info Per Serving: Calories: 242;Fat: 22g;Protein: 7g;Carbs: 5g.

# Caramel Peach & Walnut Cake

Servings:6
Cooking Time:50 Min + Cooling Time
**Ingredients:**
- ¼ cup coconut oil
- ¼ cup olive oil
- 2 peeled peaches, chopped
- ½ cup raisins, soaked
- 1 cup plain flour
- 3 eggs
- 1 tbsp dark rum
- ¼ tsp ground cinnamon
- 1 tsp vanilla extract
- 1 ½ tsp baking powder
- 4 tbsp Greek yogurt
- 2 tbsp honey
- 1 cup brown sugar
- 4 tbsp walnuts, chopped
- ¼ caramel sauce
- ¼ tsp salt

**Directions:**
1. Preheat the oven to 350 °F. In a bowl, mix the flour, cinnamon, vanilla, baking powder, and salt. In another bowl, whisk the eggs with Greek yogurt using an electric mixer. Gently add in coconut and olive oil. Combine well. Put in

rum, honey and sugar; stir to combine. Mix the wet ingredients with the dry mixture. Stir in peaches, raisins, and walnuts.

2. Pour the mixture into a greased baking pan and bake for 30-40 minutes until a knife inserted into the middle of the cake comes out clean. Remove from the oven and let sit for 10 minutes, then invert onto a wire rack to cool completely. Warm the caramel sauce through in a pan and pour it over the cooled cake to serve.

**Nutrition Info:**
- Info Per Serving: Calories: 568;Fat: 26g;Protein: 215g;Carbs: 66g.

## Poached Pears In Red Wine

Servings:4
Cooking Time:1 Hour 35 Minutes
**Ingredients:**
- 4 pears, peeled with stalk intact
- 2 cups red wine
- 8 whole cloves
- 1 cinnamon stick
- ½ tsp vanilla extract
- 2 tsp sugar
- Creme fraiche for garnish

**Directions:**
1. In a pot over low heat, mix red wine, cinnamon stick, cloves, vanilla, and sugar and bring to a simmer, stirring often until the sugar is dissolved. Add in the pears, make sure that they are submerged and poach them for 15-20 minutes.

2. Remove the pears to a platter and allow the liquid simmering over medium heat for 15 minutes until reduced by half and syrupy. Remove from the heat and let cool for 10 minutes. Drain to discard the spices, let cool, and pour over the pears. Top with creme fraiche and serve.

**Nutrition Info:**
- Info Per Serving: Calories: 158;Fat: 1g;Protein: 2g;Carbs: 33g.

## Spanish-style Pizza With Jamón Serrano

Servings:4
Cooking Time:90 Minutes
**Ingredients:**
- For the crust
- 2 tbsp olive oil
- 2 cups flour
- 1 cup lukewarm water
- 1 pinch of sugar
- 1 tsp active dry yeast
- ¾ tsp salt
- For the topping
- 1/3 cup Spanish olives with pimento
- ½ cup tomato sauce
- ½ cup sliced mozzarella

- 4 oz jamon serrano, sliced
- 7 fresh basil leaves

**Directions:**
1. Sift the flour and salt in a bowl and stir in yeast. Mix lukewarm water, olive oil, and sugar in another bowl. Add the wet mixture to the dry mixture and whisk until you obtain a soft dough. Place the dough on a lightly floured work surface and knead it thoroughly for 4-5 minutes until elastic. Transfer the dough to a greased bowl. Cover with cling film and leave to rise for 50-60 minutes in a warm place until doubled in size. Roll out the dough to a thickness of around 12 inches.

2. Preheat the oven to 400 °F. Line a pizza pan with parchment paper. Spread the tomato sauce on the crust. Arrange the mozzarella slices on the sauce and then the Jamon serrano. Bake for 15 minutes or until the cheese melts. Remove from the oven and top with olives and basil. Slice and serve warm.

**Nutrition Info:**
- Info Per Serving: Calories: 160;Fat: 6g;Protein: 22g;Carbs: 0.5g.

## Sicilian Sandwich Muffuletta

Servings:6
Cooking Time:10 Minutes
**Ingredients:**
- 1 focaccia bread
- 2 tbsp drained capers
- 2 tbsp black olive tapenade
- ½ lb fontina cheese, sliced
- ¼ lb smoked turkey, sliced
- ¼ lb salami, thinly sliced

**Directions:**
1. Slice the focaccia bread in half horizontally. Spread each piece with olive tapenade. Layer half of the fontina cheese, a layer of capers, smoked turkey, olive tapenade, salami, capers, and finish with fontina cheese. Top with the remaining focaccia half and press the sandwich together gently. Serve sliced into wedges.

**Nutrition Info:**
- Info Per Serving: Calories: 335;Fat: 27g;Protein: 18g;Carbs: 4g.

## Apple And Berries Ambrosia

Servings:4
Cooking Time: 0 Minutes
**Ingredients:**
- 2 cups unsweetened coconut milk, chilled
- 2 tablespoons raw honey
- 1 apple, peeled, cored, and chopped
- 2 cups fresh raspberries
- 2 cups fresh blueberries

**Directions:**
1. Spoon the chilled milk in a large bowl, then mix in the honey. Stir to mix well.

2. Then mix in the remaining ingredients. Stir to coat the fruits well and serve immediately.

**Nutrition Info:**
- Info Per Serving: Calories: 386;Fat: 21.1g;Protein: 4.2g;Carbs: 45.9g.

# Vegetarian Patties

Servings:4
Cooking Time:20 Minutes
**Ingredients:**
- 3 tbsp olive oil
- 2 carrots, grated
- 2 zucchinis, grated and drained
- 2 garlic cloves, minced
- 2 spring onions, chopped
- 1 tsp cumin
- ½ tsp turmeric powder
- Salt and black pepper to taste
- ¼ tsp ground coriander
- 2 tbsp parsley, chopped
- ¼ tsp lemon juice
- ½ cup flour
- 1 egg, whisked
- ¼ cup breadcrumbs

**Directions:**
1. Combine garlic, spring onions, carrot, cumin, turmeric, salt, pepper, coriander, parsley, lemon juice, flour, zucchinis, egg, and breadcrumbs in a bowl and mix well. Form balls out of the mixture and flatten them to form patties.
2. Warm olive oil in a skillet over medium heat. Fry the cakes for 10 minutes on both sides. Remove to a paper-lined plate to drain the excessive grease. Serve warm.

**Nutrition Info:**
- Info Per Serving: Calories: 220;Fat: 12g;Protein: 5g;Carbs: 5g.

# Amaretto Nut Bars

Servings:4
Cooking Time:10 Minutes
**Ingredients:**
- 2 tbsp olive oil
- ¼ cup shredded coconut
- 1 cup pistachios
- ½ tsp Amaretto liqueur
- 1 cup almonds
- 2 cups dates, pitted
- ¼ cup cocoa powder

**Directions:**
1. In a food processor, blend pistachios, dates, almonds, olive oil, Amaretto liqueur, and cocoa powder until well minced. Make tablespoon-size balls out of the mixture. Roll the balls in the shredded coconut to coat. Serve chilled.

**Nutrition Info:**
- Info Per Serving: Calories: 560;Fat: 28g;Protein: 11g;Carbs: 79g.

# Cucumber Sticks With Dill-cheese Dip

Servings:4
Cooking Time:10 Minutes
**Ingredients:**
- 3 cucumbers, julienned and deseeded
- ¼ cup olive oil
- ¼ tsp salt
- 1 garlic clove, minced
- 2 tbsp dill, chopped
- ¼ cup grated Parmesan cheese
- ¼ cup almonds, chopped
- ½ tsp paprika

**Directions:**
1. Season cucumbers and arrange on a platter. Mix dill, almonds, garlic, Parmesan cheese, and olive oil in a food processor until smooth. Spoon the dip over the cucumbers and season with paprika to serve.

**Nutrition Info:**
- Info Per Serving: Calories: 182;Fat: 16g;Protein: 4g;Carbs: 10g.

# Choco-tahini Glazed Apple Chips

Servings:2
Cooking Time:10 Minutes
**Ingredients:**
- 1 tbsp roasted, salted sunflower seeds
- 2 tbsp tahini
- 1 tbsp honey
- 1 tbsp cocoa powder
- 2 apples, thinly sliced

**Directions:**
1. Mix the tahini, honey, and cocoa powder in a small bowl. Add 1-2 tbsp of warm water and stir until thin enough to drizzle. Lay the apple chips out on a plate and drizzle them with the chocolate tahini sauce. Sprinkle sunflower seeds.

**Nutrition Info:**
- Info Per Serving: Calories: 261;Fat: 11g;Protein: 5g;Carbs: 43g.

# 5-minute Avocado Spread

Servings:4
Cooking Time:5 Minutes
**Ingredients:**
- 2 avocados, chopped
- ½ cup heavy cream
- 1 serrano pepper, chopped
- Salt and black pepper to taste
- 2 tbsp cilantro, chopped
- ¼ cup lime juice

**Directions:**
1. In a food processor, blitz heavy cream, serrano pepper, salt, pepper, avocados, cilantro, and lime juice until smooth. Refrigerate before serving.

## Nutrition Info:

- Info Per Serving: Calories: 210;Fat: 15g;Protein: 8g;Carbs: 9g.

# Bean & Artichoke Dip

Servings:4
Cooking Time:10 Minutes
**Ingredients:**

- 2 tbsp olive oil
- 15 oz canned Cannellini beans
- 1 red onion, chopped
- 6 oz canned artichoke hearts,
- 4 garlic cloves, minced
- 1 tbsp thyme, chopped
- ½ lemon, juiced and zested
- Salt and black pepper to taste

**Directions:**

1. Warm olive oil in a skillet over medium heat and sauté onion and garlic for 4-5 minutes until translucent. Add in the artichoke hearts and cook for 2-3 more minutes. Set aside to cool slightly. Transfer the cooled mixture to a blender along with cannellini beans, thyme, lemon juice, lemon zest, salt, and pepper and blitz until it becomes smooth. Serve.

**Nutrition Info:**

- Info Per Serving: Calories: 280;Fat: 12g;Protein: 17g;Carbs: 19g.

# Easy No-bake Walnut & Date Oat Bars

Servings:6
Cooking Time:30 Minutes
**Ingredients:**

- ¼ cup butter, melted
- ¼ cup honey
- 12 dates, pitted and chopped
- 1 tsp vanilla extract
- ½ cup rolled oats
- ¾ cup sultanas, soaked
- 1 cup walnuts, chopped
- ¼ cup pumpkin seeds

**Directions:**

1. Place dates, vanilla, honey, oats, sultanas, butter, walnuts, and pumpkin seeds in a bowl and mix to combine. Transfer to a lined with parchment paper baking sheet and freeze for 30 minutes. Slice into bars and serve.

**Nutrition Info:**

- Info Per Serving: Calories: 280;Fat: 14g;Protein: 4g;Carbs: 15g.

# Energy Granola Bites

Servings:5
Cooking Time:10 Minutes
**Ingredients:**

- ¾ cup diced dried figs
- ½ cup chopped walnuts

- ¼ cup old-fashioned oats
- 2 tbsp ground flaxseed
- 2 tbsp peanut butter
- 2 tbsp honey

**Directions:**

1. In a medium bowl, mix together the figs, walnuts, oats, flaxseed, and peanut butter. Drizzle with the honey, and mix everything with a wooden spoon. Freeze the dough for 5 minutes. Divide the dough evenly into four sections in the bowl. Dampen your hands with water—but don't get them too wet, or the dough will stick to them. With hands, roll three bites out of each of the four sections of dough, making 10 energy bites. Store in the fridge for up to a week.

**Nutrition Info:**

- Info Per Serving: Calories: 158;Fat: 8g;Protein: 3g;Carbs: 23g.

# Mini Cucumber & Cream Cheese Sandwiches

Servings:4
Cooking Time:5 Minutes
**Ingredients:**

- 4 bread slices
- 1 cucumber, sliced
- 2 tbsp cream cheese, soft
- 1 tbsp chives, chopped
- ¼ cup hummus
- Salt and black pepper to taste

**Directions:**

1. In a bowl, mix hummus, cream cheese, chives, salt, and pepper until well combined. Spread the mixture onto bread slices. Top with cucumber and cut each sandwich into three pieces. Serve immediately.

**Nutrition Info:**

- Info Per Serving: Calories: 190;Fat: 13g;Protein: 9g;Carbs: 5g.

# Healthy Tuna Stuffed Zucchini Rolls

Servings:4
Cooking Time:5 Minutes
**Ingredients:**

- 5 oz canned tuna, drained and mashed
- 2 tbsp olive oil
- ½ cup mayonnaise
- 2 tbsp capers
- 2 zucchinis, sliced lengthwise
- Salt and black pepper to taste
- 1 tsp lime juice

**Directions:**

1. Heat a grill pan over medium heat. Drizzle the zucchini slices with olive oil and season with salt and pepper. Grill for 5-6 minutes on both sides. In a bowl, mix the tuna, capers, lime juice, mayonnaise, salt, and pepper until well combined. Spread the tuna mixture onto zucchini slices and roll them up. Transfer the rolls to a plate and serve.

**Nutrition Info:**
- Info Per Serving: Calories: 210;Fat: 7g;Protein: 4g;Carbs: 8g.

# Crunchy Almond Cookies

Servings:4
Cooking Time: 5 To 7 Minutes
**Ingredients:**
- ½ cup sugar
- 8 tablespoons almond butter
- 1 large egg
- 1½ cups all-purpose flour
- 1 cup ground almonds

**Directions:**
1. Preheat the oven to 375ºF. Line a baking sheet with parchment paper.
2. Using a mixer, whisk together the sugar and butter. Add the egg and mix until combined. Alternately add the flour and ground almonds, ½ cup at a time, while the mixer is on slow.
3. Drop 1 tablespoon of the dough on the prepared baking sheet, keeping the cookies at least 2 inches apart.
4. Put the baking sheet in the oven and bake for about 5 to 7 minutes, or until the cookies start to turn brown around the edges.
5. Let cool for 5 minutes before serving.

**Nutrition Info:**
- Info Per Serving: Calories: 604;Fat: 36.0g;Protein: 11.0g;Carbs: 63.0g.

# Artichoke & Curly Kale Flatbread

Servings:4
Cooking Time:25 Minutes
**Ingredients:**
- 3 tbsp olive oil
- 1 cup curly kale, chopped
- 1 tbsp garlic powder
- 2 tbsp parsley, chopped
- 2 flatbread wraps
- 4 tbsp Parmesan cheese, grated
- ½ cup mozzarella, grated
- 14 oz canned artichokes
- 12 cherry tomatoes, halved
- Salt and black pepper to taste

**Directions:**
1. Preheat the oven to 390 °F. Line a baking sheet with parchment paper. Brush the flatbread wrap with some olive oil and sprinkle with garlic, salt, and pepper. Top with half of the Parmesan and mozzarella cheeses. Combine artichokes, tomatoes, salt, pepper, and remaining olive oil in a bowl. Spread the mixture on the top of the wraps and top with the remaining Parmesan cheese. Transfer to the baking sheet and bake for 15 minutes. Top with curly kale and parsley.

**Nutrition Info:**

- Info Per Serving: Calories: 230;Fat: 12;Protein: 8g;Carbs: 16g.

# Pomegranate Blueberry Granita

Servings:2
Cooking Time:15 Min + Freezing Time
**Ingredients:**
- 1 cup blueberries
- 1 cup pomegranate juice
- ¼ cup sugar
- ¼ tsp lemon zest

**Directions:**
1. Place the blueberries, lemon zest, and pomegranate juice in a saucepan over medium heat and bring to a boil. Simmer for 5 minutes or until the blueberries start to break down. Stir the sugar in ¼ cup of water until the sugar is dissolved. Place the blueberry mixture and the sugar water in your blender and blitz for 1 minute or until the fruit is puréed.
2. Pour the mixture into a baking pan. The liquid should come about ½ inch up the sides. Let the mixture cool for 30 minutes, and then put it into the freezer. Every 30 minutes for the next 2 hours, scrape the granita with a fork to keep it from freezing solid. Serve it after 2 hours, or store it in a covered container in the freezer.

**Nutrition Info:**
- Info Per Serving: Calories: 214;Fat: 0g;Protein: 1g;Carbs: 54g.

# Spiced Fries

Servings:6
Cooking Time:35 Minutes
**Ingredients:**
- 2 lb red potatoes, cut into wedges
- ¼ cup olive oil
- 3 tbsp garlic, minced
- ½ tsp smoked paprika
- Salt and black pepper to taste
- ½ cup fresh cilantro, chopped
- ¼ tsp cayenne pepper

**Directions:**
1. Preheat oven to 450 °F. Place the potatoes into a bowl. Add the garlic, salt, pepper, and olive oil and toss everything together to coat evenly. Spread the potato mixture onto a baking sheet; bake for 25 minutes, flipping them halfway through the cooking time until golden and crisp. Sprinkle the potatoes with cilantro, cayenne pepper, and smoked paprika. Serve warm and enjoy!

**Nutrition Info:**
- Info Per Serving: Calories: 203;Fat: 11g;Protein: 3g;Carbs: 24g.

# Ultimate Seed Crackers

Servings:6
Cooking Time:20 Minutes
**Ingredients:**
- 1 cup almond flour
- 1 tbsp sesame seeds
- 1 tbsp sunflower seeds
- 1 tbsp flaxseed
- 1 tbsp chia seeds
- ¼ tsp baking soda
- Salt and black pepper to taste
- 1 egg, beaten

**Directions:**
1. Preheat oven to 350 °F. In a bowl, mix the almond flour, sesame seeds, flaxseed, chia seeds, sunflower seeds, baking soda, salt, and pepper and stir well. Add the egg and stir well to combine and form the dough into a ball. Place one layer of parchment paper on your counter-top and place the dough on top. Cover with a second layer of parchment and, using a rolling pin, roll the dough to ¼-inch thickness, aiming for a rectangular shape. Cut the dough into crackers and bake on parchment until crispy and slightly golden, 10-15 minutes, depending on thickness. Alternatively, you can bake the large rolled dough before cutting and break into free-form crackers once baked and crispy. Store in an airtight container for up to 1 week.

**Nutrition Info:**
- Info Per Serving: Calories: 119;Fat: 9g;Protein: 4g;Carbs: 5g.

# Coconut Blueberries With Brown Rice

Servings:4
Cooking Time: 10 Minutes
**Ingredients:**
- 1 cup fresh blueberries
- 2 cups unsweetened coconut milk
- 1 teaspoon ground ginger
- ¼ cup maple syrup
- Sea salt, to taste
- 2 cups cooked brown rice

**Directions:**
1. Put all the ingredients, except for the brown rice, in a pot. Stir to combine well.
2. Cook over medium-high heat for 7 minutes or until the blueberries are tender.
3. Pour in the brown rice and cook for 3 more minute or until the rice is soft. Stir constantly.
4. Serve immediately.

**Nutrition Info:**
- Info Per Serving: Calories: 470;Fat: 24.8g;Protein: 6.2g;Carbs: 60.1g.

# Eggplant & Pepper Spread On Toasts

Servings:4
Cooking Time:10 Minutes
**Ingredients:**
- 1 red bell pepper, roasted and chopped
- 1 lb eggplants, baked, peeled and chopped
- ¾ cup olive oil
- 1 lemon, zested
- 1 red chili pepper, chopped
- 1 ½ tsp capers
- 1 garlic clove, minced
- Salt and black pepper to taste
- 1 baguette, sliced and toasted

**Directions:**
1. In a food processor, place the eggplants, lemon zest, red chili pepper, bell pepper, garlic, salt, and pepper. Blend while gradually adding the olive oil until smooth. Spread each baguette slice with the spread and top with capers to serve.

**Nutrition Info:**
- Info Per Serving: Calories: 364;Fat: 38g;Protein: 1.5g;Carbs: 9.3g.

# Chili & Lemon Shrimp

Servings:6
Cooking Time:10 Minutes
**Ingredients:**
- 24 large shrimp, peeled and deveined
- ½ cup olive oil
- 5 garlic cloves, minced
- 1 tsp red pepper flakes
- 1 lemon, juiced and zested
- 1 tsp dried dill
- 1 tsp dried thyme
- Salt and black pepper to taste

**Directions:**
1. Warm the olive oil in a large skillet over medium heat. Add the garlic and red pepper flakes and cook for 1 minute. Add the shrimp and cook an additional 3 minutes, stirring frequently. Remove from the pan, and sprinkle with lemon juice, lemon zest, thyme, dill, salt, and pepper. Serve.

**Nutrition Info:**
- Info Per Serving: Calories: 198;Fat: 6g;Protein: 9g;Carbs: 28g.

# Orange Mug Cakes

Servings:2
Cooking Time: 3 Minutes
**Ingredients:**
- 6 tablespoons flour
- 2 tablespoons sugar
- 1 teaspoon orange zest
- ½ teaspoon baking powder

- Pinch salt
- 1 egg
- 2 tablespoons olive oil
- 2 tablespoons unsweetened almond milk
- 2 tablespoons freshly squeezed orange juice
- ½ teaspoon orange extract
- ½ teaspoon vanilla extract

**Directions:**

1. Combine the flour, sugar, orange zest, baking powder, and salt in a small bowl.

2. In another bowl, whisk together the egg, olive oil, milk, orange juice, orange extract, and vanilla extract.

3. Add the dry ingredients to the wet ingredients and stir to incorporate. The batter will be thick.

4. Divide the mixture into two small mugs. Microwave each mug separately. The small ones should take about 60 seconds, and one large mug should take about 90 seconds, but microwaves can vary.

5. Cool for 5 minutes before serving.

**Nutrition Info:**

- Info Per Serving: Calories: 303;Fat: 16.9g;Protein: 6.0g;Carbs: 32.5g.

## Fluffy Orange Muffins

Servings:6
Cooking Time:35 Minutes
**Ingredients:**

- ½ cup olive oil
- 1 large egg
- 2 tbsp powdered sugar
- 1 tsp orange extract
- 1 orange, zested and juiced
- 1 cup flour
- ¾ tsp baking powder
- ½ tsp salt

**Directions:**

1. Preheat oven to 350 °F. In a large bowl, whisk together the egg and powdered sugar. Add the olive oil, orange extract, and orange zest and whisk to combine well. In a separate bowl, mix together the flour, baking powder, and salt.

2. Add to wet ingredients along with the orange juice and stir until just combined. Divide the batter evenly between 6 greased muffin cups and bake until a toothpick inserted in the center of the cupcake comes out clean, 20-25 minutes.

3. Remove and let sit for 5 minutes in the tin, then transfer to a wire rack to cool completely. Serve and enjoy!

**Nutrition Info:**

- Info Per Serving: Calories: 211;Fat: 22g;Protein: 3g;Carbs: 2g.

## Spicy Roasted Chickpeas

Servings:2
Cooking Time:40 Minutes
**Ingredients:**

- Chickpeas

- 1 tbsp olive oil
- 1 can chickpeas
- Salt to taste
- Seasoning Mix
- ¾ tsp cumin
- ½ tsp ground coriander
- Salt and black pepper to taste
- ¼ tsp chili powder
- ½ tsp cayenne pepper
- ¼ tsp cardamom
- ¼ tsp cinnamon
- ¼ tsp allspice

**Directions:**

1. Preheat oven to 400 °F. In a small bowl, place all the seasoning mix ingredients and stir well to combine.

2. Place the chickpeas in a bowl and season them with olive oil and salt. Add the chickpeas to a lined baking sheet and roast them for about 25-35 minutes, turning them over once or twice while cooking until they are slightly crisp. Remove to a bowl and sprinkle them with the seasoning mix. Toss lightly to combine. Serve and enjoy!

**Nutrition Info:**

- Info Per Serving: Calories: 268;Fat: 11g;Protein: 11g;Carbs: 35g.

## Turkish Baklava

Servings:6
Cooking Time:40 Min + Chilling Time
**Ingredients:**

- 20 sheets phyllo pastry dough, at room temperature
- 1 cup butter, melted
- 1 ½ cups chopped walnuts
- 1 tsp ground cinnamon
- ¼ tsp ground cardamom
- ½ cup sugar
- ½ cup honey
- 2 tbsp lemon juice
- 1 tbsp lemon zest

**Directions:**

1. In a small pot, bring 1 cup of water, sugar, honey, lemon zest, and lemon juice just to a boil. Remove and let cool.

2. Preheat oven to 350 °F. In a small bowl, mix the walnuts, cinnamon, and cardamom and set aside. Put the butter in a small bowl. Put 1 layer of phyllo dough on a baking sheet and slowly brush with butter. Carefully layer 2 more phyllo sheets, brushing each with butter in the baking pan and then layer 1 tbsp of the nut mix; layer 2 sheets and add another 1 tbsp of the nut mix; repeat with 2 sheets and nuts until you run out of nuts and dough, topping with the remaining phyllo dough sheets. Slice 4 lines into the baklava lengthwise and make another 4 or 5 slices diagonally across the pan. Bake for 30-40 minutes or until golden brown. Remove the baklava from the oven and immediately cover it with the syrup. Let cool and serve.

**Nutrition Info:**

- Info Per Serving: Calories: 443;Fat: 27g;Protein: 6g;Carbs: 47g.

## Arugula & Olive Pizza With Balsamic Glaze

Servings:4
Cooking Time:90 Minutes
**Ingredients:**
- 2 tbsp olive oil
- 2 cups flour
- 1 cup lukewarm water
- 1 pinch of sugar
- 1 tsp active dry yeast
- 2 tbsp honey
- ½ cup balsamic vinegar
- 4 cups arugula
- Salt to taste
- 1 cup mozzarella, grated
- ¾ tsp dried oregano
- 6 black olives, drained

**Directions:**
1. Sift the flour and ¾ tsp salt in a bowl and stir in yeast. Mix lukewarm water, olive oil, and sugar in another bowl. Add the wet mixture to the dry mixture and whisk until you obtain a soft dough. Place the dough on a lightly floured work surface and knead it thoroughly for 4-5 minutes until elastic. Transfer the dough to a greased bowl. Cover with cling film and leave to rise for 50-60 minutes in a warm place. Roll out the dough to a thickness of around 12 inches.
2. Place the balsamic vinegar and honey in a saucepan over medium heat and simmer for 5 minutes until syrupy. Preheat oven to 390 °F. Transfer the pizza crust to a baking sheet and sprinkle with oregano and mozzarella cheese; bake for 10-15 minutes. Remove the pizza from the oven and top with arugula. Sprinkle with balsamic glaze and olives and serve.

**Nutrition Info:**
- Info Per Serving: Calories: 350;Fat: 15.4g;Protein: 6g;Carbs: 47g.

## Traditional Pizza Margherita

Servings:4
Cooking Time:30 Minutes
**Ingredients:**
- 1 can diced San Marzano tomatoes with juices
- 16 oz pizza dough
- Salt to taste
- 1 tsp oregano
- 2 tbsp extra-virgin olive oil
- 10 mozzarella cheese slices
- 12 fresh basil leaves
- 6 whole black olives

**Directions:**
1. Preheat oven to 450 °F. Place the dough on a floured surface and roll out it thinly. Place it on a lightly floured pizza pan and drizzle with some olive oil. Puree the tomatoes, a splash of olive oil and a sprinkle of salt until smooth. Spread the tomato sauce over the base, leaving a 1-inch border and sprinkle with oregano. Arrange the mozzarella cheese slices on top and bake for 8-10 minutes until the crust is golden. Top with basil and olives and serve.

**Nutrition Info:**
- Info Per Serving: Calories: 542;Fat: 21g;Protein: 26g;Carbs: 63g.

## Strawberry Parfait

Servings:2
Cooking Time:10 Minutes
**Ingredients:**
- ¾ cup Greek yogurt
- 1 tbsp cocoa powder
- ¼ cup strawberries, chopped
- 5 drops vanilla stevia

**Directions:**
1. Combine cocoa powder, strawberries, yogurt, and stevia in a bowl. Serve immediately.

**Nutrition Info:**
- Info Per Serving: Calories: 210;Fat: 9g;Protein: 5g;Carbs: 8g.

## Pepperoni Fat Head Pizza

Servings:4
Cooking Time:35 Minutes
**Ingredients:**
- 2 tbsp olive oil
- 2 cups flour
- 1 cup lukewarm water
- 1 pinch of sugar
- 1 tsp active dry yeast
- ¾ tsp salt
- 1 tsp dried oregano
- 2 cups mozzarella cheese
- 1 cup sliced pepperoni

**Directions:**
1. Sift the flour and salt in a bowl and stir in yeast. Mix lukewarm water, olive oil, and sugar in another bowl. Add the wet mixture to the dry mixture and whisk until you obtain a soft dough. Place the dough on a lightly floured work surface and knead it thoroughly for 4-5 minutes until elastic. Transfer the dough to a greased bowl. Cover with cling film and leave to rise for 50-60 minutes in a warm place until doubled in size. Roll out the dough to a thickness of around 12 inches.
2. Preheat oven to 400 °F. Line a round pizza pan with parchment paper. Spread the dough on the pizza pan and top with the mozzarella cheese, oregano, and pepperoni slices. Bake in the oven for 15 minutes or until the cheese melts. Remove the pizza from the oven and let cool slightly. Slice and serve.

**Nutrition Info:**

# Fig & Mascarpone Toasts With Pistachios

Servings:6
Cooking Time:10 Minutes
**Ingredients:**
• 4 tbsp butter, melted
• 1 French baguette, sliced
• 1 cup Mascarpone cheese
• 1 jar fig jam
• ½ cup crushed pistachios
**Directions:**
1. Preheat oven to 350 °F. Arrange the sliced bread on a greased baking sheet and brush each slice with melted butter.
2. Toast the bread for 5-7 minutes until golden brown. Let the bread cool slightly. Spread about a teaspoon of the mascarpone cheese on each piece of bread. Top with fig jam and pistachios.
**Nutrition Info:**
• Info Per Serving: Calories: 445;Fat: 24g;Protein: 3g;Carbs: 48g.

# Walnut And Date Balls

Servings:6
Cooking Time: 8 To 10 Minutes
**Ingredients:**
• 1 cup walnuts
• 1 cup unsweetened shredded coconut
• 14 medjool dates, pitted
• 8 tablespoons almond butter
**Directions:**
1. Preheat the oven to 350ºF.
2. Put the walnuts on a baking sheet and toast in the oven for 5 minutes.
3. Put the shredded coconut on a clean baking sheet. Toast for about 3 to 5 minutes, or until it turns golden brown. Once done, remove it from the oven and put it in a shallow bowl.
4. In a food processor, process the toasted walnuts until they have a medium chop. Transfer the chopped walnuts into a medium bowl.
5. Add the dates and butter to the food processor and blend until the dates become a thick paste. Pour the chopped walnuts into the food processor with the dates and pulse just until the mixture is combined, about 5 to 7 pulses.
6. Remove the mixture from the food processor and scrape it into a large bowl.
7. To make the balls, spoon 1 to 2 tablespoons of the date mixture into the palm of your hand and roll around between your hands until you form a ball. Put the ball on a clean, lined baking sheet. Repeat until all the mixture is formed into balls.

8. Roll each ball in the toasted coconut until the outside of the ball is coated. Put the ball back on the baking sheet and repeat.
9. Put all the balls into the refrigerator for 20 minutes before serving. Store any leftovers in the refrigerator in an airtight container.
**Nutrition Info:**
• Info Per Serving: Calories: 489;Fat: 35.0g;Protein: 5.0g;Carbs: 48.0g.

# Salmon-cucumber Rolls

Servings:4
Cooking Time:5 Minutes
**Ingredients:**
• 8 Kalamata olives, chopped
• 4 oz smoked salmon strips
• 1 cucumber, sliced lengthwise
• 2 tsp lime juice
• 4 oz cream cheese, soft
• 1 tsp lemon zest, grated
• Salt and black pepper to taste
• 2 tsp dill, chopped
**Directions:**
1. Place cucumber slices on a flat surface and top each with a salmon strip. Combine olives, lime juice, cream cheese, lemon zest, salt, pepper, and dill in a bowl. Smear cream mixture over salmon and roll them up. Serve immediately.
**Nutrition Info:**
• Info Per Serving: Calories: 250;Fat: 16g;Protein: 18g;Carbs: 17g.

# Vegetarian Spinach-olive Pizza

Servings:4
Cooking Time:40 Minutes
**Ingredients:**
• For the crust
• 1 tbsp olive oil
• ½ cup almond flour
• ¼ tsp salt
• 2 tbsp ground psyllium husk
• 1 cup lukewarm water
• For the topping
• ½ cup tomato sauce
• ½ cup baby spinach
• 1 cup grated mozzarella
• 1 tsp dried oregano
• 3 tbsp sliced black olives
**Directions:**
1. Preheat the oven to 400 °F. Line a baking sheet with parchment paper. In a medium bowl, mix the almond flour, salt, psyllium powder, olive oil, and water until dough forms.
2. Spread the mixture on the pizza pan and bake in the oven until crusty, 10 minutes. When ready, remove the crust and spread the tomato sauce on top. Add the spinach, mozzarella cheese, oregano, and olives. Bake until the

cheese melts, 15 minutes. Take out of the oven, slice and serve warm.

**Nutrition Info:**
- Info Per Serving: Calories: 167;Fat: 13g;Protein: 4g;Carbs: 6.7g.

# Speedy Trail Mix

Servings:6
Cooking Time:10 Minutes
**Ingredients:**
- ½ cup chopped macadamia
- ½ cup chopped walnuts
- ½ cup chopped salted almonds
- ½ cup shelled salted pistachios
- ½ cup chopped apricots
- ½ cup chopped dates
- ⅓ cup dried figs, halved

**Directions:**
1. Place all the nuts in a skillet over medium heat and toast them for 2 minutes, shaking often. Remove and leave them to cool completely. Mix with the apricots, dates, and figs. Serve.

**Nutrition Info:**
- Info Per Serving: Calories: 348;Fat: 24g;Protein: 9g;Carbs: 33g.

# Speedy Granita

Servings:4
Cooking Time:10 Min + Freezing Time
**Ingredients:**
- ¼ cup sugar
- 1 cup fresh strawberries
- 1 cup fresh raspberries
- 1 cup chopped fresh kiwi
- 1 tsp lemon juice

**Directions:**
1. Bring 1 cup water to a boil in a small saucepan over high heat. Add the sugar and stir well until dissolved. Remove the pan from the heat, add the fruit and lemon juice, and cool to room temperature. Once cooled, puree the fruit in a blender until smooth. Pour the puree into a shallow glass baking dish and place in the freezer for 1 hour. Stir with a fork and freeze for 30 minutes, then repeat. Serve and enjoy!

**Nutrition Info:**
- Info Per Serving: Calories: 153;Fat: 0.2g;Protein: 1.6g;Carbs: 39g.

# Hummus Stuffed Jalapeño Poppers

Servings:6
Cooking Time:1 Hour + Chilling Time
**Ingredients:**
- 3 tbsp olive oil
- ½ lb chickpeas, soaked
- 1 lb jalapeño peppers, halved

- 1 shallot
- 2 tbsp tahini
- 1 tbsp lemon juice
- ½ tsp red pepper flakes
- 1 tsp cumin
- 1 tsp harissa seasoning
- 1 garlic clove, minced
- Salt to taste
- 1 tbsp paprika

**Directions:**
1. Preheat oven to 400 °F. Pour the chickpeas in a pot over medium heat and cover with water by 1 inch. Bring to a boil, then lower the heat and simmer for 45-50 minutes. Remove 1 cup of the cooking liquid to a bowl and drain the chickpeas. Reserve some whole chickpeas for garnishing. Bake the jalapeño peppers in the oven for 10 minutes.
2. Remove to a serving platter. Pour the chickpeas in a food processor and half of the reserved cooking liquid and pulse until no large pieces remain. Add in the remaining cooking liquid, lemon juice, olive oil, red pepper flakes, cumin, harissa seasoning, garlic, tahini, shallot, and salt. Pulse until smooth. Spoon the hummus into each jalapeño half and top with the whole chickpeas. Sprinkle with paprika and serve.

**Nutrition Info:**
- Info Per Serving: Calories: 250;Fat: 12.7g;Protein: 9g;Carbs: 28g.

# Roasted Garlic & Spicy Lentil Dip

Servings:6
Cooking Time:40 Minutes
**Ingredients:**
- 1 roasted red bell pepper, chopped
- 4 tbsp olive oil
- 1 cup split red lentils
- ½ red onion
- 1 garlic bulb, top removed
- ½ tsp cumin seeds
- 1 tsp coriander seeds
- ¼ cup walnuts
- 2 tbsp tomato paste
- ½ tsp Cayenne powder
- Salt and black pepper to taste

**Directions:**
1. Preheat oven to 370 °F. Drizzle the garlic with some olive oil and wrap it in a piece of aluminum foil. Roast for 35-40 minutes. Remove and allow to cool for a few minutes. Cover the lentils with salted water in a pot over medium heat and bring to a boil. Simmer for 15 minutes. Drain and set aside.
2. Squeeze out the garlic cloves and place them in a food processor. Add in the cooled lentils, cumin seeds, coriander seeds, roasted red bell pepper, onion, walnuts, tomato paste, Cayenne powder, remaining olive oil, salt, and black pepper. Pulse until smooth. Serve with crostiniif desire.

**Nutrition Info:**
- Info Per Serving: Calories: 234;Fat: 13g;Protein: 9g;Carbs: 21.7g.

# 21 Day Meal Plan

## Day 1

**Breakfast:**Vegetable Polenta With Fried Eggs    16
**Lunch:** Bell Pepper & Onion Pork Chops          82
**Dinner:** Eggplant Stew With Almonds  57

## Day 2

**Breakfast:**Feta And Spinach Frittata       16
**Lunch:**Chili Beef Stew              82
**Dinner:**Cherry, Plum, Artichoke, And Cheese Board       57

## Day 3

**Breakfast:**Artichoke & Spinach Frittata 16
**Lunch:** Rosemary Pork Chops With Cabbage Mix        82
**Dinner:**Arugula And Fig Salad  57

## Day 4

**Breakfast:**Pecorino Bulgur & Spinach Cupcakes       16
**Lunch:** Mushroom Chicken Piccata       82
**Dinner:**Zoodles With Tomato-mushroom Sauce 58

## Day 5

**Breakfast:**Pistachio Muesli Pots With Pomegranate       17
**Lunch:**Beef, Tomato, And Lentils Stew 83
**Dinner:**Gorgonzola, Fig & Prosciutto Salad        58

## Day 6

**Breakfast:** Granola & Berry Parfait       17
**Lunch:**Provençal Flank Steak Au Pistou          83
**Dinner:**Carrot & Celery Bean Soup       58

## Day 7

**Breakfast:**Basic Tortilla De Patatas       17
**Lunch:**Parsley Eggplant Lamb  83
**Dinner:**Classic Potato Salad With Green Onions         58

## Day 8

**Breakfast:**Chickpea Lettuce Wraps     17

**Lunch:**Greek Beef Kebabs     83

**Dinner:**Green Bean & Rice Chicken Soup     59

## Day 9

**Breakfast:**Za'atar Pizza     18

**Lunch:**Fennel Beef Ribs     84

**Dinner:**Quick Za´atar Spice     59

## Day 10

**Breakfast:**Vegetable & Cheese Frittata  18

**Lunch:**Eggplant & Turkey Moussaka     84

**Dinner:**Carrot & Tomato Salad With Cilantro     59

## Day 11

**Breakfast:**Parsley Tomato Eggs     18

**Lunch:**Spinach-ricotta Chicken Rolls     84

**Dinner:**Spanish Lentil Soup With Rice  59

## Day 12

**Breakfast:**Banana & Chocolate Porridge     18

**Lunch:**Greek-style Chicken & Vegetable Stir-fry     84

**Dinner:**Pecorino Zucchini Strips     59

## Day 13

**Breakfast:**Falafel Balls With Tahini Sauce     18

**Lunch:**Drunken Lamb Bake     85

**Dinner:**Pecorino Zucchini Strips     59

## Day 14

**Breakfast:**Power Green Smoothie     19

**Lunch:**Creamy Beef Stew     85

**Dinner:**Kalamata Olive & Lentil Salad  60

# Day 15

**Breakfast:**Chia & Almond Oatmeal      19

**Lunch:**Chicken & Vegetable Skewers    85

**Dinner:**Spinach & Bean Salad With Goat Cheese          60

# Day 16

**Breakfast:**Sunday Pancakes In Berry Sauce      19

**Lunch:**Chicken Tagine With Vegetables        85

**Dinner:**Bell Pepper & Lentil Salad With Tomatoes      60

# Day 17

**Breakfast:**Creamy Breakfast Bulgur With Berries      20

**Lunch:**French Chicken Cassoulet        86

**Dinner:**Baby Potato And Olive Salad    60

# Day 18

**Breakfast:**Maple-vanilla Yogurt With Walnuts  20

**Lunch:**Spiced Roast Chicken    86

**Dinner:**Tomato & Apple Salad With Walnuts     61

# Day 19

**Breakfast:**Hummus Toast With Pine Nuts & Ricotta      20

**Lunch:**Grilled Beef With Mint-jalapeño Vinaigrette     86

**Dinner:**Roasted Root Vegetable Soup    61

# Day 20

**Breakfast:**Vegetable & Hummus Bowl  20

**Lunch:**One-pan Sicilian Chicken        86

**Dinner:**Cucumber & Tomato Salad With Anchovies     61

# Day 21

**Breakfast:**Lime Watermelon Yogurt Smoothie  20

**Lunch:**Rich Pork In Cilantro Sauce      87

**Dinner:**Chickpea Tuna Salad    61

# INDEX

Creamy Saffron Chicken With Ziti 52
Creamy Sweet Potatoes And Collards 31
Creamy Tomato Hummus Soup 68
Crispy Fish Sticks 76
Crispy Pesto Chicken 90
Crispy Sole Fillets 73
Crunchy Almond Cookies 101
Crunchy Pollock Fillets 72
Crustless Tiropita (greek Cheese Pie) 28
Cucumber & Tomato Salad With Anchovies 61
Cucumber Sticks With Dill-cheese Dip 99
Cumin Cauli Mash 66

# D

Dark Chocolate Barks 95
Detox Juice 23
Dill Smoked Salmon & Eggplant Rolls 73
Dilly Haddock In Tomato Sauce 80
Drunken Lamb Bake 85

# E

Easy No-bake Walnut & Date Oat Bars 100
Easy Pizza Pockets 28
Easy Tomato Tuna Melts 70
Easy Zucchini Patties 31
Egg & Spinach Pie 26
Eggplant & Chickpea Casserole 45
Eggplant & Pepper Spread On Toasts 102
Eggplant & Sweet Potato Salad 65
Eggplant & Turkey Moussaka 84
Eggplant And Zucchini Gratin 39
Eggplant Rolls In Tomato Sauce 40
Eggplant Stew With Almonds 57
Endive & Tuna Salad With Pine Nuts 68
Energy Granola Bites 100
Energy Nut Smoothie 22
Exotic Pork Chops 90

# F

Falafel Balls With Tahini Sauce 18
Farro & Trout Bowls With Avocado 78
Fennel & Bell Pepper Salmon 81
Fennel Beef Ribs 84
Festive Pumpkin Cheesecake 97
Feta & Olive Salad 62
Feta And Spinach Frittata 16
Fig & Mascarpone Toasts With Pistachios 105
Fluffy Almond Flour Pancakes With Strawberries 22
Fluffy Orange Muffins 103
Fofu Spaghetti Bolognese 44
French Chicken Cassoulet 86

Fried Eggplant Rolls 35

# G

Garlic And Parsley Chickpeas 50
Garlic Shrimp With Arugula Pesto 80
Garlic Shrimp With Mushrooms 74
Garlic Skillet Salmon 70
Garlic-butter Asparagus With Parmesan 42
Garlicky Broccoli Rabe 30
Garlicky Zucchini Cubes With Mint 38
Garlic-yogurt Dip With Walnuts 97
Glazed Broiled Salmon 76
Goat Cheese Dip With Scallions & Lemon 97
Gorgonzola, Fig & Prosciutto Salad 58
Granola & Berry Parfait 17
Greek Beef Kebabs 83
Greek Salad With Dressing 64
Greek-style Chicken & Egg Bake 87
Greek-style Chicken & Vegetable Stir-fry 84
Greek-style Eggplants 32
Green Bean & Pork Fettuccine 55
Green Bean & Rice Chicken Soup 59
Green Salad With Lentils & Feta Cheese 63
Grilled Beef With Mint-jalapeño Vinaigrette 86
Grilled Eggplant "steaks" With Sauce 31
Grilled Lemon Pesto Salmon 74
Grilled Sardines With Herby Sauce 80
Gyro Burgers With Tahini Sauce 92

# H

Halibut Confit With Sautéed Leeks 78
Harissa Vegetable Couscous 52
Healthy Tuna Stuffed Zucchini Rolls 100
Herby Chicken With Asparagus Sauce 92
Herby Cod Stew 71
Herby Tuna Gratin 76
Homemade Vegetarian Moussaka 38
Home-style Beef Ragu Rigatoni 54
Honey Baked Cinnamon Apples 95
Honeyed Pistachio Dumplings 95
Horiatiki Salad (greek Salad) 68
Hot Tomato & Caper Squid Stew 79
Hummus Stuffed Jalapeño Poppers 106
Hummus Toast With Pine Nuts & Ricotta 20

# I

Instant Pot Pork With Rice 43
Israeli Couscous With Asparagus 52
Italian Canned Tuna & Bean Bowl 77
Italian Sautéd Cannellini Beans 54
Italian-style Chicken Stew 65

Sautéed Mushrooms With Garlic & Parsley 40
Sautéed Spinach And Leeks 30
Savory Tomato Chicken 91
Seafood Paella 76
Seafood Stew 73
Seared Halibut With Moroccan Chermoula 74
Shrimp & Gnocchi With Feta Cheese 71
Shrimp & Salmon In Tomato Sauce 77
Shrimp & Spinach A La Puttanesca 77
Shrimp And Pea Paella 78
Sicilian Sandwich Muffuletta 98
Sicilian-style Squid With Zucchini 76
Simple Braised Carrots 33
Simple Fried Cod Fillets 70
Simple Lentil Risotto 53
Simple Zoodles 29
Slow Cooker Brussel Sprout & Chicken 88
Small Pasta And Beans Pot 46
Smoky Paprika Chickpeas 44
Spanish Lentil Soup With Rice 59
Spanish-style Pizza With Jamón Serrano 98
Speedy Granita 106
Speedy Trail Mix 106
Spiced Fries 101
Spiced Roast Chicken 86
Spicy Bean Rolls 53
Spicy Grilled Shrimp With Lemon Wedges 70
Spicy Roasted Chickpeas 103
Spicy Tofu Tacos With Cherry Tomato Salsa 27
Spinach & Bean Salad With Goat Cheese 60
Spinach & Olive Penne 50
Spinach & Pea Salad With Rice 65
Spinach & Salmon Fettuccine In White Sauce 55
Spinach Cheese Pie 25
Spinach-ricotta Chicken Rolls 84
Stir-fried Kale With Mushrooms 41
Strawberry Parfait 104
Stuffed Portobello Mushroom With Tomatoes 30
Stuffed Portobello Mushrooms With Spinach 34
Summer Fruit & Cheese Salad 64
Sumptuous Greek Vegetable Salad 66
Sunday Pancakes In Berry Sauce 19
Super Cheeses And Mushroom Tart 21
Sweet Banana Pancakes With Strawberries 24
Sweet Mustard Cabbage Hash 29
Swoodles With Almond Butter Sauce 46

# T

Tahini & Feta Butternut Squash 36
Thyme Hake With Potatoes 75

Tomato & Apple Salad With Walnuts 61
Tomato & Avocado Toast 21
Tomato & Basil Chicken Breasts 87
Tomato & Roasted Eggplant Soup 64
Tomato And Egg Scramble 26
Tomato Sauce And Basil Pesto Fettuccine 55
Tomatoes Filled With Tabbouleh 39
Tortellini & Cannellini With Meatballs 51
Tradicional Matchuba Green Beans 38
Traditional Beef Lasagna 44
Traditional Pizza Margherita 104
Tuna Gyros With Tzatziki 75
Turkish Baklava 103
Turkish Canned Pinto Bean Salad 54
Turkish Chickpeas 64
Two-bean Cassoulet 48

# U

Ultimate Seed Crackers 102

# V

Valencian Arroz Con Pollo 89
Vegan Lentil Bolognese 33
Vegetable & Cheese Frittata 18
Vegetable & Hummus Bowl 20
Vegetable And Tofu Scramble 29
Vegetable Polenta With Fried Eggs 16
Vegetarian Patties 99
Vegetarian Spinach-olive Pizza 105
Veggie & Egg Quinoa With Pancetta 47
Veggie-stuffed Portabello Mushrooms 32

# W

Walnut And Date Balls 105
Warm Bulgur Breakfast Bowls With Fruits 27
Wine Chicken Breasts With Capers 89

# Z

Za'atar Pizza 18
Ziti Marinara Bake 57
Zoodles With Beet Pesto 30
Zoodles With Tomato-mushroom Sauce 58
Zoodles With Walnut Pesto 37
Zucchini And Artichokes Bowl With Farro 40
Zucchini Crisp 38
Zucchini Ribbons With Ricotta 34

Made in United States
Orlando, FL
17 July 2023

35227339R00063